STRATEGIES OF BIG BRANDS

BREAKING THE BUSINESS AND MARKETING STRATEGIES USED BY BIG BRANDS

ROSHAN RAGHAVANDER

Contents

Contents

I

AirBnB

On the 1st of December 2008, the National Bureau of Economic Research officially declared that the United States entered a recession in December 2007. And by this time, the tremors of the economic nightmare were already being witnessed not just by the United States but by countries all across the world. 2.6 million jobs were lost, several billion-dollar companies filed for bankruptcy and it cost the global economy more than $2 trillion. This financial crisis of 2008 was so bad that it was known to be the biggest economic meltdown in the US since the great depression. And it lasted for about 18 months. Now, during such a terrible time, if I asked you 'Would you like to start a business? What would your answer be? You'd call me crazy, right? Well, guess what? Airbnb was one of the few companies that were not just built during the times of recession but also became a billion-dollar company because of the paradigm shift brought along by the recession itself. So, the question is - What is so special about Airbnb? How did they succeed because of the recession? And most importantly What are the business lessons from the case study that you can apply to your business? The answer to this question lies in the teachings of the deep-rooted American culture. People, ever since childhood, children in America and even in India for that matter are taught that we should not talk to a stranger, we should not take chocolates from a stranger and in fact, any stranger who talks to you sweetly is a creep. And since childhood, we have always had a problem breaking the ice with a stranger. This is the reason why Americans back then or even present-day Indians for that matter would never let a stranger live in their bedroom no matter how much they are willing to pay. Similarly from a guest standpoint, if I asked you to stay in a stranger's bedroom, even you would hesitate, Right? Well, this is the reason why multiple startups that had the same model as Airbnb Failed people just wouldn't let a stranger live in their house. Then the question is When these people failed, what was so special about Airbnb that it became such a massive success? And here's where you need to know about a timeless business Lesson.

People always remember that every time there is a crisis of any kind whether that's a political crisis whether it's an economic crisis or even something like a pandemic it always leads to a paradigm shift in social behaviour. In this case, when the recession hit America millions of people were left jobless and they desperately needed money. Now, this money that they needed was not to buy a fancy car or a house but to feed their family 3 times a day. Therefore, it was a question of survival. The idea of Airbnb itself was born because the founders' Brian, Nathan, and Joe couldn't pay their rent and as a result of which they started hosting strangers in their house in exchange for rent at the same time people who were traveling also needed an affordable option because even they did not have a lot of money right? And that's when Airbnb connected the host with the guest and built its business model in such a way that it could generate a passive income for the host and provide a cheaper and better alternative to the guest as compared to the hotels. This is the reason why the concept of Airbnb became a game Changer and what followed next was the origin of a billion-dollar industry that redefined travel for Millennials which we know today as the short-term home rental industry. And this paradigm shift in the behaviour is what is known as the collaborative consumption movement wherein the society believes in sharing the ownership of resources rather than keeping them to themselves. And the economy that emerges out of it is what we call 'The Sharing Economy Using the valuation of Uber and Airbnb, a report from the Brookings Institution projects that the sharing economy will grow from just $14 billion in 2014 to $335 billion by 2025. And this emergence of the sharing economy is the reason why if you observe closely specifically from 2008 onwards, you'll see that multiple startups that were built on the concept of collaborative consumption have gone out to become million, even billion-dollar companies.

And as we move on to the 21st Century society is becoming more and more conducive to this kind of business. This is the first and the primary reason why Airbnb was a super success. Now, the question is - Airbnb wasn't the only startup during that time, right? Their idea was not even new. Then the question is Why did Airbnb specifically succeed? And this brings me to the second element of Airbnb and which Is designing for trust. People, back then when people were renting out places out of necessity in the initial days, things were not very comfortable because the speed of trust couldn't be established between the host and the guest. But thankfully, Joe and Brian were design students and they understood the importance of design in building human relationships. So, they took it very very seriously and started experimenting with user experience models to solve this problem. And that is when after some experimentation they found out that if the host introduced himself and described a little about himself and his family and his dog the guests feel way more comfortable as compared to just knowing about the property. And secondly, they also did a joint study with Stanford to find out exactly what factors built trust between people. And that's when they found out the more different the two people were, the more difficult it became to establish trust. For example, if you're a 23-year-old who lives in Pune and you meet a host in Delhi who is a Punekar by birth. You will begin to trust that person way more easily as compared to trusting a 40-year-old Gujarati host who lives in Delhi. But they found out that if you add social reputation to a person regardless of how diverse their backgrounds are, the speed of trust increases to a large extent. In this case, the social reputation was nothing but the reviews. And they found out that if the host had more than 3 reviews the guest was very easily able to trust her.

And for the guest, they designed a small questionnaire that could help them introduce themselves very easily and in a way that is neither creepy nor cold. And from my personal experience, I can tell you guys that this idea of the questionnaire has been a game-changer for me before writing this book. You know, earlier when I used to ask my friends for feedback about the topic I used to ask them 'What is your feedback about the Topic ?' and I used to get answers like "Good", "Best" and for some reason, people even used to say "Okay" but then I started asking more detailed questions that could help people direct their thoughts. For example, I started asking questions like "What do you like the best about the Topic ?" "If you were to change something about the Topic, what would it be?" And suddenly we started getting such insightful reviews that even today when we sit down to design a workshop or a course those reviews help us a lot in curating a better experience For my Clients. Therefore, this factor of the speed of trust separated Airbnb from the rest of the competition. Now the question is- How are these guys so sharp? I mean, how are they able to get such a deep understanding of their customers? And this is what brings me to the third and perhaps the most important element that separated Airbnb from the rest of the competition and that is its ability to build a system based on empathy. And this came from one of their investors named Paul Graham is the co-founder of Y combinator. Paul Graham specifically asked the Airbnb boys to go and visit every single one of their users at their most popular location which was back then- New York. Now, the point to be noted over here is all of this is happening at the peak of the recession wherein all 3 of them have been unemployed for 9 months they are almost broke and they have no funding. So, this trip alone was a huge burn in their pocket. But you know what guys? Despite all these difficulties, the Airbnb boys went all the way to New York and spent 4 long weekends meeting every single host to talk to them about their experiences. And guess what? They found the most valuable customer insight in every single conversation. For example, they understood that despite having a great house people did not have good camera phones to click good pictures of their house so these guys rented a camera and helped the hosts with the photos. Some of them were not able to articulate their offerings on the website, so the Airbnb boy's website sat down and wrote the description for them. And they also taught the hosts how to write good and lucrative descriptions. And most importantly after they were done, they invited the host over for a beer later on that night and sat with them and just built a relationship.

They exchanged stories, had a beautiful conversation, and even told them about the crazy Airbnb story. And you know what guys? They built such an amazing bond with the hosts that they could call these hosts up later on and tell them that you know their price is too high or that they needed to write better descriptions. And guess what? Soon enough all these listings began getting a lot more traffic and people from all across the world who were traveling to New York started to book these Airbnbs and eventually the hosts were able to make a lot more money. Soon enough, the guests to visit New York became hosts wherein they started listing their property and suddenly property listings started popping up all across the world including Germany, Spain, and even Hong Kong. This is how by turning hosts into brand ambassadors Airbnb laid a solid foundation for the most powerful method of marketing and that is word of mouth. This is how, timing, design for trust, and empathy became the perfect recipe for Airbnb's success. Today Airbnb is so huge that they've got 7 million listings in 191 countries and generated a revenue of $4.7 billion in 2019.Now, let's talk about the lessons from the case study.

Lesson number one. Every time there is a crisis or a recession of any kind ALWAYS REMEMBER that there will be a paradigm shift in the consumer behavior and the companies that are built upon this behavior are the ones that will go on to become extremely successful even if they aren't the first, even if they aren't the best.In this case, the recession gave rise to Uber, Airbnb, and the sharing economy. In case of the pandemic, if you see it boosted the sanitation industry the tech space, and the creator economy.

Lesson number two and this is something that I've said multiple times, that is market research is perhaps the most underrated and yet the most powerful tool to build a business. And what I've seen is in the race of digitalization, we often tend to underestimate the power of face-to-face meetings and what a solid rapport can do. In our case, the Airbnb boys could have easily done a Skype call or they could have used a Google Form to do their market research but despite being broke, despite being unemployed they meticulously followed Paul Graham's advice and spent 4 long weekends meeting every single host and that turned out to be a game-changer for them that helped them build a billion-dollar company. So, if you're somebody who is building a business right now and if there's any chance that you could go and talk to your customers face to face please go ahead and do that because that conversation could reveal such important insights that it could be a game-changer for your company and it could also help you separate from the rest of the competition.

II

Akasa Airlines

The aviation industry is one of the most drastically affected industries during the times of the pandemic. In the past two years, Indian Airlines have incurred a loss of 8 billion dollars. While on one side, the number of travelers is still far from pre-covid levels, the debts are piling up day by day and the aviation sector in total lost more than 39000 jobs merely due to the pandemic. But amidst all of this distress, while most companies are struggling to even survive, Rakesh Jhunjhunwala sir stands up and says that he'll be investing 35 million dollars into starting an airline. And not just that, he also aims to expand the airlines to a fleet of 70 aircraft within just four years. And this is astonishing because it took GoAir 15 years to achieve this milestone. And this begs the obvious question, What is the legend thinking? Why is he choosing this terrible time to start such a risky business? And most importantly, from the investor or a business standpoint, What are the factors that we need to take into consideration to understand the aviation market of India? The first thing that we need to understand is that Mr. Jhunjhunwala's airline is named Akasa. It will be a fleet of ultra-low-cost carriers. In simple words, it is going to be like the DMart of airlines, wherein the price of tickets is going to be even lower than the low-cost carriers like Indigo and SpiceJet. And the most important thing for an ultra-low-cost carrier is nothing but cost, cost, and cost. Now, considering the thin profit margins in the aviation industry, combined with fluctuation in demand, they need to cut costs at every single step, starting from seats, parking fees, and downtime, all the way up to the efficiency and the financing of the aircraft. So the question is, what is so special about 2021? And why is the big bull starting now? Why isn't he waiting for the industry to come back to normal? The answer to this lies in the conditions of the various stakeholders in the aviation sector. And while most of us can only see the stiff competition between the airlines, we often do not sense the stiff competition between the airline makers. In this case, the airline makers are Boeing and Airbus. And as of 2021, Boeing is in deep deep trouble, because this is what happened in 2018. 346 People were dead. We got a real problem here , This brand new plane crashed twice in about 5 months. How could this possibly happen?

Now, I don't know how many of you know this, but in 2018, two Boeing aircraft crashed in just five months, killing more than 300 people. And this is the reason why the Boeing 737 Max had been banned from flying for two years. And because of this ban, the number of orders for the Boeing 737 model fell from 837 units in 2018 to just 69 units in 2019. And this got the company from a profit of 10.4 billion dollars to a loss of 636 million dollars from 2018 to 2019, and all of this happened before covid. Secondly, it has also delayed the delivery of the 77x to 2023, which is costing the company 6.5 billion dollars in pre-tax charges. Thirdly, due to the pandemic, the other deliveries were also delayed by airlines all across the world resulting in a loss of nearly 12 billion dollars in 2020 alone. This is the deep trouble that Boeing is in right now. Where they are burning billions of dollars worth of cash every single month. And during such a time, any kind of fleet order would be a blessing for the company. And this also means that the buyer will get exceptional bargaining power to get the aircraft at an extremely low price. And this gives Akasa a huge advantage in purchasing the aircraft at a discounted rate. Now just to give you an idea about how big a deal this is, we are talking about a discount that is reported to go as high as 50% for an aircraft that caused close to a 100million dollars per unit. This means that, if Mr. Jhunjhunwala plays his cards well, he could be saving a billion dollars while purchasing the aircraft itself. And not so surprisingly, apart from Akasa, many low-cost carriers from all across the world have started placing orders with Boeing, specifically during this time of crisis. And this includes the US carrier Southwest Airlines, which has placed an order for 34 aircrafts. While on the other side, RyanAir has already placed a massive order of 75 aircraft in December 2020 itself. This is one of the most important reasons why Mr. Jhunjhunwala is planning to start an airline right now.

Now, the question is, with the aviation industry already having big guns like Indigo and GoFirst, How is Akasa going to cement its position in the aviation war? And this is what brings me to the second point and that is, the situation of the big guns right now. Indigo's combined losses for six quarters are about 10,000 crores. GoAir is now considering an IPO to revive itself from the losses and SpiceJet has seen its losses widening despite getting 150 million dollars in compensation from Boeing because of its ban. So on the outside, it looks as if when these companies start operating at a 100% capacity, they'll be very keen on recovering their losses as quickly as possible. Therefore, discounting on tickets will be very, very difficult eventually resulting in high prices. However, there is a very very important factor that needs to be taken into consideration and that is Indigo Airlines. Now people I don't know how many of you know this, but Indigo Airlines is by far one of the most extraordinary airlines in the Indian aviation market. And because of its game-changing business strategies, it has always had an advantage over its competition. In this context, Indigo Airlines has three major advantages over the rest of the competition. Number one, Indigo airlines is by far the biggest client of Airbus in India. And if you look at their fleet orders, it's quite massive. They ordered 180 aircraft in 2011, 250 aircraft in 2015, and a historic order of 300 aircraft in 2019. And if you look at it, it is more than the entire fleet of its next two competitors combined. And this means, that just like RyanAir and Southwest airlines have a bargaining power with Boeing, Indigo being one of the biggest airbus buyers, has a huge bargaining advantage over the rest of its competition. Therefore, just like southwest and Akasa plan to save billions with Boeing, even Indigo will save billions of dollars with its huge purchase order. And secondly, because Indigo gets such big fleets at such heavy discounts, it deploys sits game-changing business strategy called the sales and leaseback model. This is a technique wherein an entity sells its asset to another party and rents it back from the same buyer.

For example, now pay very close attention to this, because Indigo places such a large fleet order, it can buy a 100 million dollar aircraft at a modest price of 50 million dollars. And then, it sells this aircraft to a leasing company like BOC Aviation for 55 million dollars. Now here itself, they make a profit of 5 million dollars. And then Indigo rents the same aircraft from BOC Aviation for a period of five to eight years, such that, Indigo will pay the rent with its incoming revenue from the operation. Now, this is a great deal for the leaser also, because even at 55 million dollars, it's a bargain for them because they get to buy an aircraft at a heavy discount rate without having to place a bulk order. And along with that, they are also getting a readymade customer base that will give them recurring revenue. And this, ladies and gentlemen, give Indigo three incredible benefits. First of all, the company generates an upfront profit of 5 million dollars per unit, which could be used somewhere else, plus the leasing model eases their cash flow. Secondly, under the sales and leaseback model, as the aircraft is owned by the leaser, Indigo saves on the depreciation provision, which increases their profit and saves a ton of tax and cherry on the cake, in the leaseback agreement, is the responsibility of the leaser to bear the maintenance repairs. Therefore, Indigo further saves millions of dollars in maintenance repairs that reduce the cost of the ticket. This is the second advantage that Indigo has over the rest of its competition. And thirdly, Indigo is also looking to expand into cargo freight which will give them more cash flow that is independent of the passenger traffic. And this is a strength that even SpiceJet possesses in the Indian market. But you know what guys? There's a small catch over here. As it turns out, one of the most important people from the indigo's team who is responsible for such game-changing strategies, that is a former president of Indigo, Mr. Aditya Ghosh is now all set to join Mr. Jhunjhunwala's venture, which means what, with such brilliant minds in the game, we will be witnessing some game-changing cost-cutting strategies both from Indigo and Akasa. And as students and practitioners of business, it is going to be a delight to see what kind of strategies Akasa deploys to tackle the big guns, even with all of its limitations. This is the second factor that will decide the success or the failure of Akasa Airlines. And then some important pointers state the conducive nature of the market for starting an airline in 2021.

For example, Bangalore airport is now having a second runway. And while Delhi and Mumbai appear to be packed, Bangalore has the trio of slots, night parking, and counters available, which is very very rare. Secondly, in the next five years, India will begin to see something called secondary airports, which act as one of the most important cost-cutting elements for a low-cost carrier. I'll give you an in-depth perspective using a case study next month. But for now, just take note of this. Okay. And thirdly, under the Udaan scheme, the government aims to build another 100 airports and subsidized travel for citizens, which will eventually benefit both, the airlines and the customers. And this brings me to the most important part of the Chapter and that is, considering all these interesting strategies and the trajectory of the aviation sector and because we are now seeing IPO come in the aviation sector, what should you read about , in order to become an intelligent investor in the aviation space?

Number one, please study the concepts and strategies of RyanAir and Southwest airlines. And these are two of the best low-cost carriers in the world. And this will help you understand the intricate cost-cutting strategies that they deploy to generate profit even during times of crisis.

Secondly, if you find time, please read this book called Nuts. And this will give you an in-depth understanding of the business strategies of Southwest airlines.

III

American Express

I'm about to tell you the story of a brand that has leveraged perhaps, the most undervalued attributes of mankind and made a billion dollars out of it. And if you learn how to use these attributes you can easily go on to outperform your competition regardless of which domain you belong to. These attributes that I'm talking about are kindness and empathy. Now, in this capitalistic world while most people might consider empathy and kindness to be intangible qualities I gotta tell you that it's an open secret recipe that can enable you to design game-changing marketing strategies in the 21st Century. To tell you about it, let me take you back to 2010 America. This is when the American economy was still experiencing the wrath of the 2008 recession which caused the stock market to hit rock bottom, the giant corporations to shut down, and caused millions of job losses within a fortnight. When this happened, while the entire economy was collapsing there was one company that did not just survive but also went on to make a profit of $13.4 billion during the very same times of recession. This company that I'm talking about is the giant American retailer- Walmart. And as it turns out during the two years of recession Walmart improved its profitability by $700 million years on year. Additionally, Walmart never had a return of equity of less than 20% during the same time of recession. Now, on the outside, this might sound amazing but if you take a closer look at the impact of Walmart on retail America it's quite devastating. It has even got a term called the Walmart effect. Among the multiple studies that were conducted, it was proved time and again that every time a Walmart store opens up in a city or a town hundreds of small businesses within the radius of the store shut down within 1 year or at max 2 years. This was because

Walmart bought all of its products in such high quantities that it was able to lower the price of products to such a low level that small businesses couldn't even come close to competing with Walmart's prices. Now, just to give you an example of the same, let's say you have a small retail shop. You would buy notebooks from the wholesaler for ?30/notebook, alright? And when you buy it at ?30, you will sell it at ?40 in the market but at the same time, Walmart would sell the same notebook at ?28 per piece. Which means what? Walmart's selling price is lower than your cost price. And this made it impossible for small businesses to survive in the market. More often than not there are even protests that are held every time Walmart announces that it's going to open up a store in a town. But you know what? There was a small twist in the tale here. As it turns out another giant company stepped up and became a savior for small businesses during the times of recession. And this company lodged a campaign that was such an amazing hit that the senate of the United States itself unanimously passed a resolution to support the initiative.

And the cherry on the cake, President Barack Obama himself publically supported the campaign. The question is - What is this company and how did the American president himself end up endorsing a marketing campaign. Well, the company that I'm talking about is American Express and the campaign that it launched is known the 'Small business Saturday' This was an initiative where American Express gave away 25 dollars of special credit to 100,000 credit card members wherein they could only redeem these $25 if they shopped at a small business on a Saturday, after thanksgiving And they also gave away $100 of Facebook advertising credits to 10,000 small businesses just so that these small businesses could utilize digital marketing to maximize their profits. On top of the incentives, they also ran T.V. ads, radio ads, and even social media campaigns to educate the American population about their impact on small businesses. And you know what? Soon enough, hundreds of small business owners all across the country participated in the campaign and what followed next was nothing short of a capitalistic miracle that many considered to be impossible. Millions of Americans started walking into a small business store and rather than shopping from a Walmart, they began shopping from a small business despite knowing that they were making a more expensive purchase compared to Walmart. In its second year, 'Small Business Saturday' became even more successful wherein 5,000 small businesses participated in the campaign and 103 million Americans shopped small. And soon enough the

Small Business Saturday became such a social phenomenon that it generated over 2.7 million Facebook likes and became a top trend topic on Twitter. And #SmallBusinessSaturday became so popular that even President Barack Obama tweeted his support for the campaign. This is how capitalistic America went beyond its conventions and came together as a community to spread kindness and showed empathy toward small businesses in their community. By 2012, American Express took the campaign to the next level wherein they did not just give out credit card incentives but also provided the small business owners with social media kits, email templates, and various marketing materials to help them maximize their marketing. This further maximized their sales and within just 2 years Small Business Saturday became a part of the annual American Tradition wherein everybody starting from small business owners to the President himself participate in the campaign. And soon enough, it turned into a beautiful occasion with lots of happiness, and lots of smiles and most importantly it became an occasion of communal unity for the United States of America. In 2015, President Obama even documented taking his daughters to the local bookstore to promote the initiative of shopping at a small business. Fast forward to 2020, American Express estimates that 110 million people participated in the Small Business Saturday and sales hit a record high with an estimated $19.6 billion in spending all of this money helped keep small businesses alive even during the COVID-19 recession. This is how a bank like American Express was able to use empathy and kindness to make an economic miracle come true even during the toughest times of American history. Now, there are 3 very important lessons that we need to learn from this case study while we execute these ideas in our domain.

Lesson 1, identifying the pain and the interest of the audience is always the key to unlocking extraordinary business ideas. In this case, American Express identified the pain of the Shoppers and used its service to give them a $25 credit just so that it could motivate the shoppers to shop from a small business. Therefore, the interest of the shoppers has been addressed, at the same time, it has also catered to the pain of small business owners.

Lesson 2, in the 21st Century participatory campaigns, will always turn out to be more powerful than even an award-winning advertisement. Why? because the new age of marketing is moving from impressions to expressions. So, more than a T.V. ad it is the participation of the customers that are going to create more impact. In this case, because American Express gave out email templates and social media kits the shopkeepers automatically became the local ambassadors who participated in the campaign which eventually led to a chain reaction and got millions of shoppers on board too. This is what we call a participatory marketing campaign.

Lesson 3, And last and most importantly, always remember that empathy and compassion are the most undervalued attributes of this capitalistic world and very few people know that these are two of those qualities that are so powerful that they can turn a commoner into a king. In this case, they were powerful enough to give rise to a capitalistic miracle that America will cherish forever.

IV

Amul

On the 24th of March 2020, our Prime Minister announced a nationwide lockdown because of the pandemic, and what followed next was a nightmare that our nation was not prepared for. Millions of people, especially laborers lost their jobs several billion-dollar industries came to a standstill and it cost the Indian economy more than 10 lakh crores. One such industry that was heavily impacted due to the pandemic was the dairy industry and it cost the milk producers of India more than 112.3 crores every single day. But There was one legendary company that was so strategically able to navigate through this situation that they did not just minimize their losses but even went one step further to increase their revenue by 698 crores. This brand that I'm talking about is none other than Anand Milk Union Limited which we all so dearly know as Amul. Now, everybody knows the story and history of Amul and how it has been there for decades. But very few people know how incredible this company's business strategies are. And one such mind-blowing example of the same is how Amul reacted to COVID-19. People, you know what? Amul has done such an extraordinary job during the COVID times that in 2020 itself while the rest of the companies were struggling to even keep their supply chain going Amul went on to produce 33 new products in the market and procured an additional 35 lakh liters of milk every single day and even paid 800 crores extra to the rural milk producers of India. The question is - How did Amul manage to achieve such an incredible feat and most importantly what are the business strategy lessons that you and I need to learn from this case study to become extraordinary business leaders. The answer to this question lies in the extraordinary supply chain management of Amul. When the lockdown was announced in March the dairy industry was allowed to operate with certain restrictions because milk came under the essential goods category. But as soon as the announcement of the lockdown was done several businesses either cut down or closed their businesses and this resulted in the loss in demand for the dairy industry because these industries also included the restaurants, the catering, and the hotel businesses. And these businesses accounted for 20% of the revenue for the organized dairy sector. As a result Amul's sales also saw a decline of 10-12%.

And when the dairy companies saw this massive fall in demand they quickly cut down the milk procurement decreased their logistics and decreased their production by a large extent. This left many farmers in a helpless state because milk procurement was very less many laborers such as truck drivers and factory workers lost their livelihood because less milk meant fewer trucks and less operation of factories. But you know what guys? While the entire dairy industry was preparing for a loss in demand Amul did the complete opposite and started preparing for a surge in demand. Now the question is when it's being seen that there is a major decline in demand from the restaurants and the hotels that account for 20% of the revenue. Why would anyone prepare for a surge in demand, Isn't that like a 1000 crore gamble. Well, guess what? There was one very important variable that very few people took into consideration and that was the change in consumer behavior. Now, if you remember from what we've learned from the Airbnb case study, every time there is a crisis of any kind, there is a paradigm shift in consumer behavior. In this case, Although there was no demand from the restaurants the household consumption of milk products skyrocketed as more and more people began to stay at home. And this, in turn, gave rise to the homemade food trend because of which the demand for both, groceries and milk products Skyrocketed. And secondly, because of the pandemic, people became extremely health-conscious millions of people shifted from buying loose milk to buying packaged milk. And while other brands underestimated this consumer demand and started decreasing their supplies The managing director of Amul, Mr. Rupinder Singh Sodhi, Insisted that they keep the supply chain functioning at full capacity. And guess what? Despite the closure of the restaurants as of May 2020, during the peak of the lockdown times, the demand for milk-based products skyrocketed. The demand for cheese increased by 80% demand for cottage cheese increased by 40% and the demand for condensed milk increased by 100% the result? Well, Amul plans for operating at 115% capacity. The demand for Amul products was so high that they had to hire other plants from other companies that were lying vacant, and except for ice creams, all their plants were operating at full capacity throughout the lockdown. And on top of that, they also realized that moving trucks through the country will be very difficult because of the shortage of labor and the lockdown restrictions. So, they started using the railways to transport products quickly throughout the countries. Now, this begs the question, considering the vast supply chain of Amul. I mean, we are talking about 18,700 societies, 5000 milk tankers going to 200 chilling stations, 10,000 distributors, 1 million retailers, and most importantly more than 3.6 million farmers. The question is how did they manage to coordinate such a huge supply chain and manage their resources properly? The answer to this question lies in a strategic partnership that was established between Amul and IBM in 2009 wherein Amul invested a hefty 80 crores into transforming the information technology landscape of the company.

Now, what this means is that IBM would develop a full-fledged digital system to track every small detail of operation that is being carried out in the supply chain of Amul. And just like we get an update about our Amazon order through IBM's system, the management team of Amul could exactly tell you how many plants were working at full capacity how many trucks are engaged and in which areas and most Importantly it could also tell you when and how many trucks or plants are at idle capacity so that you can direct the workload to them to make optimum utilization of every element of the Supply chain. And this system turned out to be a game-changer for Amul during the lockdown because while on one side the supply chain of milk was overloaded the ice-cream and frozen foods vertical of the business was almost shut down. Therefore, the laborers, storage, and trucks were lying at idle capacity from the end of ice cream and frozen foods. But thanks to IBM's system, Sodhi Sir and the team were able to accurately oversee the entire operation of the supply chain. And they very conveniently diverted all the idle resources from the ice-cream and frozen foods vertical to the milk supply chain. And all of this process is said to have happened overnight. And this end-to-end digitalization made the process so efficient and gave them so much clarity about their operations that Amul was even able to provide incentives for the ground Staff. The casual workers were given 100-125 rupees cash incentives and for the workers, even food and stay arrangements were made so that they don't get sick and they don't get affected by COVID. And when they realized that the cattle feed was not

Sufficient Amul even made extra arrangements for cattle feed for Farmers. And all of this made the supply chain of Amul so efficient and effective that while the rest of the dairy industry was completely shut down Amul tapped onto their market share and procured 3.5 million liters of extra milk every single Day and paid 800 crores extra to the rural milk producers of India. A fun fact over here is that Amul even used 3rd party e-commerce sites like Bigbasket, Dunzo, and Flipkart and even landed exclusive deals with Swiggy and Zomato to sell butter, milkshake, and paneer. And according to Sodhi Sir in May itself, they got more than 60,000 delivery orders through Zomato and they sold 3 crores worth of Amul products in more than 200 cities. This was the second pillar of their historic success, which Is the end-to-end digitalization of the entire supply chain and the incentivizing of the labor forces. With that, we move on to the last part which is something that you all must have already observed and that is the humungous investment of Amul into marketing. Now, people, during the months of COVID when other brands were cutting down on their advertisement Amul increased its ad volumes by 316% compared to 2019. And they were so aggressive with their campaign that the Amul Kool ad was viewed 10 times more than the Indian Premier League (IPL) itself. And when Doordarshan started re-broadcasting the epic shows like Ramayan and Mahabharat during lockdown Amul started running their old ads to resonate with the nostalgic mood of the audience, creating an even better impact. Now, the highlight over here is that although Amul was very keen on tapping into the marketing Opportunities and even made immunity-boosting products they never went overboard with any kind of ridiculous COVID Claims unlike some other brands in our country. This is how using an extraordinary foresight of consumer Behaviour through an agile supply chain management system. using digital transformation, third party collaboration, incentivizing of labor, and strategic marketing initiatives Anand Milk Union Limited established a benchmark for crisis Management for dairy companies from all across the world to follow. And this brings me to the most important part of the chapter and that is what are the lessons that we need to learn to become extraordinary business leaders

Lesson number one, while good leaders prepare to face risk great leaders prepare to embrace risk with open arms. In this case, while most companies prepared to prevent their losses Sodhi Sir prepared Amul to operate at full capacity even during the pandemic one of the reasons was such a bold decision was the fact That he had already seen how his senior leaders kept the company Going despite the floods, despite the curfew and even during a war situation.

Lesson number two no matter how big your organization is resourcefulness is one attribute that will always save you during a crisis. The only question is how are you going to build such an agile system. In this case, it was Amul's futuristic investment of 80 crores into IBM's systems that helped them operate such a huge supply chain in such an optimized manner.

Lesson number three, And last and most importantly, every time there is a crisis of any kind, it could be a Pandemic it could be a crisis specific to your industry always remember during such a time that you can either choose to see it as an obstacle or you can choose to see it as a golden opportunity to get ahead of your competitors.

In this case, Sodhi Sir was so sharp that he realized that COVID-19 was the perfect opportunity for him to capitalize on the market on every single front. So, firstly he increased his market share and got the customers who were transitioning from loose milk to packaged milk. Secondly, all the farmers who were denied procurement from restaurants and other companies rushed to Amul, giving Amul 3.5 million liters of extra milk every single day. Hence, Amul was able to establish itself as a savior for farmers. And most importantly while the industry was ruthless in cutting down its frontline workers Amul provided the same workers with added incentives, Therefore, building a very strong relationship with its frontline Workers. This is how Amul became an opportunist during times of crisis and established a benchmark for brands all across the world to learn from.

V

Asian Paints

Asian Paints is one of the greatest companies in the history of India. And the most astounding thing about this company is that it is the only company to have grown at a CAGR of 20% since the past 60 years. And if you invested just one lakh rupees in Asian paints in 2000 today at Rs 3000 per share, your wealth would be worth at least Rs 1.87 crores, and that too without dividends. The business of Asian Paints literally doubles every three years and it has been a market leader in the industry not for five years, not for 10 years, but for the past 54 years. And if you draw a comparison of Asian paints with its competition in Tickertape, you will see that well Berger stands at a revenue of Rs 6869 crores, Nerolac has a revenue of Rs 5793 crores their combined total is Rs 12,662 crores, but Asian Paints alone generated revenue of Rs 22,044 crores. Similarly, Berger generated a profit of Rs 719 crores, Nerolac stands at Rs 529 crores their combined profit is Rs 12,049 crores but Asian Paints alone generated a profit of Rs 3139 crores.The question is how did Asian Paints become such a dominating force in the paint industry? What exactly is their secret sauce that enabled them to be a market leader for 54 years? And most importantly, what are the business lessons that we need to learn from the greatest paint company India has ever seen? Before we dive into this lengthy case study, The story of Asian Paints dates back to the volatile times of 1942, India. And this is something that you might already know that during that time, India was still under the British raj, World War Two was still going on and the government had temporarily banned the imports of paints in India. During those days the paint industry in India had a few foreign companies and Indian players like Shalimar paints were the major players in the market. But this ban resulted into a brilliant opportunity for domestic production and spotting this opportunity. Mr.Champaklal Choksey and three of his friends set up Asian Paints in Mumbai in 1942. And one of the most amazing traits of this gentleman was that he was an incredible market researcher and he spent a lot of time understanding the paint industry. This is when he understood that there were two segments in the paint industry. One was the industrial segment and the other was the decorative paint segment. In the industrial segment, it was a b2b space that is all about supplying paint to giant factories and plants. Whereas the decorative segment was a b2c as in a business to consumer space wherein you could sell paint to the common man to paint his house. Long story short, initially, the large distributors rejected Mr.Choksey so he turned to the villages wherein people painted the horns of the bulls and the South Indians painted the entrance of their house considering it to be auspicious. Looking at this demand, Mr.Choksey started supplying to the village distributors, the demand soon enough short up, and within some time, the bigger distributor started approaching Asian Paints.

And in the next 10 years with this rural to urban approach, they hit revenue of Rs 23 crores by 1952. Now the obvious thing over here is that they couldn't have become the biggest player just by selling paints for bull horns. Right? Then the question is how did Asian Paints become the biggest player in the market? Well, this is where the second phase of Asian Paints growth started when Mr. Choksey noticed another huge gap in the market. During the 1950s Mr.Choksey saw that there were two major products in the market. One was a basic dried distemper that was extremely cheap, but it had a tendency to peel off. It used to stick to the clothes and it used to stink very badly. The second product was the plastic emulsion product that was free from all of these problems but was five times costlier than tried distemper.Therefore, it was unaffordable for the common man. So you know what guys, Asian Paints came up with a game-changing product called the washable distemper that was placed exactly between dry distemper and plastic emulsions. Now, this was a revolutionary product because it has the qualities of plastic emulsion, but it was way cheaper than the emulsion product. And this product was marketed using a very successful marketing campaign which said,"Don't lose your temper, use tractor distemper." And guess what, within no time, washable distemper was a massive hit in the market, and the company started taking giant leaps. Although the firm was not very profitable during the 1950s, from 1952 to 1962, the revenues grew at a compound annual growth rate of 21%, with margins rising from just 2% to

13% by 1962. And by 1967, that is 25 years after the company started, Asian Paints became the largest paint company in India. And the most astounding thing is that even today,that is even after 54 years, Asian Paints is still the largest paint company in the Indian market.

Now, this begs the question, in this volatile and uncertain market with such a vast customer base spread across an extremely diverse country like India, how is it even possible that not a single company could challenge the position of Asian Paints? Well, the answer to that lies in three critical aspects of the Asian Paints organization. The first is a world-class supply chain that they've built over the past 60 years.And the Foundation came way back in the 1960s. During that time, large multinational corporations used to offer at least 180 days of credit period to their distribution channel and this included the shopkeepers, the dealers, the distributors, who supplied paints to the retail customers.This channel allowed the distributors to expand the credit period even as long as one full year. For example, let's say you are a paint company, and I am the shopkeeper and you gave me Rs 60,000 worth of paints that I am supposed to sell at Rs 80,000. So, I can take up to six months to sell the paint and then pay you back Rs 60,000. And this means that for you Rs 60,000 of capital is stuck and cannot be used. Now, if the same thing happens with 1000 distributors across the country, that is Rs 6 crore worth of capital of yours that will be stuck. This money cannot be used to buy raw materials. And for the next cycle, you will need another Rs 6 crores, which means that you need an exorbitant amount of working capital to even survive in the market. This is the reason why the smaller players found it very difficult to enter the market. So the entry barrier was very very high.But the one practice that was prevalent and even today it is still prevalent in any credit system is that even if the shopkeepers have sold Rs 60,000 worth of paints, then they have got 180 days to pay back, no one really bothers to pay back. And even if they did, they used to pay using post-dated checks. Now the Asian Paints team understood this very clearly. So they came out with something called 'The Regular Payment Performance Discount' wherein the regular payback was incentivized. For example, a shopkeeper would get a 3.5% extra discount if he made the payments within 30 days throughout the year. Similarly, if a dealer made payments in cash, they would get a 5% discount on his procurement price. Now, this was a very, very big deal because the paint industry by default operated at razor-thin margins at the dealer level. And these initiatives worked wonders because it was a win-win for both Asian paints and the dealers.Why? Because Asian

Paints was able to rotate its capital faster. So they were able to serve a larger network of distributors with very less working capital.And at the same time, the dealers were getting discounts and manage their working cycles better. Similarly, in the next 50 years, Asian Paints always remained a pioneer in supply chain management. In fact, Mr.Champaklal Choksey bought the first-ever supercomputer in India in 1970 for Rs 8 crore. And what blew my mind is that Asian Paints had a supercomputer 10 years before ISRO had it,10 years before IIT Powai had it and 21 years before any other company in India had it. And they use these mainframes to forecast demand by which they could run their supply chains at insane levels of efficiency.

They started branch billing on computers way back in the 1970s. And even started using GPS for tracking the movements of their trucks. And the result? Well, in 1980, the Bhandup plant used to operate with 1600 workers, but Ankhleshwar started production for the same capacity with only 250 workers. And by 1985, the same thing was done with less than 100 workers. So you see, in less than five years, they were able to improve their efficiency to such an extent that now they were able to operate at the same capacity with 1/16 of the workforce. All of this was done because of insanely superior technology. Secondly, from 1970s onwards, Asian Paints removed all middlemen like distributors and wholesalers from its distribution channel. And this meant that they were supposed to supply directly to the dealers and because of this today, Asian Paints the manufacturer reaches 70,000 paint dealers without any channel intermediation. Therefore, with only 3 to 5% average margin for the dealers, Asian Paints is able to keep 95 to 97% of the margins for itself. Meanwhile, the extraordinary levels of efficiency have taken Asian paints to such heights that even today with 125 depots in its supply chain, while Nerolac generates a revenue of Rs 40 crore per depot, Asian Paints generates revenue of Rs 100 crores per depot. Similarly, the revenue per factory for Nerolac is at Rs 700 crores, whereas Asian Paints stands way ahead at a revenue of Rs 1500 crores. This is the level at which Asian Paints operates. And this brings us to the second critical factor and that is a relationship with dealers. A classic example of the same was a distribution of something called tinting machines. For those who don't know, tinting machines are machines that could produce a large variety of shades using a small set of standard colors. For example, if you wanted saffron, the tinting machine will be able to mix red and yellow in appropriate quantities to give you the exact same saffron color that you're looking out for. So because of the usage of a tinting machine, you no longer had to store every single color bucket in your inventory. And today, you can produce 1000s of colors with tinting machines without going back to the manufacturer. Therefore, the very presence of these machines meant that the sales of the company would skyrocket. And what blew my mind is that today, while Nerolac and Berger together deploy 46,000 tinting machines through their dealer network, Asian Paints alone has 50,500 machines.

The question is, how is there such a stark difference between Asian paints and others? Well, that is not just because of the extensive network that Asian Paints has, but also because Asian Paints built a seamless system for the adoption of the tinting machines. Because back then the problem was that tinting machines were manufacturer-specific, they required significant space in the store and they were extremely costly. And while many paint companies asked the dealers to bear the heavy cost, Asian paints used to bear the initial investment, and then it would give the machine on a lease agreement to the dealers.This way, the dealers felt less burdened, and the company established a solid relationship with its dealers.Therefore, the entry barrier even for small players was almost eliminated.This is the reason why the network Asian Paints grew from just 15,000 dealers in 2001 to 52000 dealers in 2018 because even the smallest dealer in the market could afford to partner with Asian Paints. Furthermore, after some time, Asian Paints orchestrated a three-way agreement wherein banks funded the dealer and then the dealers repay the loan to the banks over time. This way, the investments were not reflected in the company's balance sheet and at the same time, financing was made easy for the dealers. And even today when I spoke to the few dealers in my circle, they told me that the Asian Paints portal is so amazing that their queries get answered usually within just 24 hours. And regardless of whatever problem the dealer faces, the company has an extensive customer support team to help them out with extreme care. And even in the tier four cities, if you order products in the evening, it will be delivered to you by noon without fail. And in tier-one cities, Asian Paints logistic system delivers goods two times a day, and in some cases, even four times every single day. Cherry on the cake is that Asian Paints has always gone beyond its call of duty to help its channel partners in case if they faced any unexpected problems.And as Jalaj Dani, an Asian Paints executive stated and I quote, "Dealers are a part of our family, if we find that they're affected due to unforeseen events like riots, floods, earthquakes, etc, we ensure that the best support is provided to them in every possible manner, including expanding the credit period, so as to help them get back on their feet."

This is a reason why ladies and gentlemen, Asian Paints has the largest number of dealers and an extensive network that is far, far superior than its competition. And the third critical factor is their incredible levels of consistency. Now, people, I don't know how many of you see this, but then in the past 50 years, the stakes of the founders have changed. And just like any other giant company, even AsianPaints had some conflicts within the company. But even then, they have been remarkably consistent with their adoption of technology. They've been recruiting the same grade of talent since the 1970s. And their marketing has constantly evolved with changing trends in the Indian culture. And last and most importantly, many companies fill theirboards with friends and cronies in order to pay lip service to the legal requirement that mandates that 50%of the board should comprise of independent directors.But Asian Paints is among the rare breed of companies whose boards are truly independent. Out of 14 directors, Asian Paints has seven independent directors who are credible individuals with extraordinary backgrounds, who always make sure that the company is always a notch ahead of its competition. And this brings me to the last part of the chapter and that is since the past 54 years Asian Paints has been a market leader that's fine. But today what is Asian Paints doing to stay ahead If it's competition in the next 50 years, to understand this, you will first have to look at the megatrend in the paint market. If you see the cost of labor involved in painting at a home has increased from just 10% of the project cost in 1980 to 65% of the project cost. This is because from 2006 to 2015, the labor costs in India have grown at a CAGR of 9% to 10%. Whereas the paint prices have increased at a mere 3% CAGR. So in the next 10 to 15 years, labor costs are expected to be around 90% of the overall paint project cost.

And when this happens, it will make more sense for you to buy paint from a store and paint a home yourself rather than employing painters and laborers. And once this happens two consumption patterns are likely to emerge. Number one, customers will be willing to pay for labor involvement only if there is service-oriented value addition, that can not be done without expertise. This is a reason why Asian Paint has already started trying several service-oriented models. They've been opening experience stores in Mumbai, Delhi, and Kolkata.They've opened color ideas stores, which provide color consultancy in mom and pop stores. They have home solutions painting service, which currently executes 20 to 25,000 projects a year. And then we have Royale Play that is high-end textured paints.And apart from that, they've even started laying the foundations into kitchenware, bathroom fitting, furniture, and even interior decoration. So to put that straight Asian Paints doesn't just want to paint your house, they want to build and sell everything that is inside your house. This is the first trend that is the evolution of a service-oriented industry in the paint market.

Secondly, the DIY model is expected to emerge. Currently, households do not adopt a DIY approach because of the lack of sophisticated tools, and number two, at 60% to 65% of the project cost, labor involvement is still affordable for many households. However, with sophisticated tools being introduced in the market, and with the labor cost shooting up to 90% of the project cost.both these factors are expected to change the trajectory of the paint industry.This is the reason why Asian Paints is now venturing into building user-friendly DIY tools in order to empower ordinary people like you and me to be able to paint our house. This is what Asian Paints is doing to prepare for the future. So if this is very, very clear to you, let's talk about the lessons from the case study. Lesson number one, no matter how big the players in the industry are, if you want to become successful, it is absolutely important to identify the gaps in the market. Lesson number two, and this is something we've seen even in the case of Toyota and Ford, that efficiency is one of the most powerful yet the most underrated aspect of a business. And in the race of scaling up, companies often overlook the inefficiencies in their system.A classic example of the same was Ford and even Gillette.Whereas on the other side, they've got companies like Asian paints, who deploy incentives in the form of regular payment discounts and invest heavily into the next-gen technology like a supercomputer to reach unthinkable levels of efficiency.

Lesson number three, while on one side, we've got companies that treat their employees as objects and exploit them in the name of efficiency, on the other side, we've got Asian Paints that goes beyond its call of duty to make financing easy for dealers, to give them extended credit period during slack time, to resolve their queries with utmost care within 24 hours, and most importantly, to go out of the way to help them out during a calamity saving them from an unimaginable amount of pain and suffering. And lastly, while good brands have a legendary leader, a great brand has a legendary culture. In this case, it was the impeccable board of directors of Asian paints, the star recruits from IIM, and the wise marketers of Asian paints, who have kept the legacy of the company not for five, not for 10 but for 70 consecutive years. If this isn't an epitome of greatness, I don't know what is. That's all from my side for today, guys.For your study materials, I'm attaching the links to them in the description.And please read this book called 'The Unusual Billionaires' because I found some fascinating insights about Asian Paints in this book.

VI

BharathPe

Everybody in the past five years we have seen a dozen players jump into the digital payments market and bharatpay in spite of being a newbie in the crowded wallet market has already reached a 2.8 billion dollar valuation in just three years of its launch and within this short span of its existence it's already serving more than 7.5 million merchants in more than 140 cities and claims to process over 110 million upi transactions per month but at the same time if you look at the other side of it according to end tracker while the operating revenue of the company went from 0 to 5.96 crores the losses of the company shot up by 839 percent going from 23 crores to 216.32 crores and for 521 their cash burn is already at 2.6 million dollars per month that's close to 19 crore rupees a month so the question is in spite of such scary figures why is bharathi considered among the top five fintech firms in the country what is their business model how on earth can barcpay become profitable in the presence of giant competitors like paytm phone pay and google pay and most importantly as investors and students of business what are the key pointers that you need to keep an eye on to understand bharatpay and the evolving fintech space of india this is a story that dates back to 2016 when the payment renaissance of india began due to demonetization and as we all saw 86 percent of india's cash was declared invalid overnight but all thanks to internet and mobile penetration paytm came as a saviour and helped us transfer money even to the smallest vendor through a qr code and as usual with such a huge untapped market several other payment gateways started offering cashback to onboard as many merchants and customers as possible but while most of us very easily became the adopters of this digital payment system behind the scenes an iit delhi student named shashwad nakhani noticed three critical problems in the system number one since each payment app needed a different qr code when you went to a kirana store at the time of making the payment it would turn out that the shopkeeper only had paytm while we had migrated to google pay or phone pay so obviously the shopkeeper would then insist that we make the payment in cash and this defeated the entire purpose of going cashless number two while payment apps charged zero percent fee on transactions for customers like you and me for merchants there was not a single wallet that was taking less than 1.5 in commissions as in if you bought groceries worth 500 rupees the profit of the vendor itself is just 50 to 75 rupees and in that also 1.5 percent of the purchase value which is 7.5 rupees used to go to the payment gateways as commissions and if you speak to your local grocery wallet they'll tell you how terrible their condition was back then and lastly the awareness of upi system which was practically free was very very less and that's when it struck him that there has to be some way of leveraging upi to remove all charges on payments this is when ladies and gentlemen on 20th of march 2018 mr nakrani and his co-founder mr ashnir grover launched bharate with a vision to revolutionize the payment systems in india and the first thing that they did was that they leveraged ups star feature which was inter-operability so now a single qr code was enough to transfer funds from your bank account to my bank account without any hurdles of a closed ecosystem and the best part of this entire transaction was that it was free for both the merchants and users like you and me and another plus point for merchants was that while most wallets and payment gateways had a minimum 2 day settlement window

Through bharatpay they got their money credited on the same day itself as a result thousands of merchants adopted bharatpay in no time so the question is if this entire transaction was being done at free of cost then how did bharat pay make money well this is where the expertise of our shark mr Ashni grover came in, Mr Grover spent years in american express wherein he met more than 100 founders who were into the payment business this helped him understand the fintech space properly on top of that since he was the cfo of grofers. he understood the problems of the merchants more than anyone else and this experience gave him two critical insights number one the margins and retail were too low to burn a hole in the pockets of the merchants with commissions, so the right way to make money was definitely not commissions number two he understood that although shopkeepers won't pay for the service they would be more than happy to pay interest on loans why because one major major problem with indian banking is that despite micro small and medium enterprises being such an indispensable pillar to our economic growth no private bank wants to lend them money due to either lack of documents or collateral and it's quite understandable because lending wouldn't make sense if there is no instrument to measure the risk of actually lending money to an individual so in spite of all these merchants having healthy balance sheets in spite of they having an incremental increase in their growth. Unfortunately very few banks wanted to lend them money and guess what this unmet credit gap of micro small and medium enterprises is one trillion dollars in india this is a reason why bharatpay tabbed on this golden opportunity to start a merchant lending system and they entered the lending space by partnering with non-banking financial companies this target segment included 65 million msmes in india that employ close to 80 million people now the question over here is that if banks couldn't lend to small merchants what was so special about bharatpay that they could tap onto this golden opportunity and more importantly how do they intend to become profitable well this is where bharatpay's artificial intelligence algorithm comes in and here's an oversimplified explanation to understand how it works just like our credit card companies nota spending pattern every time we make a payment .

Every time you make a payment at a store through the qr code the bharatpay algorithm takes note of the cash inflow at the merchant's end similarly when a merchant pays his supplies through bharatpay the algorithm keeps note of her monthly inventory value and it also notes a spending pattern and several other parameters to estimate the projected savings income consistency of income and so on and so forth and just like credit card companies look at your spending pattern to decide how credit worthy you are the algorithm of bharatpay uses this data to calculate the risk of lending to a particular merchant this way without paperwork the bharatpay algorithm can decide the credit worthiness of a merchant even if she is in the remote test corner of the country so this way all the progress that our kirana store makes is officially documented by the bharatpas algorithm and once enough data is collected tomorrow if the algorithm sees that mrs sheetal has a healthy net inflow of 3 lakh rupees per month and if she requests a loan of 10 000 rupees bharat pay will immediately process the loan without any paper or collateral similarly if a mr sunder has an inflow of 3 lakh rupees and request a loan of 3 lakh rupees since the risk is high bharate might charge a higher rate of interest as compared to mrs sheetal and once this lending procedure starts the algorithm gets smarter and smarter at risk assessment based on the merchant's loan history and credit score this is how maharate currently provides unsecured loans in the range of 10 000 rupees to 7 lakh rupees for up to 12 months and charges an interest of about 2 percent per month now one of the biggest problems with lending is the collection challenges and defaults so even if a company wants to scale its lending business through the lens and breadths of the country they need a tremendous amount of workforce for recovery but guess what , according to bharatpay its repayment rate is 96 which is among the best in the market so bharatpay is practically an option so the question is how did bharathpe achieve this incredible benchmark ?

well this is where their leverage with qr code comes in instead of requiring the merchant to pay monthly installments it deducts the amount from the transactions before the bank settlement for each day for example if the merchant has to pay back 15,000 rupees installment per month and he has an inflow of 4.5 lakh rupees per month he has an average inflow of 15,000 rupees per day so instead of asking for the payment at the end of the month before the app pays the merchant fifteen thousand rupees at the end of the day it by default subtracts five hundred rupees as daily installment and then pays fourteen thousand five rupees to the merchant at the end of the day this creates a win-win situation wherein the merchants are not burdened they don't need to be reminded about payments and at the same time bharathpe can ensure that its repayments happen without any problems this is how merchants pay back their loans in easy daily installments as small as 430 rupees per day average this is the reason why bharathi has an astonishing repayment rate of 96 and guess what as of october 2021 bharathi had already facilitated loans to over 3 lakh merchants and disbursed over 2 800 crores in loans as of october 2021 according to economic times bharati was processing loans worth 300 crores each month and today bharatpay loans are available in more than 11 000 pin codes in 24 states and has a sales force of 4000 agents to educate merchants on various financial products on top of that they have an insane retention rate with 45 of its merchants taking repeat loans and all of this is being done digitally in a hassle-free manner with no application fee and most importantly without a collateral therefore more merchants means more data more data processing means better risk assessment better risk assessment means less bad debt which means insane profitability this is a reason why bharatpe spending 2.5 million dollars a month to onboard as many merchants as possible this is how bharatpe is solving a major problem for the msmes of india using its insane artificial intelligence algorithm as a result they have witnessed a crazy growth of 10x in the last fiscal and now bharatpay aims to disburse loans worth 1 billion dollars among merchants and this brings me to the most important part of the chapter and that is considering the fact that bharatpay may soon go for an ipo what are the factors that you need to keep an eye on to decide whether or not to invest in bharatpay moving on to the pointers the first thing you need to study is the p2p lending service of bharathpe which is called the 12 person club.

VII

Boat

The boat is one of the most incredible brands in the Indian startup ecosystem and the most astonishing thing about this company is that within just five years they have achieved such a strong position in the market that if you look at the two true wireless stereo market as of q3 of 2021 where bolt stands at five point three percent noise stands at seven point seven percent realm stands at eight point one percent board stands way ahead with a market share of thirty-five points eight percent which is more than the next three competitors combined on top of that the revenue of the company has already crossed fifteen hundred crores in FY twenty-one and the profits have already shot up by sixty-one percent since FY twenty, now because the boat is now going for an IPO the question is how did boat achieve such an extraordinary position in the crowded hearable market of India? what exactly was their business strategy and as investors in students or business what are the business lessons that we need to learn from Mr. Aman Gupta and his wonderful team at the boat, one of the most important reasons for the boat's success is its genius market positioning and if you look at the rise of the boat it is very very similar to the rise of one plus phones in India now many of you must have seen that there was a time when the one plus brand was just one of the most functional underrated brands in India and it is only popular among tech enthusiasts but suddenly with the launch of one plus 7 the one plus tag became one of the most popular brands in India and you could see oneplus 7 phones everywhere in 2019. in fact at one point in 2019 oneplus was selling more phones than apple and samsung combined now the question is in spite of the phone market being so crowded with vivo oppo samsung huawei and apple how did oneplus become a legend the answer to this question lies in this pricing chart now if you look at the pricing of phones in india back in 2019 you will see that iphone was the costliest with the pricing of 85 000 rupees then we had samsung s10 priced at 55 000 rupees plus and then straight away we had oppo v1 other companies that were primarily focused on selling phones below 25 000 rupees now although they had costlier phones in india the focus of these companies was more on 25 000 rupees and below that price range now you see there is a huge gap that's left out between 25 000 rupees to 55 000 rupees which was only being addressed by samsung then as we all know samsung phones do not offer as much as a value for money as its counterparts and this audience was the most premium unaddressed and more importantly a large audience that was left untapped and here's where we saw the rise of two phones number one was xiaomi mi 9 and 31 000 rupees and one plus 7 that was priced at 35 000 rupees and both these phones positioned themselves exactly in between 25 to 55 000 rupees price range and they both had insane specs and offered way more value for money as compared to samsung phones now the question is why didn't mi become a market leader like oneplus well that is because oneplus built a crazy level of aspirational value for its brand because of getting endorsed by none other than robert downey jr himself now i don't know how many of you noted this but then in the exact same year the avengers end game hype was at its peak because when endgame was about to release in 2019 and everybody knows what an insane fan base robert downey jr has in india and this aspirational value is something where xiaomi lagged because of which oneplus won a huge market share in india in 2019.

Now i'm not saying that everyone bought one plus phones because of Robert Downey jr but the fact is that the aspirational value that Robert Downey jr's endorsement got to one plus got enough people to see one plus as a premium brand which it got enough people to buy the phone after that when people say that the tech was genuinely the best that you could find in that range it eventually led to positive word of mouth and hence oneplus 7 became one of the best selling phones in India in 2019. now if you own a one plus you must have also noticed that you considered buying an iPhone but when you saw the stupendous difference between the price of a one plus and an iPhone one plus by default looked like an obvious and the most comfortable choice of all, therefore, the one plus brand was able to build an aspirational value in the minds of the premium customers in India because of which it was able to beat Xiaomi and was able to tap into those users who were premium customers but could not buy an iPhone now the question over here is how is this related to boat and what does one plus position have to do with board well if you look closely after apple introduced the AirPods in 2016 three important things happened in the same year there was a sudden boost in the fascination of wireless earphones.

Number two the jio wave hit india in 2016 that led to the skyrocketing of the screen time of indians and most importantly many many phone manufacturers stopped shipping earphones along with their smartphones and if they did these earphones were the most basic versions in the market and all these three factors created a huge market for hearable in india so from 2017-18 onwards many many companies started jumping into the hearables market and if you look at the pricing charts of the most popular brands in 2018 this is what it looks like first we had the ultra premium wireless earphones category wherein we had bose and apple that had a base price of 17 000 and 15 000 respectively then in the premium category that is between 10 to 15k we had only jbl as a significant brand with its pod version being priced at 10 000 rupees then for sub premium that is between 5000 to 10 000 we had sennheiser's wireless earphones that started from 6400 rupees onwards and below this price point that is below 5000 there was no giant brand and yet there was a huge demand for wireless earphones in india and this is where we saw four brands come in mivi priced at three to four thousand rupees skull candy priced at two thousand rupees onwards we had both rockers at one triple nine and then we had noise shots priced at three triple nine and then we had several local brands including bolt that were priced at 999 rupees and below now the question over here is with these four competitive brands what was so special about boat that it is now market leader by such a huge margin well there are two specific reasons for that while skull candy was only popular among enthusiasts and a very limited segment of the audience the other brands like me and bolt were barely known in the market whereas boat had become far more popular because they had roped in hardik pandya in 2018 and this is where the power of celebrity endorsement comes in just like robert downey jr's endorsement brought in an aspirational value for one plus hardik pandey's endorsement by default built an aspirational value for boat as a brand as a result in the two to five thousand rupees category board became far more familiar than its counterparts now some people might say bro just because some celebrities endorsing why will we buy earphones we are smart enough to make a good choice without endorsements well you know what guys here are some basics of marketing for you a customer knowingly or unknowingly determines the value of a product based on two types of values tangible value and perceived value tangible value is the real value of the product as in if the audio sounds great in one earphone it has a great tangible value and perceived value as the name suggests is basically the judgment that you make based on how the product is portrayed for example if a restaurant looks like this you subconsciously assume that it has a clean kitchen and in our case the fact about audio devices especially earphones is that only trained yours as in only the people who are involved in video editing or sound editing can actually spot the intricate differences in audio whereas the knife ears will not be able to tell the difference in audio quality between two devices as a result you can barely spot the difference between two products as a result the entire audio market from the customer standpoint is practically commoditized and since there is no added tangible value to the product that you can spot the only value by which you will judge an audio product like your phone is by perceived value .

so if i place two earphones one of some random brand and the other that is being endorsed by hardik pandya you are more likely to trust the latter than the former even if you are not a diehard hardik pandya fan so the only delta that inclines you to purchase a product like your phone is the perceived value of the product now just to give you an idea about how super powerful this is here's some simple math merely because of celebrity endorsement if boat is able to charge an average premium of just 200 rupees extra per product here's what it looks like with 16.6 million tws units shipped this year and with boat having 35.8 market share board would have shipped close to 59 lakh units so if they got you to pay an average premium of 200 rupees per product due to celebrity endorsement boat has already made 118 crores extra in revenue fun fact is that the profit of the company in fy21 itself is 78.6 crores this is the power of building a perceived value in a crowded commoditized market this is the reason why boat obsessively focuses on presenting itself as a lifestyle brand to build an aspirational value for itself both with endorsements and design so after hardik pandya they also roped in risha panth shikhar dhavan bhumra and prithi shawn 2019 followed by neha kakar kiara advani and karthik aryan after that they also signed up shreya shair 2020. secondly boat also collaborated with celebrity designer mazhaba gupta to launch a limited edition collection of spunky headphones at the lakme fashion week 2020 and now they're also collaborating with beera which is again one of the most favorite millennial brands in india this is how just like oneplus was able to present itself as a far more premium product far more familiar product as compared to xiaomi mi 9 both through its collaborations has been able to build the same aspiration value to stand out from the rest of the crowd and we also know from the jockey case study how powerful this aspirational value building is and secondly one of the most underrated reasons for boat success was also the foundation they laid with an insane product called boat stone and these speakers are by far one of the best bluetooth portable speakers in the market and the reason why this is such a big deal is because both stone became popular without celebrity endorsements or any fancy marketing strategy during that time while jbl flip was priced at four thousand nine ninety nine rupees boat was priced at just two thousand rupees and to my knife years both sounded as good as jbl.

This is the reason why boat is standing tall in spite of powerful players like real me and oneplus in the market and even today at the entry level in the earphones market boat is still priced at a bare minimum of 299 rupees because of which a student is more likely to buy a boat and when he loves it three years later after he graduates when his purchase power increases he is more likely to buy a boat product whereas in case of oneplus the cost barrier itself is very very high and now after laying a solid foundation of positioning itself as a lifestyle brand boat is slowly expanding its price range to position itself in the upper range of four to five thousand rupees and secondly it is also getting into smart watch segment which is again a huge market to be tapped into and you know what's very very interesting to note is that just like boat created an aspirational valley for hearables after apple created a huge market for smart watches noise is now getting ambassadors like tapsi and rohit sharma and is even spending a ton of money in social media campaigns to build a spiritual value for its watches and this is boosting not just its watt sales but also the hearable sales because of which it is already the number two player in the market right next to boat so now the rivalry of noise and boat is something that's going to be very very interesting to watch this is how by building a quality product by choosing a wonderful time to enter the market by standing out from the rest of the competition through lifestyle marketing and through strategic collaborations aman gupta and team have turned both into a market leader in the hearable segment of the indian market , moving on to the lessons there are three very very important things that you need to learn from this case study lesson number, one whenever you launch a product in the crowded market always try to figure out how you are going to differentiate yourself in the presence of the big guns in this case if someone had told a man Gupta that dude there is JBL apple skull candy and so many other brands then what is so special about you then on the outside it almost looks like there is no room in the market but the moment you take a pen and paper and you start noting down their price labs you will very clearly be able to see that the 1000 rupees to five thousand rupees lab is empty and you could make your mark over there so my homework to you is taking a pen and paper and do thorough market research of the smartwatches market and you tell me how noise and boat have a solid chance of building a 1000 crore business despite the presence of giants like titan Fitbit Samsung and apple.

lesson number two celebrity endorsements although look like a cash drain in some cases even today could be a game-changer in a crowded commoditized market now considering this factor I've got one question for you me we had ambassadors like Carrie and bb endorsing their product right boat went with Hardik Pandya karthikaryan and the rest.

VIII
BSNL

Since the past 1.5 years we've been hearing the news about the government's plans to shut down bsnl and ever since we started following the news we've always seen bsnl as a loss incurring company which incurred thousands of crews of losses every single year in fact in the past 10 years itself bsnl has incurred a combined loss of more than 80 000 crores and considering the case of air india and government bureaucracy in general we by default assume that bsnl is also one of those ill-run businesses that the government just cannot handle isn't it well guess what in fy 21 while the market went crazy to see that reliance jio generated a profit of 12 000 537 crores very few of us know that there was a time when bsnl generated a profit of 10 000 183 crores and that too in a single year and from 2001 to 2008 bsnl generated a cumulative profit of 46 668 crores which was more than the next three telecom operators combined and that too in spite of all the subsidized schemes that it rolled out for rural areas and for farmers and not just that it once had a market share of 70 and literally acted as the backbone of the indian telecommunication industry so the question is what exactly went wrong with bsnl that it suddenly went from being a dwell of india to a sick company in less than a decade was it yet another government mishandling or was it deliberately paralyzed by the private sector and most importantly as citizens of india what are the lessons that we need to learn from the tragic downfall of bsnl. To understand the fall of bsnl we first have to understand why is it critical for a nation like india to mandatorily have government companies operating in certain sectors even though they incur heavy losses well in this case there are three important reasons that very few people understand the first reason why a government company is essential is for accessibility you see if a company like airtel wants to serve a particular region then the most important factor is going to consider is profits so if there are only 100 farmers living in a particular village with only 10 of them who can offer to pay for airtel then for airtel setting up a tower spending a ton of capital and human resource does not make any sense at all because eventually it will incur losses but if you look at it from the common standpoint while for ltl they are just customers for the government of india they are citizens of the country who need to be taken care of who need to be uplifted so they can eventually go on to contribute to the economy of the country why because only when they have access to basic facilities like telephone electricity and water can they actually become resourceful to the economy of india in fact many of you must have even heard about something called the krishi sim card that offers dirt cheap internet and calling to farmers and this is also the reason why even today you will see that bsl's network is available even in the remotest parts of our country whereas your idea jio and airtel do not work in those regions especially a region like ladakh and this brings me to the second reason and that is regulation which means tomorrow if jio and airtel join hands to become a do a pulley they might start increasing the price of their data and now that internet has become super important to us even if these companies double the charges of the internet we will have to pay them anyways but in this case if a company like bsnl exists it will by default give out service at a nominal rate that way the people who cannot afford a jio or airtel will always have a company like bsnl to fall back on and lastly in case of a natural calamity like that of uttarakhand or even a wartime situation again while airtel and jio might not consider it their agenda to set up towers bsnl is obligated to set up their infrastructure at the earliest because it is not a question of profits but a question of citizen safety and in case of a war scenario it is a question about national security itself now although this could be done with strict regulation on private players it is always safer to have an in-house organization for these critical requirements these are the reasons why even if bsnl bleeds hundreds of crows of losses it is very very important to keep the company alive but in case of bsnl let alone losses the company was a market leader with 10 000 crores in profits and it was only after 2008 that bsnl suddenly started incurring losses so the question is how this is a story that dates back to early 2000s during this time landlines were the primary mode of communication and during this time bsl occupied nearly 70 to the market and with evolving tag bsnl also started laying the foundations for 2g internet connections at the remotest corners of the country whereas other private players found it commercially unviable to do that during that time and in spite of reaching the unviable locations bsnl managed to earn such hefty profits that they posted profits of 5976 crores 10 0183 crores and 8939 crores during 2003, 2004 and 2005. until this time the company was operating almost like an autonomous body with very less scrutiny from the government committees but this is when a news brokered about the telecom minister of india the central bureau of investigation interrogated former telecom minister diana de in the illegal telephone exchange case on wednesday maran who was the indian telecom minister between 2004 and 2007 of using his influence in colluding with senior officials of the state-run bsnl to draw 323 high-speed lines to his residence well it is alleged that the exchange was set up to upload signals of channels of the sun tv network a multi-lingual television empire owned by kalani maran long story short according to the cbi Dayanithi maran used his official position and got private telephone exchanges installed at his residence these 700 high speed lines were used for business transactions of the sun network which was owned by his brother kalani this case was a very very big deal not because of the laws but because fraud and ministry and government and keeping huge phone systems off record is also a national security risk this was where the government started getting involved in bsnl's matters and this is where a man named a raja took over the reigns from maran in 2007.

During this time BSNL was in discussion about rolling out something called the wimax technology this was a telecommunication technology that was aimed at providing wireless data over long distances basically wireless broadband this would have helped bsnl roll out speedy internet connections all across the country but guess what this is where one of the biggest scams in indian history came to light which was the 2g scam three days before parliament resumes the decade's biggest scam has triggered a political war parliament said to resume in three days the report is likely to trigger yet another political battle the jpc has put the blame squarely on then telecom minister a raja claiming he misled the prime minister on procedures followed now when this happened although it did not affect bsnl directly it was very evident that a lot of frauds might be taking place within the company so after 2007 onwards the garment started inquiring every small tender that bsnl ruled out this is where the company started to slow down starting from its tender system now for those who don't know about the tender system here's a very simple explanation to understand the same the way the system works is that let's say the government wants to build a bridge so what will it do, it will roll out a tender inviting all the construction companies in the country by stating all the requirements of building that particular bridge then multiple companies will come together and they will start presenting their plans and cost of building the bridge then after these proposals are submitted the government will check what is the background of the company, which one of these companies has actually completed similar projects in the past, what is a methodology of execution and most importantly what is the cost and time of execution of the project and based on these parameters the company is given the contract by the government to execute the project in this case instead of a bridge it was about laying down the communication technology like wimax to enable wireless broadband all across the country but this is where the setback started coming after the marant incident and the 2g scam the government started digging for corrupt practices that could have happened in the tender system and not so surprisingly according to economic times a string of shell companies and dubious companies were being shortlisted and at the same time several reputed companies with proven track record of offering wimax services were disqualified in the first round itself these companies included soma networks and cisco back telecom and even unwire india and the moment these type of news started coming out CBI got into the case and soon enough according to some employees BSNL was not allowed to procure equipments and materials and orders were delayed and cancelled and the entire company started to slow down according to economic times during this three year period that is between 2007 to 2010 while indian telecom industry was growing at the fastest pace in history while every other private player was aggressively scaling up their infrastructure and were pouring in crores of rupees into accreditation BSNL was not able to place any significant orders for equipment so practically with each passing day BSNL was losing its market share to private sectors and while the company was at the brink of sinking into losses in 2008, 2009 somehow a new ray of hope came up in 2009 a project worth 10 billion dollars was taken up by BSNL to lay down 93 million gsm lines all across the country and this could have enabled BSNL to provide top-grade voice and data facilities all across the country and had this project gone through it seemed like bsnl would have been the undisputed king of telecom in india and this project at that time was the world's largest telecom contract but guess what in 2010 the central vigilance commission started suspecting irregularities and again when dig deeper they pointed out that the disqualification of important vendors like nokia, zte and alcatel had left only two players in the bid which were ericsson and huawei and since they were the only contenders left BSNL could not get the best price as there was no competition with the contract at all and because of this irregularity, again the entire 10 billion dollar tender was cancelled and BSNL was asked to start all over again and while BSNL was still cluelessly trying to issue tenders they had run out of mobile network capacity in most regions of the country and during the exact same time airtel, vodafone, idea and other players started to rule out 3g services and eventually started eating into BSNL's market share as a result during this time from 2007 to 2010 the profits of the company started sliding from 3009 crores in 2007 to a loss of 1822 crores in 2010 and guess what due to this stalling according to the employees of BSNL from 2006 to 2012 during the most important growth period of indian telecom BSNL made very few to none significant purchases into development of its infrastructure.

This was the first and perhaps the most important reason for BSNL's downfall which was power hungry greedy ministers who wanted to fill their pockets at the cost of a national asset and here's where things started getting worse as the mobile revolution picked up BSNL's most important source of revenue that is landline phones started to go obsolete the number of landline phone users had dropped from 24 million in 2016 to just 19 million in july 2020 and here's where the second blow came up when jio wave emerged in 2016. the world is at the beginning of a digital revolution so ladies and gentlemen today i have great pleasure in announcing a revolutionary concept for the indian market all voice calls for jio customers will be absolutely free reliance jio has become the largest telecom operator in india adding 5.6 million mobile subscribers in november now while most people think free data and calling was the sole reason for jio's growth very few people understand that it was actually a massive advantage that 4g as a technology gave to jio both in terms of cost and service the question is how now let's take an oversimplified case to understand how 4g is different from 2g or 3g if yash and i are talking to each other in the early 2000s the process would look something like this when i press the call button on my phone a digital signal is sent from the antenna on my mobile phone to the nearest cell tower from there the signal is transmitted to a switching center now my switching center contacts other centers in the complex network to identify the center closest to yash and once yes switching center is identified and notified it sends a signal to the cell tower that is nearest to yash which then transmits it to his phone and his phone starts ringing and when answered the connection is established through a complex underground network this path is called circuit and this process is called circuit switching now for data the case was a little different here a different communication method called packet switching was used in this method if you are sending an email your entire email is broken down into multiple packets wherein each package could be containing a single word or sometimes even a single letter but with this data the address of the receiver is also mentioned then once the email is grouped in packets these packets are routed through a huge network wherein each packet might take a different route and sometimes they might even go all across the world so by breaking the communication information down to small packets it allows the same path to be shared among multiple users in the network now in case of both 2g and 3g both voice network and data network had to be maintained separately but this is where jio came up with the revolution and the advantage that jio had over any other telecom player was that it was a purely 4g network so while others had to run one network each for voice and data jio had to maintain only one network for data because even their calls were routed through the data network this paradigm shift and approach lowered the cost of equipment by a very very large extent as a result it lowered the operating cost for the 4g network and in comparison to jio our poor bsnl did not even get the approval for 4g and was using decade old and energy inefficient equipments and occupied a large real estate footprint, this drastically short of their cost while jio was using the same margin of cash to acquire millions of customers with each passing year and finally it was only in 2019 that BSNL got the spectrum allocated and now they are moving to 4g and BSNL is yet to start with 4g rollout in 2022 and lastly because of the cash crunch human resource management of BSNL started to shake. So this is how a golden goose of the Indian economy was paralyzed to go from around 10,000 crores in annual profits to a loss of 15,500 crores in 2019-2020. The first thing you need to understand is that while businesses function to profit from the customers, government companies function for national duty and economic upliftment of its citizens so don't ever blindly compare them with other companies and say that government companies suck.

IX

BurgerKing

Burger King is one of the most successful food chains in the world. In its 70 years of existence, Burger King has gone from being a modest Burger Outlet to becoming the second-largest fast-food chain in the world, with more than 17000 Outlets all across the world. And even during the pandemic, It has been extremely profitable with a profit of 823 million dollars. But while most of us are familiar with the glorified success of Burger King, very few of us know that In 2009, the brand image of Burger King was in deep deep trouble. While on the one side, McDonald's was expanding rapidly capturing every inch of the market. On the other side, Burger King was in a mess. They had changed 13 CEOs In just three decades. The stores were shutting down rapidly. The shares had dropped by 18% and profit had fallen by 10% to just 44 million dollars. But something magical happened in 2010 when an investment firm called 3G Capital took over the company and appointed one of the youngest CEOs in fast-food history, who went by the name Daniel Schwartz. Back then, Daniel was only 32 years old. And the weirdest thing was that he did not have any experience in the restaurant business. He spent most of the time in core Finance, but as usual, while most of the industry experts undermined his capabilities, This guy did such an incredible job that when the same Burger King went public again in 2012, in just 18 months, the stock price shot up by 100%. The question is, how did such a young man with no experience in the restaurant business achieve something so extraordinary? What exactly was his business strategy? And most importantly, as future Business Leaders, what are the lessons that we need to learn from this incredible Businessman?

The first thing that Daniel did was something that no ordinary CEO would ever do. And that is, scrubbing the floors and cleaning the toilets. Yes, You heard that right? When Daniel took over the leadership of the company, Since he had no experience in the restaurant business, He decided to get down to the ground and walk with the Burger King employees to try and understand what exactly was the fundamental problem with the operation. And this involved doing everything from making burgers to cleaning the toilets. And in this wonderful process, Daniel learned that there were four fundamental problems with the operation of every Burger King Outlet. Number one, the menu was extremely cluttered with a lot of options that confused the customers. And despite having so many options, no signature dish was popular enough to attract loyal customers. Number two, although Burgers as an individual product were a very good value addition to the menu when the employees were making these burgers, the kitchen got cluttered. As a result, there were a lot of sauces and a lot of ingredients. Eventually, this reduced both the efficiency and the accuracy of making burgers. Thirdly, this inefficiency increased the wait times, and it gave the drive-thru customers a terrible experience. Now, this was a very, very big deal because you see the drive-thru customers contributed to more than 60 percent of the revenue for both McDonald's and Burger King. And from the consumer standpoint, if the order gets delayed by an average of just one minute three terrible things happen. Number one, the customer who's fifth in line has to wait for 5 extra minutes in hunger, which is a terrible time to annoy anyone. Number two, during peak times, when the cars get lined up at the store, If another customer wants to eat at the Burger King store, He will skip and move on to the next Outlet merely by looking at the long line. As a result, The number of burgers sold decreased by a large extent at every single Outlet. And last and most importantly, in the race of having a diverse menu, despite all the inefficiency, very few products on the menu were high-profit margin products. Therefore, when these inefficient practices were repeated for a million orders all across the United States, it cost Burger King millions of dollars in profits. So you know what? Daniel Schwartz took a bold step and decided to eliminate a dozen items from the menu. And he presented only Whopper as the signature dish of Burger King. And since then, starting from the marketing campaigns, all the way up to the menu, even the Instagram post, Whopper has always been presented as the signature dish of Burger King. This is the reason why, if I asked you to name two other burgers that Burger King sells other than the Whooper, you will have a hard time remembering them despite making countless visits to the Burger King store. Now this seemingly simple move, brought along an insane amount of benefits for the Burger King brand. Number one, out of the 2.4 billion hamburgers that were sold, 2.1 billion of them, that is, more than 87 % of the burgers that were sold at Burger King were just Whoppers. Secondly, because 87% of the orders were of the same Burger, there were very less sauces and very less ingredients. As a result, There was no confusion inside the stores.

This skyrocketed the efficiency and brought down the wait times to a large extent. Apart from that, the supply chain inventory also became extremely lean and extremely efficient. And last and most importantly, the most amazing thing about the Whooper is that it is a high-margin product. Now, although Burger King doesn't reveal how much profit it makes with every Whopper, It is said to be around 50 to 80%. And just like that, when such a high degree of efficiency and profit margins were repeated for millions of orders throughout the United States, it started to give out millions of dollars in profits. This is the primary reason why Burger King became an extremely successful brand after 2010. But Daniel Schwartz did not stop there. He further went deeper into the cause and found out every little cause the company was incurring, starting with the office supplies to the executive travel. That is when he found out that there were already two years of office supply, and there was a lot of unnecessary spending that needed to be cut down. So he started cutting down on things as small as pen and paper also. Apart from that, He made a bold statement and sold the corporate Jet and asked the executives to use Skype to do the meetings. And even by a modest calculation, they estimated saving was at least 5321 dollars per online meeting. That's 3.9 lakhs per meeting. And after this groundwork was done, one final thing needed to be fixed and that was the marketing of the Burger King brand. But at the outset, no company, especially after becoming as efficient as Burger King would ever think twice before shooting up their marketing budget, right? After all, marketing is one of the greatest investments a company can make. But in the case of Burger King, they wanted to achieve external visibility and at the same time, spent very less on marketing. Now, this looks impossible, right? Well, guess what? Burger King deployed a marketing strategy that was based on a fundamental attribute of human psychology and that is, conflict breeds attention In simple words, the reason why Big Boss is a hit is that conflict breeds attention. The reason why serials are a hit is that conflict breeds attention. And the reason why news anchors bully their guests during prime time is that conflict breeds attention. So you know what? Burger King purposefully started trolling and calling out their rival McDonald's in the social media posts and the Billboards inviting a conflict. And soon enough, McDonald's started to respond.

As a result, The conflict started breeding attention. And not so surprisingly, hundreds of blogs started reporting about the marketing war that was happening between Burger King and McDonald's. And people like you and me started retweeting their ads. And a large chunk of the customer base even participated in the campaign like the burn the ad campaign and this participation of the customers indicated the extraordinary impact of this marketing campaign. This is how Burger King gets billions of dollars worth of publicity through organic blogs, International media, and social media Impressions. And the best part is they only have to spend a fraction of their marketing budget to create the conflict. And then, the attention that the conflict breeds eventually leads to the Snowball Effect, creating billions of Impressions on social media, and giving Burger King the publicity that it never paid for. These are the reasons why Burger King today is not just one of the fastest-growing chains in the world, but also one of the most profitable food chains in the world. Now this brings me to the meat of the matter and that are the lessons from the case study and there are three important pointers that we need to learn.

Number one, great leaders never shy away from getting their hands dirty, and they will go to any extent to understand their business to understand their company better. In this case, It was the humility and audacity of Daniel Schwartz to go and do the menial jobs at the store despite being the CEO.

Lesson Number two, micro causes and micro inefficiencies are more often than not, the heaviest expenses that go unnoticed, and they often lead to a chain of expenses and inefficiencies that will drag your business down without even you knowing it. So always try to keep the processes lean and the cost low, no matter how big your company is. For this, If you are at a sea-level position or the management level, I would highly recommend you to do a quarterly review of the micro expenses at your company. And when you are done calculating, show it to your employees and tell them how important it is to spend cautiously.

And lastly, conflict is a marketing superpower that breeds attention. So as consumers make sure that you don't become a spectator of someone else's stupid conflict. And from the business standpoint, you need to study why a big boss is the work of a genius.

Chik

The FMCG market is by far one of the most competitive markets in the world. The margins are thin, the supply chain is complex and customer retention is very very challenging. So much so that even after pouring in crores of rupees many companies often incur losses and even quit the market altogether. This is why for decades, this industry has always had only a handful of players who can afford to pour in crores of rupees just to start a venture. But you know what, an ordinary middle-class Indian came out with a simple but brilliant idea that ended up changing the dynamics of the entire FMCG market. And this idea gave rise to what is now about to become a billion-dollar company. And not just that the concept of this idea is now being applied by billion-dollar companies like Coca-Cola and Procter & Gamble also. The question is- What is so amazing about this idea that it redefined a billion-dollar industry? And more importantly, how can you apply this concept in your business. This story dates back to late 1980s India. Back then India was a fairly underdeveloped country and if you ask your parents, they would tell you that back then even shampoos and perfumes were considered to be luxury products. And as far as brands were concerned most brands didn't even bother to cater to the needs of the lower-middle-class people because every brand had a certain segment of the audience below which they could not do viable business. Now just to give you a better understanding of the same, if you were to draw a pictorial representation of the purchase power or affordability of the audience. For any product, it would look like a pyramid. A very simple example of the same is the mobile phone market. On top of the pyramid, you've got this bunch of people who can afford iPhones and ultra-premium Samsung phones. And then below that, you've got people who buy OnePlus phones. followed by people who buy Oppo & Vivo. And on the lower end, you've got Jio phones and Nokia phone buyers. and these are the products that will cost you between ?1000-?3000. And below this price point of, say, ?1000 you won't find any reputed company manufacturing phones. Because for any mobile manufacturer, it isn't viable to make a phone and sell it at a profitable margin below ?1000. And this segment of the audience, that is, the lowest strata of the customer base is what you call the bottom of the pyramid. Similarly, if you look at the shampoo market in the 1980s it looked something like this. On top, you had these luxury brands, the imported brands. And after them, the only strong contenders were Sunsilk and Clinic Plus which only catered to the needs of the upper segment of the pyramid. And the least you could find was a 100 ml shampoo bottle that would cost you ?40. Now the point to be noted over here is that we are talking about a time wherein even the salaries of white-collar employees were in the range of ?1000-?3000 per month.

And for them, a shampoo bottle of ?40 was a very big deal. But the shampoo companies didn't even bother to sell to the rest of the population because they believed that they couldn't do viable business. And that is when the hero of our story, Mr. Chinni Krishnan had an idea. He was an ordinary middle-class person with an extraordinary inventor's mindset. And he had this philosophy that everything that a rich person can afford should be accessible and affordable to a poor person also. So one fine day he observed that the pricing of a 100 ml shampoo bottle was ?40 and in one bottle you could wash your hair about 20 times considering 5 ml per wash. So essentially, the cost of one wash was ?2. So practically speaking, a rich person paid ?2 per wash and that is when he thought that this ?2 price is something that even a lower-middle-class person can afford. It's just that he can't afford to pay for the entire bottle at once. So why not divide the same bottle of shampoo into small segments and make it affordable for the lower-middle-class people. And that is how ladies and gentlemen, the idea of sachets came into existence. Now, Chinni Krishnan Sir did this not just for shampoos but for many other products like salt and talcum powder also. Initially, the idea was not very successful but his son C.K. Ranganathan took it forward and formed a company called CavinKare. And he did a thorough market survey and found out that rural families wouldn't spend more than ?2 per month on sachets with an estimate that a customer would wash his/her hair once a week. So they launched 50 paise sachets in Tamil Nadu in

1983.

And in just one year they ended up selling 10 lakh sachets. Fast forward to today, CavinKare which started with only ?15,000 of capital is now an 1100 crore empire. But the story doesn't end here. The idea of sachets gave the FMCG market 3 incredible superpowers and these are practical techniques that even you can use for your startups. Number one, tomorrow if a company wants to launch a new product or a new flavor of shampoo, it does not have to spend exorbitantly to manufacture millions of 100 ml bottles and then wait for the customer's reaction. Now, they could just spend a fraction of that money to make sachets and they could give it away for free as complementary products and see if the customers come back to buy more. The second superpower that this idea gave was through upsells. For example, if you see the Head & Shoulders sachet it will cost you about ?4 for an 8.5 ml pack which is about 47p/ml But at the same time if you buy a 180 ml bottle it will cost you ?150 which is about 83p/ml. If you see, that is about a 36% increase in profit from sachet to a bottle. And when you factor in millions of bottles that are being sold that's a million-dollar profit. So this is how brands first sell smaller packets and once they gain the trust of the customers they increase the margins on bigger packs which translates into a million-dollar profit. And third and most importantly, the concept of the bottle of the pyramid is today being used by multiple brands to penetrate both, into the lower strata of society and to make their products more affordable for a larger segment of the audience. A classic example of the same is a ?20 bottles of Coca-Cola. Now, if you take a step back you'd observe that since the time the ?20 bottles came out you hardly ever bought the 600 ml version of Coca-Cola. And that is because the quantity is perfect to suffice your need and it is also super affordable.

Today, Procter & Gamble comes out with smaller versions of its products. and nearly every product, starting from soaps to talcum powder comes in mini versions which state the incredible power of this simple idea. And here's where all of us need to understand that regardless of how big the players are in a particular industry ideas as simple as sachets can also bring about a revolution because they make a product-market viable. And these kinds of ideas open up gateways of business opportunities that even the big players never even bother to look into. And that is where you as an entrepreneur could find your pot of gold. At the end of the day always remember, that the greatest ideas are born not because someone has a billion dollars or some rich connections but because while the world is busy in its hustle and bustle someone cares to pause to observe the little things in our life that we all take for granted. And this gives rise to an idea that changes the world forever.

XI
Coco-Cola

Coke is nothing but sugared water and a lot of sugar is not good for your body, so do not consume Coke in excessive quantities it's bad for health; everybody knows about it. But have you ever wondered, despite this brand merely selling sugared water how is it that they can generate billion-dollar profits every single year? And not just that. Coca-Cola is a company that has survived for more than 111 years which includes 7 revolutions and 2 World Wars. The question is How is it possible that a company selling sugared water could make a billion dollars despite having competitors which are much tastier than Coca-Cola and much healthier than Coca-Cola. And a simple example of that is the lemonade business in India. The answer to that is that Coca-Cola deploys a genius marketing strategy because of which Coca-Cola can make a billion dollars in profits merely by selling sugared water. So if you're here to learn something incredible Let's do a deep dive and try to understand one of the greatest marketing strategies ever known to mankind and that is Coca-Cola. In 2005, there was a scientist called Reed Montague conducted a very simple experiment to try and understand exactly the difference between Coca-Cola and Pepsi and which one was more preferred by people. So he conducted this simple experiment with 3 iterations. In the first iteration, he placed two bottles one of Coke and the other of Pepsi and he took off the label so that people couldn't identify on the outside which one is Coke and which one is Pepsi. So, when he called the subjects to come and taste both the colas he scanned their brains through an fMRI scanner. And the first iteration was when people came and tasted both the colas from the bottles which were not labelled.

They were not even able to identify the difference between both the colas. And the fMRI scanner also did not show any difference in the reading. So he sends them back and calls them in for a second iteration This time, he puts the labels back on so that people can identify which one is Coke and which one is Pepsi. This time when the subjects come and taste Pepsi nothing happens. But the moment they tasted Coca-Cola, the fMRI scanner showed a significant difference in the reading. That's when Reed Montague thought, 'Maybe there's something to the recipe. So let's send them back and call them in for a third iteration.' This time he swapped the logos, which meant that the bottle that contained Coca-Cola was now labelled as Pepsi and the bottle that contained Pepsi was now labelled as Coca-Cola. This time when the subjects came and tasted the cola from the Pepsi labelled bottle nothing happened But the moment they tasted the cola from the Coca-Cola labelled bottle the fMRI scanner showed the same significant difference in the reading. And that is when Reed Montague understood that it's not the cola, it's not the bottle, it's not the subjects it is just the flash of the red colour logo of Coca-Cola that made that significant difference in the reading. Now, to put that straight people in front of the scenes it's just the 3-second logo flash that made a significant difference in the reading and altered the very perception of people whereas behind the scenes it justifies the billion-dollar budget that Coca-Cola takes out every single year to establish itself as the brand icon of happiness.

Now, people, the question is what do we exactly mean by a brand icon of happiness. So for that let's try to understand the fundamentals of marketing. So every product, people, has two kinds of values The first value is the Tangible value which is the real value of the product and the second value is the perceived value. Now, just to give you a simple example of the same take, for example, a restaurant. Now, when you go to a restaurant the aroma, the room freshener, the ambience, and the lighting are what are going to make up for the perceived value of the product. It is going to enhance your perception of the experience the tangible value of the product is how well the food is cooked So if I serve you rotten chicken in the best restaurant in the world you're still not going to like it, right? Because the true value of the product is nothing but the product of the tangible value and the perceived value. So even if one of them is bad the value of the product goes down. Similarly, if I were to serve you the best food in the world but I put dead cockroaches around the table you're still going to feel disgusted, right? Now, the question is you still have the best food on the table and the cockroaches are not even inside the food. Why do you still not like experience? And the answer to that is even though the tangible value of the product is great the perception of the product has been degraded to such an extent that the experience is completely ruined. So every company needs to make sure that it can build great products hence bringing up the tangible value of the product and it has to make sure that the marketing strategies are so well designed that they can enhance the perception of the product in the minds of the people. Now, when it comes to Coca-Cola, the tangible value of the product is sugar and by default, scientifically speaking sugar is bound to give you pleasure whereas when it comes to the perception of the product Coca-Cola does an extraordinary job by associating itself with the emotion of happiness. Now a classic example of the association with emotion can be seen when Coca-Cola penetrated the Indian population using its remarkable marketing strategy. So to put that straight, when Coca-Cola came to India they were facing a hard time because they did not know what type of commercial to bring in which is going to resonate with the entire country because we are such a beautifully complex country that when you go from one state to other the tradition changes, the culture changes, the language changes lifestyle also changes. So, how does a brand come out with a commercial which is going to resonate with the entire country?

And that is when after doing deep research they found this beautiful recipe for something called the game of cricket. Because Coca-Cola, after doing deep market research, understood that in India, regardless of your religion, caste, race, or sex in the game of cricket everybody is an Indian and everybody is going to cheer, "Sachin! Sachin!" And guess what they hired Sachin Tendulkar as their brand ambassador and came out with a beautiful campaign called "Coke ki Khushi, Cricket ki Khushi" they came out with a bunch of commercials which portrayed the true essence of the game of cricket and this is what the commercial looks like. If you look closely at that commercial, it is not even talking about the product until the last 3 seconds because you know that while good brands sell you products, legendary brands sell you emotion and that is the secret behind Coca-Cola's genius marketing strategy. So, to put that straight, there are a few lessons that you need to learn as an entrepreneur if you want to do the same for your product. Number one, like I said while good brands sell you their product legendary brands will always try and sell you an emotion. Number two, it is okay if you don't talk about specifications. All you have to do is tell a great story. And if you do that you're going to resonate with your customers more than anybody else. Number three and most importantly even if you're selling sugared water, you could still make a billion dollars.

XII
Dell

Dell and ibm are two of the most iconic companies in the computer revolution of the world and while most of us see them as just another computer company very few of us know that dell and ibm were involved in an iconic business war that changed the computer industry forever while on one side there was ibm with a revenue of 4 billion dollars way back in 1984 itself on the other side at the same time dell was a baby company that was founded by a 19 year old kid with just one thousand dollars in investment but in the next 14 years something extraordinary happened and you know what in just the first half of 1998 dell reported operating earnings that were greater than the personal computer earnings of compaq gateway hp and ibm combined and by 2001 dell also became the largest computer manufacturer in the world the question is how did a 19 year old kid end up beating a giant like ibm what was so special about this business strategy and most importantly what are the lessons that we need to learn from the iconic case study of michael dell , this is a story that dates back to late 1970s during this time personal computers were relatively alien to the american society but by 1981 small startups like apple and radioshack started recording a decent amount of sales in the market this is when ibm being a pioneer in the computer industry decided to tap into the market and launched its first personal computer in 1981 and just two years later it was already dominating the market with a 42 market share with a world-renowned corporate sales force and service organization ibm even commanded 61 of the market for mainframe computers and produced many of the components for its mainframes but while launching a pc however ibm purchased many of its confidence from outside the organization it bought the operating system from a startup called microsoft and adopted the microprocessor architecture designed by a company called intel and in the next two years ibm used its huge sales force to sell personal computers to large corporate accounts soon enough the computer market started catching fire in the b2b space and since ibm sales people had very strong relationship with the industry ibm was undoubtedly the first choice to buy computers in the business to business space and then to serve small businesses and customers ibm built a robust supply chain to reach every nook and corner of america this was executed through a network of distributors and dealers who were known as value-added resellers these resellers not only sold pcs to the customers but also guided them through the purchase of what was still an unfamiliar product to the society this way ibm had established a full-fledged widely accessible supply chain to sell its personal computers now the catch over here was that the market of personal computers was growing so rapidly that if you look at the charts from 1982 to 1984 the computer market almost tripled in just two years to 12.8 billion dollars from just 4.5 billion and by 1988 it was already a 20.6 billion dollars market and because of such an explosion of a new fund product in the market even ibm was not able to cater the demand of pcs this is the reason why soon enough other companies began to offer something called ibm clones this is where compact came in and it entered the market with a low priced portable clone in 1982 and merely by capitalizing on a small gap compact made 100 million dollars in revenue in the very first year itself this is how rapidly the computer market was growing and one of the many many clones of the market was none other than a baby company called dell computer corporation which was incorporated in 1984 and just like ibm all the makers of ibm clones built the same supply chain of going through resellers and retail stores to reach the customers but you know what guys dell was no ordinary clone and like i said before within the next 14 years dell beat every single player in the market to become the most profitable computer company in the industry.

Now the question is with so many competitors and giants like ibm and compaq in the industry out of nowhere how the hell did dell become a market leader well this is where michael dell's business acumen comes into play michael was a curious and opportunistic boy whose first computer was the apple ii and the first thing he did when he got the computer home was to open it up and see how the computer was made back then the architecture of computer was fairly simple but very few people were actually educated about computers soon enough dell started reading and became proficient enough to take an ibm pc dismantle it and started buying parts to enhance pcs like more memory disk drives bigger monitors and even faster modems within some time he even started selling it at a profit and started placing bulk orders with distributors to reduce the cost and to increase the profits and people look at the passion that this guy had way back in 1982 barely in the age of 17 this guy skipped school to visit the national computer conference to understand the computer industry properly this was an eye-opening experience for him when he got the macro picture of the entire computer industry including the latest tech in the market and the sales prices of different components in the market and that is when michael dell found three market indicators that presented a game-changing opportunity for dell computers the first thing he found were the anomalies in the sales and markup of the machines he saw that an ibm pc was typically sold in store for three thousand dollars but the components could be purchased for just six hundred to seven hundred dollars and the best part was that the technology was not even owned by ibm secondly the resellers were operating in the computer stores didn't even know much about personal computers in fact they had previously sold stereos and cars and just happened to sell computers because it was apparently the next big thing so the dealers used to pay 2 000 for an ibm pc and sold it at three thousand dollars making a crazy profit of one thousand dollars per machine on top of that they offered little to no support to the customer and yet they were making tons of money because people really wanted to buy computers at that point michael was already buying the exact same components that were used in these machines to upgrade his computers and that is when he realized that he could directly compete with the computer stores not just on the basis of price but also on the basis of quality and third and most importantly ibm was selling a six hundred dollar machine at three thousand dollars not because it wanted to make hefty profits but because a major chunk of this money actually went to the resellers and the retailers and that is how based on these market insights michael dell built a revolutionary supply chain that changed the computer industry forever this model was called the dell's direct model to tell you about it here's how the phase one of the direct model worked out like we saw before ibm and ibm clones were selling their computers through resellers so they couldn't bring their price of the computers below two thousand dollars but michael dell knew the cost of all the parts and the perfect vendors to buy them from and he already had customers whom he could sell it to so he literally assembled the computer for six hundred to seven hundred dollars and seemed to have sold it within a bracket of one thousand to two thousand dollars which was impossible for ibm or others to reach and because of this huge price difference the world starts spreading out and within some time even business people attorneys and doctors from that area started buying from tel by this time michael realized that he was ready to get into this business full time so on 2nd of january 1984 he officially incorporated the company with pcs limited and rented a small place hired a few people to assemble the pcs and within a few months they were already selling 50 to 80 000 a month of upgraded pcs and add-on components now the question is michael was selling 50k worth of pcs that was fine but ibm was a national player right and they were using resellers to reach the lens and breadths of the country then the question is without e-commerce without resellers how did michael dell sell to the entire country of america well this is where the second phase of dell's direct model comes in and again just like the previous phase it was based on some very deep market insights that very few people paid attention to number one dell noticed that as the computer market started growing rapidly ibm was again not even close to meeting the demand in addition the distribution of these pcs had led to a tremendous imbalance in the demand and supply for example a dealer would order 100 computers and would receive only 10 so the next time to get what he wanted he would order 1000 pcs and he would get 633 but during that time he would have needed only 100 pcs and because of this massive mismatch of inventory and supply the resellers would often end up paying just for the excess inventory as a result they started selling these extra pcs at a dirt cheap cost and this is what then became to be known as the ibm gray market so you know what dell purchased all these computers that dirt cheap cost upgraded them and started selling them again in the market secondly the chipset technology became accessible and affordable enough to enable smaller players like dell to make their own computers and lastly in the race of meeting the exceeding demand ibm and compact were engaged in selling to the masses so much that they started moving far away from their customer disability as in they used to make computers that they thought were best suited for the customers and they just expected the sales to pick up and since the market was so huge the sales actually picked up but michael understood that this would result into a deviation from what the customers actually desired and most importantly it left a huge untapped market for customized computers that would be needed both for businesses and individuals and based on these three insights michael dell began the second phase of the dell corporation that turned dell computers into the largest manufacturer of pcs in the world with over 1 billion dollars in sales and they deployed the following strategies to achieve it number one instead of going by conventional challenge for sellers they set up a highly talented sales team that could cater to the exact needs of different types of customers they set up two types of teams for that the first team would cater to the business to business segment and the second team would cater to the ordinary customers and in the business segment the sales staff were specifically hired based on who had a background of the client's domain for example one department was an expert in dealing with federal and state government the other was a specialist in dealing with educational institutions and the other was specialized in dealing with hospitals and so on and so forth this way the sales staff didn't have to keep beating on the bush trying to understand the intricacies of eight different industries and they could quickly and accurately solve the queries of the customers to complete the sale on top of that the sales team was compulsorily asked to set up their own computers with the exact specification that they needed now although many people did not like it it gave them a real sense of what an uneducated customers would go through while setting up his system this is the reason why dell's sales team was one of the best performing sales teams in the industry secondly when the sales team started directly talking to the customers from different domains they started collecting important inputs based on which the engineering team used to work on to make the perfect pcs that could fit the requirements of different clients and this was applicable both for custom clients and mass customers thirdly they deployed the iconic just-in-time system to minimize the inventory and maximize cash flow and profits for those who don't know while most companies often stock up thousands of pcs and move it out of the inventory as soon as the sale happens in the just in time system the pc starts getting manufactured only when the customer places the order this way the inventory cost is minimized and the overall cost of production comes down because of which there is less wastage and maximum profits and if you want to know more about it in depth go to our chapter on toyota's just in time model and lastly no matter what happened because ibm was considered to be gold standards dell always tried to beat ibm with every single product just to make a name in the market as a result not so surprisingly dell started to build a supply chain that was a revolution in the computer industry and here are the numbers that blew my mind while ibm and dare started with more or less the same days of supply and inventory at 30 to 40 days because of the just-in-time system the days of supply and deals inventory started dropping drastically going from 35 days in 1994 all the way down to just about five days in 1998 and during the same time compact was still at 34.2 days ibm was at 49.4 days and hp stood at 70 long days of inventory this is the reason why by 1998 the retail on invested capital of dell was absolutely crazy while ibm had a return on invested capital of 13 percent hp stood at 16 percent compact stood at 35 percent but dell was way ahead with a written on invested capital of 186 percent soon enough dell computers started winning performance awards they began receiving five star ratings for quality support and service and all the key magazines began recommending dell for the best value and highest performance as a result by december 1996 dell sales on web reached 1 million dollars a day and by may 2000 the company's online sales generated 40 million dollars in daily revenue which is about 50 percent of the total sales of the company this is how dell set a world-class benchmark for other computer companies to follow and beat the giants like ibm and compact to become the largest computer manufacturer in the world and this brings me to the most important part of the chapter and that are the lessons from the iconic case study of dell versus ibm there are three lessons that we need to learn from the iconic rivalry of dell and ibm lesson number one no matter how young you are no matter how small a player you are in your industry if you keep learning about your industry your chances of finding an opportunity will keep increasing with each passing attempt but most founders don't succeed because they don't obsess over learning about their industry but in our case michael dell in spite of being just 17 he had the audacity and curiosity to attend the computer conference to open his new apple ii computer to go and talk to the resellers and retailers and the insights that he gained through these interactions is what gave him the foundations to build his billion dollar business lesson number two if you want to make a name for yourself always try to compete with the best in the market in this case while ibm clones were just trying to eat the breadcrumbs of the market michael dell went after the 4 billion competition ibm itself and slowly and steadily he started raising his bar to beat his competition and lastly always keep reading about the emerging markets in your vicinity and keep a close eye on those markets that are growing so fast that in the biggest players cannot cater to the demand in today's world those markets are the creator economy the b2b software space the renewable energy space the ai application space and even the fintech space because these markets will give you a wider scope to fail and rise up in spite of you not being the best in the market.

XIII
D-Mart

DMart has been one of the most disruptive companies in the food retail industry of India. Ever since it went IPO in 2017, In just four years, the demand share price shot up by 580 percent going from just 616 rupees to more than 4200 rupees in 2021. And the most astonishing thing about DMart is that in its 19 years of existence, it had not closed a single store until the pandemic hit. And despite having giant competitors like future retail and reliance retail, its profits have skyrocketed by 1700% going from just 60 crores in 2012 to more than 1000 crores in 2021. And this begs the question, how did the mind become such a dominating force in the retail industry? How did they compete and beat the giants like reliance retail and future retail? And what are the lessons that we need to learn from a retail mastermind like Radhakishan Damani? The first and perhaps the most important element of demand growth is nothing but price, price, and price. And if you ever visited a demand store, you will not be seen that the store is not fancy. The items it sells are not fancy, nor is it located in a fancy location like a mall. And yet, our parents have gone out of the way just to shop at DMart, our moms would schedule all of their work just to make time to go to the market. And despite having a Kirana store right outside. If something is out of stock, they will tell you to note it down and we will go and buy it when we go to Dmart. Now, this extraordinary level of effort that they take is because DMart prices are always 6% to 15% lower than the MRP. The question is, how does this 6% to 15% discount make such a big difference? it would make sense if there is an 80%. discount at Zara's and then somebody is taking so many efforts. But why so many efforts for penny discounts like 6% to 15%? And now if I'm bringing a 15% DMart discount on groceries, you will see that the savings shoot up to 243 rupees, which means that merely by visiting the demanding store four times a month, a lower-middle-class family's savings could increase by 30%. And this is a big, big difference. This is a reason why DMart commands an extraordinary level of brand loyalty from the Indian middle-class consumers. Now this begs the question if DMart could offer such low prices, why couldn't the shopkeepers do so and what was so special about DMart's business strategy this is what brings me to the second part of the episode and that is deep discounting. Now if you watch the Walmart episode, you already know about deep discounting, but if you haven't done it yet, here's how this million-dollar strategy plays out. Let's take the example of one liter of ghee. Now Gowardhan ghee sells at an MSRP of 579 rupees per liter. So, if 1000 packets get sold for 579 rupees, each with a profit of 87 rupees assuming a 15% profit margin for the retailer, then the total profit is about 87,000 rupees, but if the same key is sold at 529 rupees, although the profit is only 37 rupees, due to the discount, the volume of the sales is expected to shoot up to 1500 packets giving a profit of 55,500 rupees. Now, although this might look like less profit, it has some incredible benefits that very few retailers understood back then. Number one, it results in more volume in sales, which means more people come to the store to buy ghee and since demand has a tonne of other products also, it is more likely that people will buy something else also along with the ghee and this is what we call as the product assortment strategy. Number two, the inventory starts moving at a flash speed. So if you're a retailer, like DMart, you will quickly sell your ghee and you will get fresh stock on the shelf. This means that there'll be no expired products, very less wastage and customers would love to buy from you because you only sell fresh stock most importantly, you as a retailer get a better bargaining power with your sellers if your inventory moves faster. For example, if other players buy 10,000 units, you can buy 20,000 units from your suppliers because of our accelerated sales volume. And using this bigger purchase order, you could ask the seller to reduce the price by another 10%, which would give you a 10% extra profit, even with the best prices in the market. Now for a small store, that's only a 10% increase in margin, but when DMart scaled it up while applying this technique, they became so powerful that they started dominating the sellers and started crushing the other retailers. For example, in the present day, if the wholesaler sells 2000 packets of ghee to a small retailer at 499 rupees with 200 rupees of profit, DMart will place an order for 20,000 units and it will ask the seller to sell it at 399 rupees. And because it's such huge purchase order, it gives the seller more profit at once. So they agree. Now normal retailers price their 499 rupees purchase at 579 rupees which are the MRP, DMart sells its products at 499 rupees, which means that the selling price of demand is lesser or equal to the cost price of the retailers making it impossible for them to compete with DMart. And hence, DMart makes a healthy profit of 100 rupees per unit despite offering the lowest prices in the market. This is a superpower of discounting. Now the question is whether DMart can beat all of its small retailers. That's great, but how is it competing against the giants like big bazaar and reliance retail? And this is what brings me to the third segment of the episode and that is DMart's competitive strategy against the giants. And this strategy could be described in just three words careful, nonfancy, and ownership. Now Mr. Damani has been extremely careful about the expansion of the DMart stores and you will see that despite being in the market for 19 years, they only have 220 stores, whereas the big bazaar has 284 stores, reliance retail has more than 11,000 stores, and even more retail has 645 stores across India. And the reason why DMart expands so slowly is that they take the time to understand its customers, build operational efficiencies, and form a solid relationship with its suppliers. This is the reason why until 2020, DMart had never closed a single store since its inception in 2002. And when they did recently, they have done that to use the store for their online win. Whereas if you look at its competitors, they have been on a seesaw ride opening and closing several stores across the country. Secondly, because DMart is very careful and usually certain about its profits, they follow the store ownership model, and this allows them to save a tonne of money on rental costs. Now although on the outside, it feels like buying and constructing a store is way more costly as compared to renting it. The numbers tell a different story. If you look at the 2017 numbers when future retail was at its peak, you will see that future retail spent around 8% on rentals, the hyper city spent 5%, and reliance spent 3.4%. But if you look at DMart, they spent only 0.2% of their total expenses on equivalent rent. Now, this is some next-level cost-cutting. And thirdly, these stores that you usually see are not located in a fancy location. They're mostly present in suburbs, in tier two and tier three cities where the cost of real estate is extremely low. And this is the reason why you will hardly see or perhaps never see a DMart store in a fancy mall. And this cost-cutting results in insane levels of profits. Now, just to give you an idea of this in 2016, which is just before the e-commerce wave, when future retail had revenue of 12,914 rupees per square foot, reliance retail was at 13,901. But if you look at DMart, DMart was way ahead with a revenue of 25,844 rupees per square foot. And not just that, even in terms of profitability, while future stood at 252 rupees per square foot. reliance was at 213 rupees per square foot, but DMart was at 965 rupees per square foot. This is the insane difference that is created due to the perfect combination of location, ownership, and deep discounting. Ultimately, all these factors together turn DMart into a dominating force in the Indian retail space. Now, this brings me to the most important part of the episode and that is the lessons from the case study and the important observations that you need to make before you invest in DMart or similar companies. Before we move on, Moving on to the lessons from the case study, there are two lessons and two observations that you need to make about DMart and similar companies. Number one, discounting is a superpower that turned DMart into a legend. But while most of us think that Mr. Damani was able to do it only because he was rich, we miss out on the fact that this concept of discounting came from the legend Sam Walton who was not even close to being a millionaire. So like Dhirubhai Ambani once said, ideas are nobody's monopoly. So if you can't do it alone, build a cooperative society, acquire capital and then do it. But the one thing that you should never do is shying away from ideas just because they look difficult. Number two, the Indian middle class is the most underrated customer segment in the market. And while most businesses focus on selling to the cash-rich audience, the disposable income of the middle class even today is a billion-dollar market that is just waiting to be tapped. Apart from that, I wanted to make these two observations in the Indian retail space. I'll attach both of these links in the description. So do check them out and study them intricately. Number one, if you compare the numbers of the retail players on the ticker tape, you will see some insane differences in the expenses and the revenue. And look at this guys, the revenue of Avenue which is the parent company of DMart is three times more than future retail. And yet, the operating cost of Avenue is 60% less as compared to the future. Number two, draw a comparison of two scenarios. Number one is before the eCommerce boom in 2016 and after the acceleration of e-commerce in 2021. For this, I'm going to attach a research report from HDFC which has an in-depth analysis of the retail market in India and over here what I want to highlight specifically is figure number 22 that you will find on page 10 if you see as compared to 2016, reliance retail grocery wing is catching up very quickly and it is almost equal to DMart today and this is because of reliance retail's online presence while on the other side. If you look at the rest of the competition, they're not even close. Now what remains to be seen is how is DMart ready going to tackle the likes of the big basket, reliance retail, and Groofers and both these documents are very good data points to start with to understand the retail space of India.

XIV
Dominoes

Domino's is one of the most incredible companies of the 21st century. While most of us know Dominoes only because of its 30 minutes of free delivery policy. Very few of us know that from 2010 to 2017 Domino's stock has performed so well that its stock price has gone up by 2000%. And it has outperformed even giant companies like Amazon, Apple, Netflix, and even Alphabet. And the best part is.... this meteoric stock rise was neither a bubble nor did a billionaire tweet about it. Instead, it was a result of one of the most strategic, calculative, and perhaps the boldest moves made in corporate history. The question is What exactly was this strategy and more importantly how can entrepreneurs like you and me apply this to our company. This is a story that dates back to 2009 when the brand image of Domino's was completely down the drain. The stock was selling at a rock bottom price of just $6 per share, the store sales were going down drastically and Domino's ranked last in the consumer brand preference survey. All of these things made it very very clear that Domino's was failing real bad. This is when the CEO of the company back then, Patrick Doyle decided to take a closer look at the situation and soon enough they found out that multiple blog posts were saying how bad their pizzas were; some of them said that the crust of the pizza tasted like cardboard while the others said that the sauce tasted like ketchup. And this was followed by a series of social media posts that consistently appeared online. Now, if you take a step back and try to understand the situation; the situation is very very delicate. The stock price of Domino's was already hitting a rock bottom, and the American economy was still recovering from the 2008 crisis during this time Domino's, as a publicly listed company, was already walking on a very very tightrope. Now in this case, what any normal company would do is they would engage in great PR they would make sure that all the bad reviews are overshadowed, and then, in the background they would make a few changes and maybe even give out free pizzas, just to get positive reviews. Or worst case, they would just ignore this altogether thinking that after all in 2009 what could a blog do to a billion-dollar company. But you know what? Domino's opted for the most lethal weapon in advertising that nobody ever dares to use, especially when the company is failing. And this weapon was brutal honesty. Patric Doyle, CEO of the company took full responsibility for what was happening and they publically admitted that they were not doing a good job. They called upon actually disappointed customers and got them to taste the pizzas to give them feedback. And it was perhaps the most difficult day at work because every person who walked in just put out some brutal phrases and told them how pathetic their pizzas were. But the team of Domino's listened to them very very patiently and took notes diligently. But what followed next was nothing short of an adventure.

For the next 18 months, every single chef of Domino's worked a day in and day out without taking a weekend off. just to try every possible combination of ingredients to make the best pizzas they possibly can. And they changed their pizzas from top to bottom. And in the process of experimentation, they also realized the fact that in the race to provide customers with 30 minutes delivery the company's supply chain itself was compromised. The majority of its ingredients were frozen, canned, and even pre-made just so that they could cut down on cost and make it easier to assemble a pizza in record time. So the chefs and the management got together and changed the entire supply chain of the company. Now, this was an extraordinary move because we are looking at a complete revamp of processing, inventory, storage, and transportation that is going to be executed to a chain of more than 4200 stores that are spread across 9.93 million square kilometers which is practically 3 times the size of India. But to everyone's surprise, they managed to pull it off within just 18 months. And guess what? On top of that they launched a campaign called the 'Oh yes we did' campaign. wherein they documented their entire journey of how they went from making terrible pizzas to making the best pizzas in the United States. There is also a very sweet video online wherein the head chefs of Domino's personally go to the houses of their harshest critics and they surprised them with their new pizza wherein they had incorporated all of their feedback and each one of these critics was mind blown that the head chef of Domino's himself had come down to deliver pizzas. They tasted the pizzas, they loved it and they were smiling and most of them couldn't even believe that such a huge company would take their feedback so seriously. Apart from this they also included a special section on the website wherein they posted Facebook posts and tweets of the customers who expressed their delight after having the new pizzas. This is how Domino's reinvented itself and did everything in its capacity to get back to making the best pizzas in the United States. And the results? Well, while the pizza delivery business itself saw a decline of 3% the same-store sales of Domino's increased by 14.3%. which is the largest quarterly increase in fast-food history. Domino's stock rose by 44% in just one month following the campaign. And by the end of the quarter, the stock had reached a 75% increase. The campaign has earned 2 billion free media impressions to date and the stock price just kept going and going for 7 years and rose by 2000%, outperforming Apple, Amazon, and Netflix. This is how Domino's set a benchmark for other brands to learn how to embrace criticism and how turn it into a business opportunity. Now, there are 3 very important lessons that we need to learn from this case study.

Lesson 1, customer criticism is a part of the business although sometimes there might be meaningless hate, as a business owner it is your responsibility to filter through the chaos and identify the weakness before it paralyzes your business. In this case, the CEO could have easily ignored the blogs but because he decided to fix it, Domino's still existing. Lesson 2 the cost of rectifying a mistake is always far less than paying the price for it when it's already too late. In this case, if Domino's had considered revamping the supply chain to be a million-dollar expense it would have cost them their entire business but because they saw it as a million-dollar investment it allowed them to rise from their ashes. And last and most importantly every brand needs to realize that the future of marketing is not about discounts and fancy packaging. Although they are important, at the end of the day the brand needs to connect with its customers at a personal level and thanks to social media it has become easier now than ever. The moment the customers realize that they are a part of your journey and the fact that their contribution matters you will go on to achieve an extraordinary level of brand loyalty which is by far the most powerful asset that you could possess as a brand. And the best way to establish this connection would be to tell a beautiful story. In this case, it was the 'Oh yes we did' campaign.

XV
Dream 11

Ever since the indian premier league has started the indian business ecosystem has been pouring in thousands of crores into sponsorships but while it's quite normal to see a company like pepsi or tata pour in hundreds of crows to sponsor the ipl in 2020 it was mind boggling to see that a 12 year old startup like dream 11 won the bid to sponsor the ipl for an astonishing 222 crores and since then dream 11 has become one of the fastest growing sports fantasy platforms in the country with more than 140 million users as of 2021 and guess what dream sports is now valued at 8 billion dollars and is now one of the rare consumer focus startups to actually post a profit as of 2020 there are profits to that 180.8 crores and the revenue has already crossed 2 000 crores the question is what is this dream level model how are they able to generate profits in spite of spending hundreds of crores into marketing and most importantly how did this company very very cleverly escape the garment regulation that could have banned it for being a gambling game moving on let's first try to understand how does the dream 11 model work let's say shubham wants to try his hand on dream 11 and now that it's the ipl season shubham is a chennai super kings fan and he's excited about the csk mi match so he selects the cskmi match and is given a hundred crore virtual ports to select his team of 11 members this purse is capped and is the same for everyone who's wanting to play on dream 11. now obviously the better the player the higher will be the amount that shubham has to pay to get the player into his team and this is where the strategy comes in in this case if mayan rising dhoni and rohit sharma both have a dream level price tag of 11.5 crore although shubham would want to have both of them in his team he wouldn't be able to do so because he would be left with very little money to purchase other players another catch we hear is that shubham although a csk fan can not pick all the 11 players from csk at max he can pick 6 members from csk and a minimum of 5 meaning he will either have to select 5 or 6 players from mumbai also now please note this very very carefully because it's very important for the discussion ahead so coming back the teams have to be logged in before the start of the game the toss is where shubham would actually get to know the playing 11 and he would quickly make the changes to his team bases on who is in and who has been benched now shubham enters his team into contests these contests are a pool of different people who enter the contest with different permutation and combinations of the 22 available players this contest starts from as low as 10 rupees but could go all the way up to thousands of rupees now let's say shubham who's a little skeptical enters the contest with an entry fee of 50 rupees and just like shubham there will be thousands of players who will enter the contest now dream 11 basically acts as an organizer for these contests such that all of these players are categorized on the basis of the amount and the participants then play the game so there'll be a 50 rupees contest a thousand rupees contest and so on and so forth for 50 rupees let's say the number of participants is 3 lakh and only the top 50 of the participants get a payout and for this there's a sliding scale of payouts from rank 1 to rank 1.5 lakh so the first ranker gets the highest amount and from there onwards the amount keeps descending and whether shubham ends up in the top 50 or not depends on how well the players he chose actually played in the match and eventually the number of points this team makes decides how much money shubham will make these point systems are pre-set by dream 11 so you get a different point for a catch a different point for a weekend a different point for the number of runs your player scores and you can see all of these in real time along with your ranking and from there onwards you have nothing in your control all you can do is just wait and hope that your players play well this is how based on the choice of players some dream 11 members will lose while some will win if this is very very clear to you let's try to understand how do these fantasy sports companies like dream 11 actually make money the answer to this is pretty simple roughly 20 percent of the total amount collected for a contest goes to dream level as commissions so if the entry fee for a contest is 50 rupees and 3 lakh people enter the contest then the total money collected amounts to 1.5 crores out of which 20 percent is usually dream 11's cut so in this case if 1.5 crore is collected 30 lakhs by default is dream levin's cut and the rest of the amount that's 1.2 crores is disbursed to the winners as payouts so when you as a user enter various contests you make money in some you lose money in some and regardless of whether you make money or not dream 11 always walks away with a hefty profit now the question over here is isn't this just like gambling i mean even over here users select a particular player and they do that because they hope that the players will play well and when they do these players actually win and just like in betting while the money of the players placing the bet is left to chance the bet organizer wins by default so if it so obviously looks like gambling to us and considering the fact that betting is banned in most of the states in india how is this company operating all across the country and that too being a sponsor to the biggest sports events in india the answer to this lies in a rajasthan high court case when a man named chandra shankara filed a complaint with the rajasthan high court and he stated that the public is being defrauded in the name of dream 11 and that it amounts to gambling and betting and should not be allowed in india but guess what the rajasthan high court dismissed the petition by relying on the judgments of the punjab haryana and bombay high court the high court observed while dismissing the petition and stated and i quote it can be safely deduced that the result of the fantasy games is not determined merely by chance or accident the skill of the participant determines the result of the game and has a predominant influence on the outcome of the fantasy game this is what the court said in fact this was even taken to supreme court and the outcome was no different the petitioners contended that fantasy sports companies like dream 11 are pure gambling and not games of skill now in order to understand this argument we first have to decide on the definition of gambling gambling is often defined as betting gaming or participating in an activity that will be a game of luck and not the sport of skill to win a much bigger amount of money or any other prize by wagering some amount of money now for dream 11 the defense was that it takes analytical skills strategy and historic knowledge about the players before picking them and putting them in a team together it's not mere chance and it's not done knowing the outcome of the game and here's where the feature that we discussed earlier comes into play you see guys when you're playing on dream 11 you aren't betting on one team alone the 11 players that you select will be in a 5 6 combination meaning you've got five players from one team and you have to pick six players from the other team or vice versa and the argument over here is that with the knowledge of the player's past performance and on the basis of the record in certain games a judgment is supposedly made by the players of dream 11 like chris gayle usually gets out very quickly in the finals or dhoni plays insanely well at chennai so by observing these kind of records it's argued that the players of dream 11 are using their skill and knowledge to end up on the winning side and with this in consideration the rajasthan high court observed that and i quote whether any particular team in the real world match wins or loses is also a material as the selection of the virtual team by the participant involves choosing players from both teams playing in the real world and that's exactly what the supreme court also stated this is how the case was closed and dream 11 was legally safe but the problem was that from the marketing standpoint the damage had already been done despite the judgment going in their favor it was still perceived to be a gambling game as soon as this news broke out in fact google play store doesn't even host dream 11 on their platform and you might have downloaded the app through an apk from the dream level website this is because the play store has strict guidelines on the apps that indulge in gambling directly or indirectly so now the question is how did dream 11 fix this dent to their reputation very very simple they robed in the legend mind raising dhoni himself and when dhoni endorses a particular brand we all know what is the effect of it along with that dream 11 also launched a campaign with the tagline kelo di marxe very evidently highlighting the need for strategic thinking this is how dream 11 got back into the game and along with dream 11 many such sports fantasy companies have jumped into the cricketing craze to make as much money as possible and the dream sports 8 billion valuation makes it quite obvious as to where this industry is heading now the question is should you play dream 11 or not well people if you ask me here's my two cents i don't know if dream 11 is a game of skill or a game of chance but what i know for sure is that the amount of time and money that you're pouring into dream 11 if the same thing is channelized towards acquiring a skill it is bound to give you way more returns and the probability of getting return increases and the same thing is what i say about network marketing also there is no question about whether that is a scam or not the only point is when there are far better ways to make more money and that too more calculatively why do you need a network marketing scheme or a dream 11 like app to make money and if you're just doing it for thrill then that's completely your call and just like what i say for crypto only put in as much money as you can offer to lose so tomorrow if you put in thousand rupees and you lose it it should no way affect your life or your family's life if that is clear then it is pretty much okay to play dream 11 but if you ask me i would always go for a skill than going for a fantasy sports app.

XVI
Gillette

Gillette is one of the most revolutionary companies of the 20th century. It is one of those very few companies that have survived for more than 120 years which includes more than 7 revolutions and 2 World Wars. But what is more fascinating about Gillette is not the growth of the company, but the fact that Gillette gave the world a billion-dollar idea. And this idea laid the foundations of success for some of the biggest ventures on the planet which include PlayStation, Xbox, Kodak, and even Amazon Kindle The question is - What exactly is this strategy? and how did a razor company go on to inspire legendary products like PlayStation and Xbox? And more importantly, how can you apply this strategy to your startups. The answer to this question lies in the history of the Gillette company which dates back to the late 1800s This was the time wherein the trend of dense beards was fading away and the trend of clean shave mustache look was on the rise. But back then shaving was not an easy task it was even considered to be a dangerous undertaking In the late 1800s if you wanted to shave you had only 2 options. The first option was a straight razor and the second option was a safety razor The straight razor are the ones that looked very similar to the ones you might have seen in Game of Thrones. And they were considered to be very risky because they were super sharp and people were kinda scared to get them too close to their face or their neck. On the other hand, the safety razor was like a one-time purchase but once you bought it you had to frequently keep sharpening it and that was a very very tedious procedure. So, the men of the 19th century had to seek professional help and they visited the barbershop 2-3 times every single week One fine day, a traveling salesman was getting late to work and he got extremely fed up with using his life-threatening razor. And he had completely lost his patience to keep sharpening the safety blade every time he wanted to shave. That's when he thought, why not have a razor with a detachable, disposable blade that can just be thrown away after every shave and can be replaced by a new one. And that is how the ideation of the modern-day razor blade happened. This angry, pissed off salesman was none other than Mr. King Gillete himself and his vision gave birth to the revolutionary invention of disposable blades which then went on to change men's grooming forever King Gillette collaborated with his friend and got a patent for their razors and their blades, which is why nobody in the market could mimic their iconic design. And that is how for the next 15 years Gillette remained a market leader and became a million-dollar company But you know what? Things started to change in 1921 and this is when the patents of the Gillette razor blade expired within just one year every single Gillette competitor was making a similar pair of a razor blades and this put Gillette into deep deep trouble this was reflected in their sales numbers also From 1921 onwards, the sales of Gillette razors saw a massive decline of 20% in just one year, which is like a crazy downfall for a company that had been a market leader for more than a decade. Now, here's where they needed to do something magical to save the company from failing. And that is when they came out with a pricing model called the Razor Blade model this model went on to change the very dynamics of the razor business forever. This model was based on a very simple philosophy wherein they said, 'Let's sell the razors at an ultra-cheap price with low margins and then sell blades at a higher margin. So that, when the customer keeps buying the blades we can have a recurring profit from each customer' Basically, in one line it meant, "Give them the razors and make them come back for blades" So Gillette started selling razors at an ultra-cheap rate to compete with the competition and sometimes they even sold it at a loss, just so that they can get people into the "Gillette Ecosystem". And guess what? Within a year the sales of Gillette razors shot up and after 1922 when the razor blade strategy was fully implemented, the sales of Gillette razors skyrocketed by a humongous 127%. I repeat, Gillette went from seeing a 20% decline in its sales to seeing a massive increase of 127% in just one year because of the execution of the Razor Blade strategy that is how Gillette established a legacy in pricing, and today, even after 100 years, it still serves as an inspiration for some of the most iconic brands of the 21st century And the Razor Blade model, even today, is taught extensively in B-schools all around the world Today

Sony uses his pricing model and sells it's PlayStation consoles at a loss, just so that they can make recurring profits through CDs and PlayStation Plus subscriptions Sony incurred a loss of about 60$ which is about ?4200 for every PS4 console they sold, just so that they could make billions through CDs and subscriptions. Kodak sold cameras at a dearth cheap cost just to make customers come back for the film rolls and Amazon Kindle today is being sold at almost 0 profit just so that Amazon can make billions out of its e-book sales. This is the power of the Razor Blade model So now the question is how can you apply this model to your startup Well people, as far as I am concerned there are 3 important lessons that you need to keep in mind while you apply this strategy for your startup The first thing that you need to understand is that getting your customers into your ecosystem will always give you an unfair advantage over your competition because an ecosystem always results into massive customer retention. Secondly, while you apply this model you need to find the points of maximum reluctance and then you have to work on minimizing it For example, you would be more reluctant to buy a PS4 console as compared to buying PS4 the games after buying the console. Therefore, selling consoles at a loss and hiking the price of the games will give you exponential returns as compared to doing it otherwise. Thirdly, you need to be careful to not be so dependent on this model that you end up neglecting the very possibility of disruption because this is exactly what happened with Kodak Now I don't know how many of you know this but then Kodak was so stuck to making money by selling their film rolls that in spite of being one of the first companies to file a patent for digital cameras, they did not realize that the film roll itself will seize to exist with the rise of the digital revolution. And the fact that by sticking to the razor blade model, they were practically digging their own grave. And last and most importantly, every entrepreneur needs to realize that pricing is a double-edged sword. When used right, it will give you incredible returns but if you don't keep the track of the changes, it can even kill your business.

XVII
Google

We all have experienced the magical effect of Google in our lives. What was once just a plain wide web page has now become such an integral part of our lives that now it's hard to imagine a world without Google. As a result, Google has emerged as one of the most successful companies on the planet with its stock price skyrocketing by 5000% and a market cap of one trillion dollars. But the most surprising fact of all is that back in the day, Google was neither the first search engine in the market Nor was it the most profitable company in the market. In fact, in 1998 Google was bleeding money. While it was just a small start-up. On top of that, They had killer Rivals like gotocom which made 231 million dollars in Revenue in the very same year through search ads. When Google did not even have a concrete business model, then the question is, how did Google become so successful? What exactly was your business strategy? And as students of business, what can we learn from this legendary Penny? This is a story that dates back to September 1998 When Larry and Sergey founded Google based on an algorithm called Page Rank, and they developed it as Ph.D. students at Stanford. Now, during that time, the problem with search was that majority of the search engines rank the pages majorly based on the text that they contained. And because of this, it allowed spammers to game the system by filling their pages with commonly searched keywords. For example, when you searched for Honda, Instead of giving you Hondacom as a search result, It would show you an adult site that just copies and pasted, the word Honda 50 times, but PageRank dived much deeper and evaluated the sides by Authority and influence based on several other relevant websites that God link to them in the form of backlinks. Now, although Google's algorithm was far superior to most of the algorithms in the market, They struggle to make money. Because, unlike today, the standard wisdom back then was that there was no money in search results. Web sites like Yahoo Used their homepage to place banner ads and generate billions of dollars in profits. This is where Google had the first chance to make a million dollars by displaying the same banner ads as Yahoo. But Larry and Sergey hated the idea because it degraded the customer experience. So while other companies were making a million dollars both due to their business model and due to the com bubble, Google was bleeding money and was wandering around without a business model.

That is, when Larry and Sergey started studying there, I will go to come back in the day, Although it did not have a great search algorithm, eight minutes 68 million dollars in profit in 1999 Why? Because instead of building their search engine from scratch will grow as the founder took an existing search engine called Tommy's engine, and introduced The Twist called the paid search, along with that bill, also introduced a game-changing pricing model called the cost per click pricing. Now, this model was extremely successful back in the day, because it solved three major problems in the market. Number one, in an attempt to downplay the spammers, companies like Honda were very keen on paying more money for their keywords, such that they could get the top spot and not those spammers. And when they paid for the advertising, it automatically pushed down the spammers. Secondly, these keywords were placed in an auction. Therefore, it created competition among The advertisers, which generated a ton of profits for the website. And thirdly, in other search engines, advertisers had to pay for an impression, whereas, in go to, they only had to pay for the click, instead of paying for the advertisement every time it appeared in front of the users They needed to pay only when someone clicked on it. Now, this was a revolutionary idea back then, because it gave the advertisers of confidence in conversion and the uncertainty of wasted money on marketing was Eliminated. This is when Larry and Sergey started dissecting the model of gotocom. And when they did, they identified two major problems with the model. The first problem was that because the model was solely based on who pays more money, a large company could abuse its power by the keywords of other companies. Also, for example, Samsung could buy all the keywords related to Vivo. So even if someone is searching for Vivo, Samsung sponsored content would pop up. And This was unfair to the small businesses. Secondly, the small businesses were discouraged from placing their ads, merely due to the price domination of the large players there for Larry and Sergey work, day in and day out to come out with two major improvements that turned Google into a trillion-dollar company. The question is, what exactly were these improvements? Number one, they came out with the idea of something called the quality score that would filter out content in such a way that the ranking will not just be based on the option Paid but also based on the relevance of the ad concerning those searches. So if you're looking for a Honda, Tesla cannot sabotage on displacing and present itself on top. Secondly, they came out with the idea of using a variant of a unique auction model called the weekly auction model. This is a model that was proposed by a Nobel Laureate named William We crave, and this is how it works out. Let's say there are four bidders, Mahindra, mg, Tata and Toyota, and the Two bids are 10 Rupees, 20 rupees 30 rupees, and 10000 rupees, respectively. And they are bidding for a keyword called XUV. Now in the standard model or the first prize Model. Toyota will win the auction, and it has to pay 10000 rupees. Now, although Toyota could have got it for 31 rupees, It has to overpay because of its assumption that the keyword XUV will be costly, whereas in the second prize model or the wickery model, Although Toyota still wins the Auction, It only has to pay one rupee more than the second-highest bidder, which in this case is the startup. So Toyota only has to pay 31 rupees. And in the case of Google, Toyota has to pay the price quoted by Tata.

That is, the second-highest bidder data have to pay What was quoted by mg That is the third-highest bidder, and so forth. This way advertisers don't have to overpay for the keyword, and they also get insights into the competitive prices in the market, which in turn helps them optimize the future bits Along with this, using the quality score, Google ensures that they don't just rank the ads based on the bids, but also based on the quality of the content that the bidders are putting forward, Such that the sponsor with the most relevant content always shows up on top, even if they've paid less money. And these two features, ladies and gentlemen, turned Google into a revolutionary search engine that was far superior to the rest of the competition, because it did not just have the amazing feature of Sparkling of gotocom, but also saved advertises a ton of money due to the second price auction method. And most importantly, due to the Quality score, despite being the highest bidder, a company could not overpower another bidder solely based on money. And this eventually encouraged authentic advertisements and eliminated the abusers and spirals. This is how lazy and German in 2002 Google launched Its pay-per-click auction-based search advertising product called Old the Google AdWords select. And from that year onwards, the revenue of the company started skyrocketing. They made four hundred million dollars in Revenue In 2002 15 billion dollars in 2003 32 billion dollars in 2004. And finally, when they went IPO in 2004, the company reached a valuation of twenty-three billion dollars. And the rest is history. Now, another important question that needs to be asked to be here is that during such times of Ruthless competition, when Had a predator like Microsoft and a giant like Yahoo As their competition, What was so special about Google that they were able to keep innovating to stay ahead of these well-established companies? And this is what brings me to another important attribute of Google as a company. And that is their culture of innovation. Did you guys know that some of the most game-changing projects at Google, like Gmail, Google, suggest, and even Google news? They were all just side projects, and none of them were officially allocated to any team in the company. All of them were designed by enthusiastic employees who just happen to do something extraordinary that their manager Never asked them For. The question is, how and why Would these employees work so hard on something that the company is not even asking for? Well, that is because of a wonderful company practice called the 20% Rule. And because of this rule, every employee had to dedicate 20% of their time to projects that interest them, even if they have not been officially allocated by the company. And this was based on the philosophy that even if it leads to 1000 failed projects, even if one of them turns out to be successful, it is enough to make up for the one thousand failures. And this is exactly what happened because today, Gmail alone is being used by 18 billion users. And it is said to generate a billion dollars in profits for the company,

Therefore, because of such wonderful practices, not just Sergey and Larry, but the entire organization was not just a bunch of workers, but a bunch of Learners who kept learning and trying new things every single day. And this is what brings me to the most important part of the chapter. And that are the business lessons from the case study and the study materials to help you dive deeper into the concepts of the case study.Data is annual is probably the code of the century. In this case, Google's data analysis and Engineers played a crucial role in helping Build, the most formidable products and services in the market. So if you're Keen to understand how you can optimize your company's data, do check out upgrades data, and science programs that will also help you understand data, draw inferences and effectively use the observations to help you bag your dream job. Now

Let's talk about the lessons from the case study and the study materials to help you dive, deeper into lesson Number One, never be discouraged If there's already a big player in your Market. You should be happy because it allows you to dissect their strategies and learn from their mistakes that which will enable you to build an even better business. If you look back at the tech Revolution, Napster did not succeed. Spotify Did Myspace not succeed, Facebooked It. Why? Because the founders of these companies did not make the mistakes made by the first Moors. In this case, It was the dissection of gotocom that motivated Sergey and Larry to design the quality score system and use the We cream order to benefit the advertisers. And this eventually had them build a far superior search engine, not just in terms of tech, but also in terms of business, because they use the cost-per-click model. Secondly, as a leader of your organization, If you want your company to achieve greatness, you have to find a way to develop a culture of learning and failing such that you build a foundation for failure. And eventually, you build a culture wherein ideation Beyond work, Never stops, And even at things cool, no matter who we work with, whether that is a freelancer and intern, or even me, or Posh.

XVIII
Haldirams

Haldiram is one of the most iconic brands in Indian business history. And while most of us are taught about American icons like Domino's and McDonald's, very few of us know about the world-class business strategies developed by the homegrown brands of India. And Haldiram is one such brand that started as a small sweet shop in Bikaner, but today, it has expanded its presence in more than 80 countries, employs more than 1500 people. And in FY 19 alone, Haldiram generated a sales revenue of $1 billion. The question is while we see 1000s of sweet shops every single day, What exactly was so particularly special about Haldiram that they were able to build a billion-dollar business? What exactly was their business strategy as students of business? What are the lessons that we need to learn from this iconic brand? This is a story that dates back to 1990 Bikaner. When Haldiram was just 11 years old. He worked at his grandfather's bhujia shop and being a marwadi, he soon enough started finding ways to make money for his family. Back then bhujia in Bikaner was an extremely commoditized product, which means that since there were hundreds of bhujia shops in Bikaner, there was hardly any difference between their products. Therefore, the competition was solely based on the price and not on quality. During this time, Haldiram would take up odd jobs such as chopping and cleaning the kitchen, and he gradually began to take interest in the making of the bhujia. Originally, the tasty bhujia was made by one of the daughters-in-law of the family. And soon enough haldirams grandfather realized the potential of this product, and he took it to the market. And as soon as this product hit the market, the bhujia started selling very well. And as soon as they started making more money, the entire family was extremely happy. But

Haldiram was the only member who was not at all satisfied neither with the penny profits nor with the taste and quality of their product. because deep down he still felt that bhujia was not good enough. And he wanted to make something that was far away from the rest of the competition. And he wanted his product to be not just yet another bhujia among the hundreds of bhujia in the market. And right away, driven by this insane obsession for a high-quality product, this little boy started working very hard and started experimenting with different ingredients in search of a mind-blowing product. And that is when many, many iterations later Haldiram was able to make three changes to the bhujia that changed the destiny of his family forever. The first change he made was that instead of making bhujia out of besan, he started making it out of Moth Ki Dall. And this made bhujia extremely delicious, turning it into a delicacy overnight. In addition to that, instead of making them soft, he started making them into a fine crispy mixture so that it could give people an enhanced experience of eating bhujia and at the same time, it could make the customers feel something different from the conventional bhujia sold in Bikaner. Secondly, because this bhujia was extremely commoditized he started selling his bhujia at a 150 percent extra cost at 5 paise per kilo as compared to the market price which was just 2 paise per kilo. And lastly, he named his bhujia Dungar Sev which was named after that then Maharaja Dungar Singh.

And these three changes gave Haldiram three superpowers over his extremely crowded competition. Firstly, the name danger by default made this bhujia sound like a delicacy that people would want to try. And this is because, although the name danger did not have any connection to the Maharaja, it acted as a brand ambassador for the bhujia. Therefore, the perceived value of the product was enhanced to a large extent. Secondly, because of this increased perceived value, people do not mind paying three paise extra because they by default assume that they were buying a premium product. And third and most importantly, we people pay the premium for the bhujia after perceiving it as a better product. When they tasted it, the bhujia genuinely turned out to be delicious. As a result, the demand for Haldirams dungar sev skyrocketed within just a few weeks. If you see, this is a textbook execution of one of the most powerful principles of marketing which says that brand perception plus a tangible value delivery results in brand value. In this case, by hearing the name of danger Maharaj, haldirams bhujia attracted more customers due to the enhanced perceived value after that, when it tasted great customers and wholesalers do not mind paying three paise extra per kilo. So if you see, the three paise extra or the 150 percent premium cost was the brand value of Haldiram's bhujia. And this turned Haldiram's bhujia into a leading product in a highly commoditized bhujia market. And within no time, hundreds of kilos of Haldiram's bhujia started to be sold. This was the founding pillar of the incredible Haldiram story. The second pillar of Haldiram's growth was led by Mr. Shiv Kishan Agarwal in the late 1960s. And he belonged to the third generation in the Agarwal family. Until this point, the family has separated into three discrete businesses which were in Bikaner, Kolkata, and Nagpur and when Bikaner and Kolkata were doing very well, Shiv Kishan was struggling to sell bhujia in Nagpur because of the demand for snacks, in general, was not very high in Maharashtra. Therefore, he decided to take a step back and got back on the ground to do thorough market research about the food habits of the Maharashtrians and that is when, after making countless visits to the most popular stores in Nagpur, Shiv Kishan identified three major opportunities in the market. The first thing he realized was that Maharashtrians had not been exposed to more than a few savory snacks. And this presented him with a huge opportunity to be a first-mover in the market. But at the same time, just like any other first mover, the trust factor or the hesitancy of the people was a major obstacle to market penetration. The second gap he identified was in the sweets market, and he noted that the most popular shops in Maharashtra mostly sold only bhalushahis Gujarati pedals, Mysore Pak, and ladoos. This is when he realized that the Maharashtrians had a sweet tooth that could be exploited further. And thirdly, Shiv Kishan realized that because the variety of sweets available in Maharashtra was very less, there was immense scope for hundreds of sweet delicacies from other regions that could be leveraged for market penetration. So guess what? He started by making his favorite sweet using thickening of milk, sugar, dry fruits, cashew nuts, and saffron. And this is what ladies and gentlemen gave rise to the iconic Kaju Katli in Maharashtra. And Shiv Kishan started aggressively promoting the dish by giving out free samples and by encouraging every customer to taste the dish. Soon enough, word of mouth spread, and the sweet began to achieve extraordinary levels of popularity. In fact, in one of the interviews, Shiv Kishan said that it first started with people buying 100 grams then it went up to 200 grams, and gradually people started buying 500 grams of Kaju Katli per customer. The flavor was so well accepted and loved that they were flooded with demand for Kaju Katli. Soon enough, he introduced the logos to the delights from

Bikaner and Calcutta like malai ladoo, rasgulla, and ras malai.

And not so surprisingly, his Maharashtrian customers couldn't get enough of Haldiram bhujia wala sweets. And within just three years, their sales shot up by 400% going from just 100 rupees per day to 500 rupees per day, which in today's world is, by the way, equivalent to 12,000 rupees of sales per day. Now, while most of us would be extremely satisfied with this crazy amount of sales, Shiv Kishan did not stop there. After serving the market further, he realized that South Indian snacks like Dosa and Idli were extremely popular in Nagpur. So he immediately started a South Indian restaurant for customer acquisition reasons. And when more and more people started visiting his restaurant, he slowly introduced Samosas and Kachoris. And this time, it did not take a lot of time because samosas and kachoris became standard fast foods in Maharashtra. This is how Shiv Kishan achieved market penetration in a seemingly unknown market with his brilliant business strategies. Now in business terms, what he did was that he build a golden bridge to move the customer sentiment from skepticism to delight. So initially, he was an unknown vendor selling unknown dishes which people are skeptical about. As a result, market penetration was extremely difficult. So what did he do, he first started selling known dishes and establishing trust with the customers. And as soon as he owned the trust of the customers, he brought in the X-Factor that no other known vendor had. And that were the brilliant dishes, which were completely unknown to the audience. As a result, the customers embraced his dishes with open arms. They were super delighted because a trusted guy was brilliant enough to present many new dishes. While the rest of the known guys were presenting the same old stuff. This was the magic of Shiv Kishan's execution. And this is what brings me to the third pillar of haldiram's growth which was nothing but packaging and location. And these two changes were brought about by another third-generation member named Manohar Lal Agarwal. And when executed, it led to exponential sales because of something called brand recall value. Long story short, when you see a lot of guys delivering food, and wearing tomato t-shirts, you automatically tend to believe that Zomato is a trusted brand. When you see a lot of images of the same book cover on social media and many other places, that might likely be the first book you read. A very simple example of the same would be Dale Carnegie's How to Win Friends and Influence People, and the subtle art of not giving an F. Similarly, when you see a lot of people buying or gifting Haldiram bhujia Wala sweets, they automatically become mini-banner ads to make you feel that the Haldiram brand is extremely trusted. And this strategy, ladies and gentlemen, was a game-changer back then because, in the 1980s, nobody in the market took packaging seriously. So when Manohar Lal executed this strategy, Haldiram bhujia Wala was not just shipping 1000s of products, but they also shipped 1000s of mini billboards that made the brand stand out and established trust both with the customers and the sellers. And when this was combined with the strategic placement of stores in densely populated places like the railway station, the sales numbers went crazy. To tell you about it, In just five years, by 1981, the production of Haldiram had shot up by 400% to 3000 kilos per month, and people from all across the country came in and asked for Haldiram bhujia Wala specifically, and soon enough, the brand logo started traveling through the length and breadth of the country. And this is when people of Bikaner and Nagpur view that Haldiram bhujia Wala was not just a small sweet shop, but an iconic brand in the making. And from here onwards, despite many challenges, there was no looking back for the Haldiram brand. As a result, today Haldiram is a humongous brand valued at $3 billion with its signature dishes, making an impact not just in India, but in 80 countries all across the world. And this is how three generations of the Agarwal family laid a solid foundation to build a 5000 crore business empire. And this is what brings me to the most important part of the chapter and that is, the lessons from the case study and the study materials to help you read further about them. Before we move on, I wanted to tell you about this one skill of Haldiram founder that I was personally fascinated by. And that was his focus on accounting and inventory management.

Because these two factors are extremely critical for any business irrespective of its size. Now let's talk about the lessons from the case study and the study materials to help you dive deeper. Lesson number one, while most people think that there is no scope for brand building in a commoditized market, you need to realize that a commoditized market is perhaps the best place to build a brand because once you do it, you're going to stand out and that is going to skyrocket your sales in no time. In this case, it was haldirams acumen to build a brand name for his bhujia among the hundreds of bhujia sellers in Bikaner. Lesson number two, while most of us love to play on our strengths, sometimes we need to realize that to play our strengths, we first need to cater to the demand in the market. In this case, you see, even after 20 years of running a family business just around bhujia, it was Shiv Kishan's strategic approach to first establish trust with the customers by selling sweets. And then he came full circle by selling South Indian snacks eventually selling North Indian dishes like samosas and kachori. And this eventually helped him stand out from the rest of the competition. And lastly, we all need to realize that healthy obsession often turns work into art. And regardless of what you do, if it is pursued with a certain degree of craftsmanship even if you're selling something as seemingly insignificant as bhujia it can help you build a billion-dollar business.

XIX
Havells

The story of havells is one of the most iconic tales in the Indian business history , In the past 20 years havell's stock price has shot up by seventy thousand four ninety percent going from just 1.58 rupees to 1082 rupees in 2022 and a mere 10 000 rupees investment in havells in 2001 would be worth 18 crores including stock splits and excluding the dividends and the most astonishing thing about this company is that it was made legendary by an ordinary drawing teacher with a salary of just 90 rupees who then turned to trading and went on to become one of the most iconic businessmen in the Indian business history this man that I'm talking about is none other than khimat rai Gupta so the question is what is the story of havells what are the business strategies that turned havells into a gold mine for its investors and most importantly what are the study materials and lessons that we need to learn from this iconic rise of havells, This is a story that dates back to 1948 when a businessman named Haveli Ram Gandhi registered a company called havells. Haveli was an astute businessman and imported several electrical products like switchgears starters and meters and after importing them he then re-branded them as havels and sold them in the market soon enough he even began manufacturing them and started selling them in the local market and because of the consistent quality of its products havels became a renault name in the market and coincidentally there was another dutch company by the name havel so people presumed havels to be a foreign company and this also gave it an aspirational value but unfortunately after his wife's death and son's suicide heavily lost the zeal of running the business and while haveli was dealing with this tough phase of his life on the other side of the country during the same time from 1958 to 1971 an uncle nephew duo were running a company called gupta g and co this company was very well established but the problem was that they were just middlemen they neither had the financial clout to buy directly from the manufacturers nor did they have an established distribution network to sell to institutions or customers directly so they were essentially middlemen who bought products from wholesalers and then sold them to smaller retailers this nephew was none other than khima rai gupta himself or he's referred to as qrg realized that although their business was going very well it was in such a vulnerable position that if tomorrow the retailers found a better way to connect with the manufacturers their business would vanish right away why because their value addition to the supply chain was nothing more than just logistics and when he did his research he realized that the actual gold mine was in manufacturing so qrg started thinking about building a factory such that they could increase their profits as well as become an important stakeholder in the supply chain the only problem was that building a factory was an extremely cost intensive process that would have been very heavy on his bank balance but it so happened that one of his clients turned out to be havels during that time as it turned out havels lost a very big government order and the company's financials were in a terrible state so although they had a great name in the market the management was looking to sell the company so you know what mr indar mata who was managing the business of havels during that time offered qrg to buy out the company and this is where qrg's business acumen came into play since he was anyways in the pursuit of getting into manufacturing he decided to go ahead with the business deal but the catch over here was that qrg said that he would pay 7 lakh rupees not to buy the company but just the brand name and the goodwill of havels which means what he wouldn't buy any of the physical assets of the company like a factory or a warehouse but only by the brand name havels that's it now the question over here is why would someone pay such a huge amount of money just for that brand name i mean it obviously wasn't like the apple of electricals during that time right well listen to me very very carefully while most of us think of 7 lakh rupees as an overrated price tag for a brand name if you look closely you will see that it is actually a bargain why because had he gone ahead with establishing a new company let's call it indie electricals qrg would have to spend a ton of resources into actually pushing it into the market which means what since nobody knew the name of indie electricals he would first have to convince the distributors and retailers that this product will sell in the market this will need a huge sales force and then he even has to pay the distributors extra margin as in an incentive so that they would buy the products after that chemotherapy would have to spend a ton of money into marketing with the hope that people will go and ask for any electrical products at the retail stores and after the sales are done then come establishing of trust with customer experience and only when this entire cycle is complete will the distributors actually keep pushing indies products by which they can slowly decrease the margins and establish themselves in the market all of this would anyways have costed qrg an enormous amount of money and most importantly a lot of time to establish the brand recall value but merely by buying the brand name of havels all of these initial costs dropped down drastically and since havels had been in the market for 23 years and had a good name in the market most people already knew the havels brand distributors anyways placed orders and most importantly the retailers were already happy to take the products so the 7 lakh rupees that he paid was not just for the name but for this intangible benefit of the cost of building trust in the network and the time to establish the brand recall value . It took mankind not one not two but seven years to become profitable in spite of having all the modern tools of distribution and even celebrity endorsements this is the reason why qrg paid 7 lakh rupees just to get the brand name of havels and then came step number two wherein instead of building giant factories he first outsourced the manufacturing and just sold the products with a label of havels this way although he had to pay margins for the outsourcing he did not have to take the risk of setting up giant factories and bear the heavy cost of land machines labor etc and as far as the distribution network was concerned since qrg enemies traveled to different cities to meet their distributors slowly he began expanding his network to establish the supply chain all across the country eventually once the business stabilized he used the profits to acquire acres of land to build great factories for manufacturing electricals and they used more or less the same strategy to acquire towers and transformers limited to make electric meters and standard electricals that enable them to diversify into different categories this is how the foundations of the harvest brand was laid in the 70s and 80s and this brings us to the second phase of havels wherein they made a strategic entry into the consumer durable space during the 1990s which was right after liberalization during this time the indian market had opened up and lots of companies entered the consumer durable space most of these companies tried to sell products at the most profitable rates possible but you know what guys haven't actually took a completely different approach and they started selling products directly in the premium segment with their first targets being ceiling fans and lights now the question over here is while most brands were fighting in the affordable segment with an already tough competition why would a brand choose to enter in the premium segment isn't that like directly losing out in the pricing war straight away well this is where another important business insight comes in which is brand perception leads to brand value to understand this concept the classy example would be the case of bhatta and nike now people if you were to spend 5000 rupees into buying a single pair of shoes and i gave you two options one is a 5000 rupees nike shoe and the other is a 5000 rupees bata shoe my question to you is which one would you buy in most cases people would choose to spend 5000 rupees on a nike but will never spend beyond 3000 rupees on a bata shoe why because if you're a 90s kid you would remember that since childhood bata has always been a budget option and nike has always been a fancy premium option so knowingly or unknowingly we have allocated the cost of bata shoe to a maximum of just 3 000 rupees but since nike is perceived as a premium product the company is able to push its price range so hard that they start selling shoes at 2 900 rupees but push it all the way to sell a 19 000 rupees jordan and even a 31 000 rupees airmag and in spite of being at such a high price range people still flock to buy a nike shoe and you must have seen the same thing happen with apple wherein the cheapest product is always just about the budget range and the most expensive product often touches unimaginable price points so the moral of the story is that once you establish yourself in the premium segment you can actually break through the price brackets of a budget product and push your price range insanely high eventually bagging extraordinary levels of profit margins this is the reason why not just travels but many of the brands often deliberately choose to be in the premium segment in spite of the market being flooded with players in the affordable segment and even today if you look at the price point of havel's fans in comparison to others while orient fans maximum price point stands at 12 000 rupees bajaj touches 7 000 rupees cromten touches 15 000 rupees but havel's fans go all the way up to 34 000 rupees and even touch 61 000 rupees in fact they even did something very similar by acquiring crap tree which was again a premium brand in the switches segment this was the second pillar by which harvest was actually able to stand out from the rest of the crowd and was able to achieve extraordinary levels of profit and this brings us to the third pillar of havel's growth and that is their marketing love and needless to say havels has obsessively focused on communicating its message in the most creative in the most humorous and most importantly in the most memorable manner possible and all thanks to their strategic appearances between cricket matches and specifically the ipl they are fresh in our memories even years after seeing them and this brings me to the last and perhaps one of the most critical reasons for their massive expansion and that is their diversification time and again have us very strategically and carefully diversified into electric meters by acquiring towers and transformers limited into acs and refrigerators by acquiring lloyd into affordable consumer durables by acquiring standard electricals and into switches by acquiring cratery and the best part is that in spite of the insane growth in spite of they experiencing rapid expansion time and again and in spite of making extravagant acquisitions like sylvania they have virtually stayed debt free most of the times and even today they have one of the healthiest balance sheets in the industry and this brings me to the most important part of the chapter and that are the lessons and moving on there are three lessons that we need to learn from the iconic rise of havels lesson number one brand value and the time that a brand spends on the market has some intangible benefits that makes it extremely valuable because it saves the acquirer a ton of time efforts and gives them the trust of the formerly built network in this case qrg was a master in leveraging the brand value starting from havels to craftory to stand electricals and even lloyds lesson number two always choose your segment in the market very very carefully before entering because within some time your brand perception will often bind you in a price bracket and this price bracket can change your fortunes both for good and bad in this case we saw how qrg carefully chose to place the havers and craftery brand in the premium segment in spite of the market being flooded with affordable players and then he let standard electricals play in the affordable segment this way he was able to catch hold of both the premium and the affordable market lesson number three even if you're selling something as uncool as wires mcv's or fans if you know how to tell a memorable story to your audience you will achieve an extraordinary level of brand recall value which is an invaluable asset for any company and lastly time and again try to use diversification to stay relevant and risk your brand regularly and carefully without straining your balance sheet.

XX

HDFC

Hdfc is one of the most extraordinary players in the indian banking industry what started as an ordinary bank with a handful of visionary ambitious bankers has now turned into the largest and perhaps the most powerful private sector entity in the indian banking space and if you look at the stock price of hdfc in the past 21 years it has shot up by more than eight thousand percent going from just 17.86 rupees in jan 2000 to more than 1 400 rupees today and what's mind-blowing is that this return rate in the past 20 years is more than the stock returns of reliance microsoft and even amazon in fact in the past 10 years the revenue of the company has shorter by 350 going from thousand one eighty five closed in twenty twelve to one lakh fifty five thousand eight eighty five crores in twenty twenty one the question is how did hdfc become such a powerful entity in the indian banking space how did it break the monopolies of the nationalized banks in india and most importantly what are the business strategy lessons that we need to learn from the legendary leaders of hdfc bank people the first thing that we need to understand is how does a bank work in the first place in simple words a bank collects money from people like you and me the businessman and the corporates by providing us with saving accounts and current accounts these are the most valuable assets to a bank because they have to pay very less interest to both these stakeholders furthermore using this deposited money the bank offers services like home loans and car loans for which they charge an interest to the borrower therefore the profit of the bank equals the interest collected from the borrowers minus the interest paid to the depositors now the catch over here is that back in 1990s even though hdfc had the license of rbi even though it was backed by mr deepak parikh himself considering all the scams that were going on no one trusted a new bank therefore in its initial days hdfc did not have enough deposits because of which it could not offer lucrative services to the borrowers so you know what the legendary team of hdfc went on to do some extensive market research to find out the gaps in the market and one such gap they found was the pain of the cooperative bank transactions to tell you about it back in 1998 cooperative banks were restricted to one state and their customers and branches were only in that particular state so the moment they had to do any interstate transfer they were dependent on another bank in another state for example let's take the example of two people mr gopaldas and mr sham sunder mr gopaldas is a maharashtra cooperative bank customer who buys 10 lakh rupees worth of cement from sham sundar who is from gujarat gobaldas pays by check so sham sundar goes back to gujarat and deposits the cheque in his abc bank this abc bank clears the cheque and pays sham sundar but charges a processing fee plus takes three to four days to deposit the money why because they had to send the cheque to their maharashtra partner bank to clear the cheque so for three to four days 10 lakh rupees of sham sudar was stuck with the bank plus he has to pay a processing fee now when this happened with sham sundar for two to three clients shyam sundar needed 30 lakhs of extra working capital just because of the tedious procedure of the bank this is the reason why most suppliers were not at all willing to accept a cooperative bank's check as a result the cooperative banks were losing these big ticket accounts of local businessmen but here's where hdfc offered a simple solution hdfc said that because it has branches all across the country it will issue checks at par to all cooperative bank customers by which when gobaldas writes a check to sham sundar for 10 lakh rupees instead of sending the cheque back to maharashtra sham sundar can deposit this cheque at his local sdfc branch in gujarat and hdsc will clear the check without any fees or delay this is how cooperative banks could pay their suppliers all across the country because of which they were able to retain their high ticket customers but in return hdfc asks these cooperative banks to keep interest-free deposits with hdc bank so for example if 10 cooperative banks deposited 20 lakh rupees with hdfc hdfc had two crore rupees of low risk interest-free capital that they could use to give out car loans home loans and other services eventually to make a profit the second gap that the legendary team of hdfc spotted was the functioning of the stock market to tell you about it back in 1998 just like today back then we had five entities in the stock trading system the buyer broker of the buyer stock exchange broker of the seller and the seller and before 1990 all these transactions used to happen physically through share certificates but as the computer revolution picked up in 1990s the process of trading started to change and we saw the rise of dematerialization of stocks wherein instead of being physically traded the transfer of stock started to happen electronically but the catch over here was that although the share transfer happened electronically the funds were still being transferred physically for example if you are mr partel and you are a buyer from maharashtra using sbi if you want to buy 10 shares at 500 rupees per share you have to give a check of 5000 rupees to the broker who had an icici bank account he then gave another check to the stock exchange for 5000 rupees which had an account in canada bank and then assuming that the exchange has a seller it will then carry out the exchange by giving a 5 000 rupees cheque to the broker of the seller and lastly the broker of the seller then gives another check to the seller that is mr singh after this transfer was done the shares used to be electronically transferred immediately to the buyer but the problem with the system was that this was a very very inefficient system and it caused three major problems to the entities of the supply chain number one each one of these transactions used to take two to three days sometimes even five to seven days to be carried out this was because each entity in the supply chain had a different bank which had different transaction times secondly this process became even more complex when a broker had multiple customers who again had different bank accounts with different processing times and thirdly from the seller's end the broker had to settle the transaction for the volume of shares sold by mr singh so he had to pay 5000 rupees to mr singh even if the money did not hit his bank account yet this meant that the broker had to have a huge amount of working capital with lacks of rubies in his account which will only be used to pay back the sellers and lastly while this transaction was being carried out the exchange had no way to figure out if the broker had enough balance to execute the trade or not which is why to mitigate this risk the exchanges had to send data on dues of various brokers to the bank at the end of the day to check whether the brokers had enough money to honor their trade or not in this case every single day in the evening canada bank used to send the data saying mr singh and mr sheikh have one lakh rupees and they are supposed to execute trade worth 80 000 rupees and 1.2 lakh rupees respectively this further made the process extremely inefficient tedious and costly but this is why ladies and gentlemen hdse bank came up with a revolution and opted in for a software solution called the micro banker which was developed by a company called iflex solutions micro banker was a fully integrated online banking automation system whereas other banks either saw online banking as way ahead of its time or they stuck with offline banking or they had a hybrid of both online and offline and this gave hdfc the superpower to transfer funds electronically with minimal human interaction and what followed next was nothing short of a revolution now hdfc could make sure that not just the shares but even the funds could be transferred electronically to the entities of the supply chain in the stock market and hence the transaction time reduced from 5 to 10 days to just two to three days and this gave the entire supply chain three features that was nothing less than a superpower to the stakeholders first of all all the buyers and sellers could carry out the transaction within two to three days making this entire process extremely effective in terms of both ease of calculation and strategy secondly the exchange could immediately check if the brokers had enough funds to carry out the transaction or not because of which it saved them a lot of headache and thirdly the broker needed very less working capital to operate for example instead of having three lakh rupees he could operate with just one lakh rupees because the funds were coming in and moving out very very quickly and because of this they had enough time to settle the transaction this is how hdfc revolutionized the stock market system in india now some people might say yeah bro so what what is the big deal with using computer and internet for banking well for those people i gotta tell you guys that this was not like ordering pizza online we are talking about using a new age technology to carry out critical transactions and that too in the stock market this requires a ton of efforts into reskilling your employees setting up new systems and procedures that no one has ever used in india and most importantly it comes at the cost of putting the company itself at risk because you're dealing with critical transactions but in case of hdfc the meticulous execution of this strategy paid off dividends that were far beyond anyone's expectations and guess what this resulted into a viral opening of hdfc accounts from 1999 onwards not only did all the brokers switch to hdfc but also asked their customers to switch to hdfc accounts and starting with the nsc in 1998 the hdfc bank became the clearing member of all major exchanges by fy2000 and in total 800 broker accounts and a majority of custodians were using hdfc bank services by fy2000 and by late 1990s hdfc bank had captured 80 market in the settlement business in addition to that hdfc even started offering lines of credit to brokers to settle their excess transactions giving them one more reason to win the big ticket accounts of the stock brokers of india this is how lees and german hdlc bank ended up getting the most valuable current accounts in saving accounts giving them a huge chunk of funds to then be utilized for financial services and lastly they even carried out a similar process to tap into huge corporate accounts by digitizing their employee salary system and because of this hdfc got crows of rupees in its bank account in the form of current accounts of large corporates and on the other side they also achieved extraordinary penetration into retail banking because all the employees of these companies also shifted to hdfc accounts this is the reason why from 1994 to 2000 in just six years hdc went from being an ordinary bank to becoming a legendary company in the indian banking sector and this brings me to the most important part of the chapter and that are the lessons from the case study moving on there are three very very important lessons that we need to learn from the rise of hdfc lesson number one whenever you are a new player in the market before jumping into the mainstream market always trying to find the gaps in the market and we even saw this in case of asian pins in this case it was the cooperative bank's pain of transactions that hdc leveraged in order to get low risk industry deposits which then laid the foundation for its growth number two as the legend guy kawasaki once said innovation always happens when a company jumps to the next curve and reinvents an existing process in this case the legendary dream of hdfc had the audacity to jump to digitalization and number three please read this book called the unusual billionaires and this book called the bang for your buck both of these books have given me some fascinating insights about hdfc bank and lastly always remember no matter how big a company you are if your processes are inefficient even the smallest player in the market with a better process could actually become the biggest threat to your company in this case it was the complacency of the nationalized banks of india that was disrupted by the likes of icici hdfc and axis bank eventually turning these newbies into legends leaving the bureaucrats struggling in the market so always keep your evaluations tight and kill your inefficiency before someone else kills your business

IKEA

Ikea is one of the most innovative companies of the 21st century and the most astonishing thing about ikea is that in spite of furniture being a highly localized business ikea has been the pioneer in turning the furniture business into a global success and today ikea draws in a revenue of 45 billion dollars from 445 stores spread across 30 countries and what's more important to note is not the growth of the company but the fact that ikea taught the world how to use the most powerful psychological tactics to exponentially increase sales and today you are going to learn one such strategy that makes ikea stand apart from the competition and no matter which business you are in no matter which field you are in you can use these powerful psychological strategies to double your profits at zero cost the question is what is this strategy how does it make ikea stand apart from the rest of the competition and most importantly how can you use them to double your profits the answer to this lies in a fascinating experiment conducted by dan ariely with the students at the mit in the first iteration, dan went to his class of 100 students and asked them to choose between two subscription plans for the international magazine called the economist now let's do this experiment together so you tell me which one of these options would you choose okay so the three options were the digital version for 59 the print version for 125 and thirdly the print plus digital version for the same 125 as it turns out 16 students wanted the digital version zero percent wanted the print version for 125 and 84 of them chose the print plus digital option so for the second iteration he makes a small change he thought since nobody is buying the second option then why keep it there in the first place right so he removed the 125 print option and presented the same question to another class of 100 students now technically by eliminating the option that nobody chose the results are not supposed to change right well guess what in the second scenario the results changed drastically and this time only 32 percent of the students opted for the print plus digital version and 68 of them opted for the just digital version subscription and that is when dan realized that there was something magical about this unnecessary option that made such a huge difference in the choice of the customers and that is what we call as the decoy effect the decoy effect says that consumers change their preferences between two options when presented with a third option which acts as an unattractive option just to make the other options look extremely lucrative now when i say decoy effect most people think about the popcorn example wherein in the movie houses you get popcorn of small medium and large at a price of 300 rupees 650 rupees and 700 rupees and because of the decoy effect people tend to choose the 700 rupees option now although this is technically correct it is the worst possible example to use why because if you look at the underlying message that is being communicated to the customers this is what the options indirectly tell the customers option a overpay for the popcorn option b extremely overpay for the popcorn and option c extreme overpay for the popcorn with a little extra popcorn and the basic flow over here is that the prices over here can in no way justify the value for the popcorn therefore by default making the purchase of that popcorn becomes a painful experience this is the reason why we often feel guilty for buying popcorns and if you are a person like me you and i we will not even think about buying a popcorn at the theater now when this is done in a close and compulsive environment like a theater it will definitely work but if the same is done in the free market this strategy will backfire in a terrible way and if you give your customers this kind of a painful experience while paying for your product the customers will never buy from you eventually it will result into extremely heavy losses so the question over here is what exactly is the right way to apply the decoy effect and that is where ladies and gentlemen ikea's genius application comes in to tell you about it this is how ikea applies the decoy effect ikea places three cabinets for you cabinet a b and c a cost forty dollars b cost sixty dollars and c cost sixty five dollars option a is a very small cabinet with very smooth movement but it's got very small space plus the material used would be very ordinary option c will be a large cabinet with premium handles premium material and most importantly it will offer a large storage space along with that you will also get a 10 worth of compartment as complementary if you buy option c and then you've got option b which is as large as c but it is made out of ordinary material does not have premium handles and you will not get complimentary compartments and here's where the catch comes in if you look at the underlying message that ikea is trying to communicate using its products here's what they say option a says here's a budget product with a great value for money option c says here's a premium product plus large space plus delightful complimentary product so very very high value for money and lastly you've got option b which is almost the same price but without premium build quality without complementary compartments so not so much of a value for money as compared to option c so this way option b acts as the decoy so that when you compare option b with option c , option c looks like an amazing deal now while most sellers only think about the people who directly buy option c ikea understands that a 22 year old boy who just moved into the city will not be able to afford a 65 product which is why he would buy the 40 product but when he does ikea wants to make sure that he does not regret the purchase so even though it's a low margin product in the race of upselling ikea will never ever try to rip off its customers who've got low purchase power and the best part is the decoy effect over here doesn't just make option c look great it also makes option a look great because the customers feel like they would have overpaid by choosing option b which is 50 more costlier as compared to option a so by default the budget buyer buys the smaller drawer set and the premium customers they buy the 65 product why because they compare it with the decoy and this clean execution of the decoy effect gives the ikea brand three wonderful superpowers number one irrespective of their purchase both types of customers get value for their money secondly the premium customers have been tactfully influenced to buy the 65 product and because the 60 product was such a bad deal the premium customers actually feel very good about the purchase and most importantly when the 22 year old boy is extremely satisfied with his 40 purchase tomorrow when he grows up and makes a handsome income he will again choose ikea but this time as a premium customer because he was given the value for money that he was promised even at the 40 price tag therefore customer retention of the ikea brand increases by a large extent this is how you actually apply the decoy effect so while most sellers often use pricing strategies with the sole intent to upsell the ikea team constantly keeps learning and carefully deploys its strategies in a way that it drives profits but at the same time it retains its brand value and the most amusing thing over here is that ikea does this literally for every single one of its 12 000 products starting from affordable drawers all the way up to the premium beds and even wardrobes now again this might look very easy to some people but here's something that nobody will tell you if you take a step back guys you will realize that it is extremely difficult to maintain this fine balance between profit and brand value especially when you're as big as ikea with 4 45 stores spread across 30 different countries with 2.1 billion visitors who are coming from different cultures from all across the world and the only reason why they're able to execute this strategy is because of ikea's powerful philosophy of democratic design and lifelong learning culture every time ikea enters a country the ikea team specifically studies every little aspect of that place starting from the average balcony size all the way up to the average spoon size this is done just so that ikea could fit into the cultural framework of any country therefore even when you apply this strategy always make sure that you constantly keep learning about the customer's reaction and keep a very close eye on the customers culture purchase power and their spending habits because only then you will be able to understand how to strike a balance between profit and brand value and this brings me to the most important part of the chapter and that is as a businessman or a business woman what is the step-by-step process to apply the decoy effect and what are the study materials to help you dive deeper into the superpower of pricing moving on to the application here are five very very important steps that you need to follow when you apply the deco effect to your products step number one do a thorough research and find out which is the most popular and profitable product in your store step number two if it is a premium product find a budget substitute for the same product such that people who cannot offer the premium one can still fulfill their need with a budget product why because budget customers will soon become your premium customers therefore engaging with them should never ever be underestimated step number three would be to create a decoy and the point to be noted over here is that your decoy must not be a degraded version of your premium product however the premium product should have a way better offering than your decoy so if you're selling drawers it's okay to have a non-premium material but it shouldn't be like the drawers are rigid and they're very badly functional why because people even the decoy is going to reflect your brand value so always try to make the premium product more attractive with complementary offerings rather than purposefully degrading the decoy step number four would be to price your products in a way that the premium product looks way better than the decoy and the budget product or option a looks like the obvious choice for the customers with a lower purchase power this way your high margin product will become extremely lucrative driving very high sales and at the same time the budget customers will also be very happy to get the value for their money in fact those people will be even more happy because they didn't have to pay 50 extra just to get a bad deal on the decoy and lastly do not add more than five products and make sure that the price of the decoy is very close or even equal to the premium product now the disclaimer over here is that in the green for more profits please don't misuse the decoy effect because people always remember in the free market the customers are just one step away from leaving you forever this is how ladies and gentlemen you can apply the decoy effect to your products and when done right it can increase both your conversion rates and your profit margins by a large extent meanwhile if you are someone who wants to dive deep into the philosophies of pricing and consumer psychology i would highly recommend you to read this book called misbehaving by richard thalor which has now become my standard recommendation and the second book is this book called nudge written by the same author.

XXII

Indigo

The indian aviation space is one of the toughest places to do business in in the past 10 years itself india has seen the fall of giants like kingfisher jetairways saharaair and even the iconic deccan air and even while existing airlines have been struggling to make a profit indigo had been insanely profitable for 10 consecutive years till 2018 and even if you draw ticker dip comparison you will see that in 2015 while jet airways was still a dominating player while jet generated a net loss of 2097 crores spice jet generated a loss of 687 crores indigo was way ahead with a profit of 1 300 crores and today indigo is so far ahead of its competition that if you look at india's non-stop domestic market share while spiced stands at 11.7 percent air india stands at 10.2 percent goer stood at 8.8 percent whereas indigo was way ahead with a 52.7 market share which is more than the next five competitors combined the question is with indian aviation being such a tough market to operate in with giant computers like jet airways deccan airways and air india how did indigo become such a strong monopoly and most importantly how on earth had this company been profitable for 10 consecutive years the answer to indigo's massive growth could be summarized by louis pasteur's coat wherein he said chance favors the prepared mind to tell you about it back in 2005 when indigo just entered the market the indian aviation space was being dominated by the likes of jet airways deccan air and air india this is when both kingfisher and indigo started their operation but if you look at the growth of these companies after 2005 there is something very interesting to note until 2007 all these companies are operating with losses that were proportionate to their scale while kingfisher incurred a loss of 408 crores spices stood at a loss of 132 crores jet airways stood at a loss of

423 crores whereas indigo entered a loss of 234 crores but suddenly after 2008 something crazy happened and out of nowhere kingfisher's losses shot up by four times to one thousand nine hundred crores spiegel's losses shot up to 340 crores jets loss was relatively stable at 400 crores but somehow indigo managed to pull off a profit of 82 crudes and after that shock while kingfisher and jets started failing indigo's profit again shot up by 400 to 484.7 crores and from there onwards indigo's market share started increasing rapidly eventually turning it into a monopoly in the indian aviation business now the question over here is how did these giant players suddenly fall down and moreover how did a baby company like indigo end up becoming a monopoly well that is because indigo very very carefully avoided the mistakes made by these airlines and on top of that it deployed some game-changing business strategies that change the indian aviation space forever to understand this let's try to understand the three fundamental truths of indian aviation number one in spite of the airline business being an extremely capital intensive industry needing thousands of crores of investment the cost of flying in india is already at the border line of affordability for most people so if you want to survive in the indian aviation space you cannot raise your prices beyond say 5000 or 6000 rupees if you want a decent amount of customers so the filter of cost is the only thing that matters to most customers as in even if the flight is carried at 2 AM if it's 1 000 rupees cheaper people will still opt in to lose their sleep rather than paying more secondly the flying market in india is still at the baby stages in spite of having more than three times the population of the us as of 2017 while india's air traffic stood at just 161.5 billion the u.s was way ahead at 632 million and lastly in spite of your charges being at the threshold of affordability it is very very difficult to pull off a profit in india why because the most expensive element in your balance sheet is completely out of control and that is the fuel cost that is around 35 to 45 sometimes even 50 percent of your operation cost and this price keeps fluctuating based on the geopolitical situations so the only way you can make money in the indian aviation space is by increasing your margins without increasing the cost of your tickets and indigo was an absolute master at it the first thing indico did was that it surprised the entire industry by ordering 100 aircash with airbus in a single order in the very first year of its operation and this deal had an order value of 6 billion dollars which was one of the biggest aircraft deals in aviation history now on the outside most people thought it to be crazy but in reality it was a genius deal made

at a strategic time and mr rakesh gangwan the co-founder of indigo made this big decision for three specific reasons number one back in 2005 airbus almost completely lost the indian market and the indian companies started buying from boeing this was because airbus aircraft met with a series of accidents in india and this included the air crashes in 1988 1990 and 1992 but after fixing all these problems and the safety issues airbus was desperately finding a way to come back to the indian market and during this time when indigo placed such a huge order of 100 aircrafts airbus was by default willing to sell them at a dirt cheap cost now although the exact prices are not revealed as far as the data from the order of southwest airlines and ryanair indicate the discount could have gone as high as 50 percent secondly the airbus aircrafts were way more efficient than boeing aircrafts and lastly indigo used something called the sails and lease back model that drastically reduced its cost of operation and here's how this model worked out this is the technique wherein the airline buys the aircraft from the manufacturer and sells its asset to another party and then rents it back from the same buyer now let's take a contrived example to understand this when indigo places an order for 100 aircrafts it gets a massive discount by which a hundred million dollar aircraft could be bought at a modest price of 50 million dollars and then indigo sells this aircraft to a leasing company like boc aviation for 55 million dollars now here itself they make a profit of 5 million dollars so after the sale is done indigo rents the same aircraft from boc aviation for a period of five to eight years such that indigo will pay the rent for its incoming revenue from operation now this is a great deal for boc because even at 55 million dollars boc aviation gets a 100 million aircraft at 55 million without the risk of placing a bulk order and with that they are also getting a ready-made customer base that will give them a recurring revenue and at the same time if you see for indigo it's an amazing deal because it gives indigo three incredible benefits over its competition first of all the company generates an upfront profit of 5 million dollars which could be used for cash flow and indigo can stay cash rich while other players struggle during crunch times secondly under the sales and leaseback model indigo stated that not all these aircrafts will arrive at once but with a gap of 6 to 8 weeks so that they can steadily accommodate the flights as per the market conditions on top of that any technical glitch or issues with the engines were to be taken care of either airbus or the engine supplier this way indigo neither had to pay the cost of maintenance staff nor did it have to pay for maintenance cost of the aircraft and lastly indigo could easily use way more air cars with very less capital compared to the competition now the fun fact is that even kingfisher used the same sales and leads back model with airbus but even then kingfisher failed miserably and indigo succeeded at the exact same time in the exact same market the question is why did this happen well that is because of a fundamental truth of the indian flyers market and that is customers love living king size but they don't like paying king size to tell you about it kingfisher and jet airways both these airlines wanted to give a king size life to their customers so they gave out in-flight meals in-flight entertainment system and i even remember my dad used to get headsets for free at kingfisher flights whereas indigo decided to eliminate all these perks and decided to give the customers only what was absolutely needed to travel and that is a seat and a little bit of legroom why because food and entertainment would need equipments that would require more fuel to carry and operate eventually increasing the cost reducing the efficiency and complicating the workflow because that would again need additional maintenance and in order to minimize the travel time kingfisher opted in for something called the point-to-point model of operation whereas indigo opted for something called the hub and spoke model of operation and here's how these two models worked out let's say we have six destinations a b c d e n f now if you have to offer a flight connecting all these destinations using a point-to-wide model here's how it would look like you would need a flight from a to b b to c c to d d to e and e to f and then you would need to connect a to c a to d a to e and so on and so forth so in total if you want to connect all these six destinations you would need 15 planes but in the hub and spoke model this becomes very simple instead of connecting all these destinations with a separate flight you create a hub o in between these six points such that if you want to connect a to c this is how it would work out there will be a plane a which will carry all the passengers who want to go to b c d e and f and then when plane a lands at the hub the passengers will go to their respective flights which are b c d e and f and those planes will then fly back to their respective points now on the outside this might look a little complex to you but you know what guys here are the four major benefits of using the hub and spoke model number one you only need six planes in this model as compared to 15 planes in the point-to-point model secondly by using the hub and spoke model the planes are more occupied because now you are serving the same number of customers but with only six flights thirdly due to the presence of the central hub maintenance becomes extremely easy and lastly it is very very easy to expand your network all you need to do is just add another spoke by adding another plane to the network and that's it you can connect all these six destinations with the added point whereas if you want to add another destination to the point-to-point model you will need another six planes to do it therefore the hub and spoke model is that model that can connect people from anywhere to everywhere in the most efficient manner in this case if you see because of using a point-to-point model while kingfisher held a market share of 19.99 with 66 aircrafts indigo almost had the same with 17.6 market share but it was able to serve them with just 38 aircrafts this is the reason why kingfisher and jet airways in the race of providing comfort and convenience were not able to pull off a profit whereas indigo although initially in laws began expanding rapidly without bleeding cash this continued from 2006 to 2008 and then came the most horrific time in indian aviation when the oil prices started shooting up from july 2007 to 2008 the oil prices skyrocketed from just 76 dollars per barrel to 132 dollars per barrel and when this happened every single airline started bleeding money this is the reason why if you see from 2007 onwards the losses of airlines touched crazy levels kingfisher went from 498 to 1900 crores in loss spies it went from 132 to 340 crores in loss jet was steady at 400 crores in loss but then it hit rock bottom to 12 36 crores by 2011 but you know what guys this is where indigo became an opportunist and like we saw on the graph while every other airline was bleeding money indigo went from a loss of 234 crores to a profit of 82 crores which then shot up by 400 to 480 crores and then touched an insane mark of 700 crores all of this happened because indigo's operational costs were low and they were able to rotate their cash better because of which they were able to pull off a profit when every other player was bleeding and from here onwards for the next 10 years indigo reached record levels of profit and today it stands as a market leader with a market share of more than 54 and in addition to its models of operation while kingfisher was bleeding indigo used it as an opportunity by directly poaching the kingfisher pilots , this was because kingfisher was not able to pay its pilots due to its losses and indigo all thanks to its cash reserves offered the pilots a bonus that was almost equal to the pending salaries at kingfisher this way according to the reports somewhere between 200 to 300 pilots joined indigo in just 6 months this is how indigo saved a ton of money on training and onboarding of pilots and became even more profitable in the coming years similarly they also did not make the mistake of spies jet or jet airways with unstable leadership while spy said has been sold and bought many times jet airways at one point didn't even have a full-time ceo for 15 months whereas mr aditya ghost led indigo for 10 long years from 2008 to 2018 and the result of all these strategies is as astounding as it could be from 2012 13 to 1617 indigo's average expenditure on establishment cost was just 11.01 of the overall operational cost whereas spicejet goer and jet airways spent 17.9 11.2 and five five percent respectively india also had some of the lowest number of employees per aircraft in the industry in 2011 while jet needed close to 180 employees per aircraft kingfisher needed 110 spy jet needed 120 whereas indigo needed just 96 employees per aircraft the fun fact is that air india needed 250 employees in 2012 and when it comes to customer service and hospitality indigo has been extraordinary with the lowest complete percentages and cancellation rates in the industry this is the reason why from 2012 onwards if you draw a decorative comparison of all these airlines while kingfisher went out of business indigo started achieving record levels of profit and by 2015 while jet generated a net loss of 2097 crores spicejet generated a loss of 687 crores indigo was already generating a profit of 1 300 crores now although jet tried to come back it sunk down by 2019 but indigo kept going going and going and today it commands a market share of more than 50 in the indian aviation space with an absolute monopoly in 194 routes out of the 531 routes that it operates eventually indigo remained profitable for 10 consecutive years which is absolutely remarkable in an industry that is considered to be a graveyard of regional airlines this is the iconic story of indigo airlines with that let's move to the most important part of the Chapter and that are the lessons from the case study like we saw the one thing that helped indigo grow while all other competitors were sinking during the bad times was its cash flow management the asset led approach that indigo pioneered more than a decade back is now being replicated by companies in multiple industries in various forms companies like furlenko beoku big spoon everest azure strategy and several others are now leasing assets instead of buying them outright this eventually fuels their growth while managing their cash flows better the best part about this shift is that investors like you and i can now benefit directly from the shift in corporate strategy and we can actually create our own stream of fixed passive income moving on there are three very important lessons that we need to learn from indigo lesson number one if you're in the business to serve the common man of india always remember people are always willing to live king size but not pay king size so always think twice before pampering your customers too much and as much as it is important to provide the best quality service to mankind always remember no matter how noble your work is if there is no cash flow you cannot sustain in the market and we saw that in the case of jet airways and kingfisher number two while good brands learn from their mistakes great brands learn from their competitors mistakes in this case while indigo learned the cost of flamboyance from kingfisher and jet airways it also learned from deccan air that there is a difference between cheap and affordable because deccan often messed up with timings and customer service in the race of keeping costs low similarly indigo learned the hub and spoke and sails and leads back model from american european legends like southwest airlines and ryanair and last and most importantly as louis pasteur said chance favors the prepared mind in this case it was the ultra low cost of operation of indigo and the cash reserves of the company that helped it turn the tables as soon as the 2008 crisis happened and this turned indigo from a baby company to a monopoly in the indian aviation space.

IPL

Ipl is one of the richest sports properties in the world the indian premier league has just sold its tv cricket rights for a staggering 2.6 billion dollars you heard it right star india has bagged this huge deal with 16 347 crore rupees hi everybody the indian premier league is by far one of the most remarkable achievements in the indian sports industry but while most of us only know it as the iconic summertime sports sensation very few of us know about the business intricacies of ipl that makes it a capitalistic miracle for the economy of india and the most astonishing thing about ipl is that even during the pandemic while most of the companies were incurring heavy losses in 2020 season in spite of the ticket sales hitting rock bottom due to coved in spite of vivo retracting from its title sponsorship bcci's revenue from ipl shorter by almost 100 going from 2200 crores in 2019 to 4 000 crores in 2020 season and today the brand value of ipl stands at an insane mark of 4.7 billion dollars which is almost 35 900 crores and if you compare the broadcasting rights of ipl at the world level as of 2020 while nba stood at 2.1 million dollars per match bundesliga stood at 3.9 million dollars per match whereas the indian premier league stood way ahead at 8.5 million dollars per match so the question is with so much of money flooding into the ipl ecosystem how does this ecosystem of indian premier league work how do ipl teams make money in spite of losing the competition and most importantly as students of business what are the study materials that can help you understand this billion dollar global sports industry this is a story that dates back to 2007 and this year was very very special in the history of indian cricket why because yuvaraj singh had just mesmerized us with six balls and six sixes movement and the indian cricket team had just won the t20 world cup and the very next year itself the 2008 recession happened because of which businesses all across the world started incurring heavy losses and the 2008 crisis costed the global economy close to two trillion dollars but amidst all of this chaos bcc and lalit modi spotted some critical market indicators that made the market extremely conducive for a domestic cricketing league in india number one because india had won the t20 world cup indians had fallen in love with the new t20 format number two since this game lasts only 3 hours fans can easily watch the entire game unlike an odi which lasts for 8 hours or test cricket that goes on for 5 long days and lastly during the summers indian audience especially the kids desperately needed something for entertainment because they were on summer vacations and they also observed that the league games were always a big big hit all across the world which eventually drew both great revenues and a passionate audience classic examples of the same being the premier league in england which gave us manchester united and the nba championship in the us which gave rise to some of the richest players in the world like shaq and michael jordan therefore bcci wanted to build a similar product for indian teams in india and this is how the idea of the indian premier league came to life and little did they know that in the next 10 years this venture will go on to become one of the biggest sensations in sports history so the question is how does this business model of ipl function well let's try to understand the ecosystem of ipl very very clearly the first set of stakeholders who actually bring the game to life are organizers and administrators in this case ipl's organizers until 2021 was a company called img or international management group and the administrator is still the board of cricket of control in india which is known as bcci then after these two we have the third stakeholder which are the leagues which in this case is ipl so ipl is practically your bcci asset then we have the fourth and the fifth type of stakeholders who are the franchise who participate in the league and the home stadiums that provide the venue for these franchise to play the game these franchises are nothing but your teams like chennai super kings mumbai indians and the rest then the franchise rope in the sixth type of stakeholders who are the players and as you already know the player selection process happens through an auction now whenever these teams play in the stadiums the great revenue is shared between the home team away team and the stadium then we come to the most influential and the most casual stakeholders in the ecosystem who are the streaming platforms and the broadcasters of the indian premier league and the reason why they are so so powerful is because they help the leagues and the players get directly in contact with the lifeblood of the game who are the fans and the members of the stakeholder group includes hosta for streaming and sony or set max for broadcasting and finally we have the most important stakeholders of ipl who are the fans who watch the game for entertainment now based on the number of fans in the demography of the fanbase we have the 10th type of stakeholders which are sponsors and as we all know these are the companies that actually want to leverage the viewership of ipl to give visibility to their product or services now initially fans are just viewers but as the number of fans and the attachment of the game of the franchise increases this industry attracts a secondary stakeholder which are merchandise maker this is where the franchise owners can actually decide whether to license the brand and take a portion of the sales or to set up an in-house merchandise department to sell products directly to the fans apart from that we also have fantasy games like dream 11 that actually use the game to build a business around the fans of the games all you need to know is that these are the primary and the secondary stakeholders of the indian premier league and this brings me to the most important part of the chapter and that is the economics of ipl now let's start with the first stakeholder since bcci is the administrator of the league bcci uses the league as an asset and sells media and digital rights for the ipl to broadcasters and streaming platforms these broadcasters in turn sell ad spaces to brands which wish to get visibility for their products or services so if you saw during the 10 year period of 2008 to 2017 sony owned the broadcasting right to ipl and it bought the broadcasting rights from bcci for 911 crores per year then sony gave away its ad spaces to sponsors who paid to show ads between the matches these ipl ad spaces command a huge price and fall somewhere around 15 to 18 lakhs for every 10 seconds and this is where we saw the commercials of dream 11 nimbus pepsi and so on and so forth so sony's revenue is equal to the number of ad slots sold multiplied by the amount paid per ad slot minus the cost of the broadcasting rights then once the expenses are factored in we'll get the profits generated by the broadcasting partner and similar is the equation of the streaming partner also so initially when the league is not at all popular the broadcaster has to take a very big bet and selling the ad slots in the initial stages is very very difficult but as the popularity of the league increases the broadcaster keeps on increasing the price of the ad slots by which these broadcasters and streaming platforms make an enormous profit and the value of ipl has increased by such an insane rate that when the deal with sony expired star network paid 3270 crore each year for the next five years for the exact same broadcasting rights and this makes it a total of 16 350 crores that's a crazy growth of 258 percent now this money that is obtained through the sale of these rights is then distributed between the franchise and the bcci earlier franchise were entitled to a more than 50 media rights money but with time the franchise share has now come down as of 2021 bcci kept 50 of the money while the franchise distributed the remaining 50 among themselves and in this also around 45 of the money is distributed equally among the teams while the remaining 5 is distributed on the basis of the team's performance in the season this is the economic relationship between bcci the franchise the broadcasters the streaming service and the advertisers and now we come to the individual team partners this is where we have a company like air cell that did not air commercials but just placed its logo on the chennai super king's jersey these are called the individual team sponsors and these companies do not just pay money to appear on the jerseys but can also use the intellectual properties of the franchisees like the players images or using the logos of the teams in their advertisement now out of the revenue that the franchise generates all franchise must pay a 20 cut to bcci each year as a fee this fee is then used to organize matches pay associations and for other organizational purposes now this individual sponsorship is a very very big deal because based on the fan falling and the viewership of the team matches the individual sponsors may choose to pay more or less to these franchise for example if you look at the fan base of all the franchise in the ipl as of 2021 csk have emerged as the strongest franchise with 26.8 million fans followed by mumbai indians at 24.8 million fans then by rcb with 13.3 million fans these three franchise combined accounted for 75 percent of the total fan base in india while the remaining five teams combined contribute to the balance of 25 so obviously according to the success of each team in the tournament and more importantly based on the fan following of the players in the team the brand value of teams itself varies very very vastly this is the reason why while csk and mi command a brand value of 79.5 million and 76 million dollars respectively the not so popular teams like rajasthan royals have a brand value of just 34.4 million dollars this is how the ecosystem of ipl works and as a result of this capitalistic miracle in 2015 alone the indian premier league contributed to 11 500 crores to the gdp of india and this ipl is just a glimpse of the fast-growing domestic indian sports industry and in the next 10 years it is expected that these indian leaks might go on to become some of the most valuable leagues in the world.

XXIV

ITC

Now and then we keep hearing about the pathetic state of farmers in our country. And despite employing more than 50% of the workforce, the condition of the Indian agricultural sector has been so bad that every day 28 people dependent on agriculture commit suicide. And every time we hear this news 99% of us curse the government, we feel sorry for the farmers and we just move on until another news comes in. And in this process of shallow activism, we never try to understand exactly the problem of the farmers on the ground. But you know what, while every single media house and politician has been using the state of farmers for their advantage, the Indian tobacco company has been working on a revolutionary business strategy, and has improved the lives of 4 million farmers across 35,000 villages in India. And the best part is that they have achieved this not by doing charity, but by deploying a world-class business strategy that has even doubled the income of farmers. And if you understand the strategy properly, you will not just be able to tap into a million-dollar business opportunity in the Indian agricultural space. But you'll also be able to understand how can companies like zomato and grofers become profitable in the next five to 10 years? So the golden question is, what exactly is this strategy? How will it help zomato and grofers become profitable, and more importantly, what are the business lessons that we need to learn from this wonderful case study? This is a story that dates back to 1999 when the agricultural export division of ITC was not performing well at all. During that time, soybean was a primary export commodity of ITC, and in 1999 4 million tonnes of soybean or 80% of the produced soybean produce of India came from rural Madhya Pradesh. 80% of this produce was turned into a soya meal that was used in poultry and cattle feed. And eventually, ITC exported soya milk to countries such as China, Pakistan, Bangladesh, and the even United Arab Emirates. And the remaining 20% became edible oil, which again was a highly nutritional high demand product. So the soybean industry overall was supposed to be very, very profitable. And the farmers who produced soybean were supposed to be extremely rich. But guess what? The soybean farmers in Madhya Pradesh were leading a miserable life, most of them struggling in debt when they didn't even have enough capital for the next season. And at the same time, even companies like ITC that were procuring these crops were not able to make healthy profits. So the question was when soybean was in such high demand in the international market, how is it possible that neither the farmers nor the export companies were able to make healthy profits? Well, as it turns out, it was because of a major inefficiency in the supply chain of soybean. And this is how it worked out. On paper, there were three elements in the supply chain, the farmers, the apmc, or the agricultural produce market committee, and then we had export companies like ITC and the wholesalers. So ideally, the farmers were supposed to produce their crops and they were supposed to take them to the apmc. APMC was nothing but a body of licensed traders set up by the government to ensure that farmers are not exploited by open trade. It's also called the mandi. So at the mandi, only government-licensed traders could buy the produce from the farmers, and no other trader was allowed. So theoretically, these traders were supposed to auction the crops, and the highest bidder procured the crops from the farmers. This way, the farmers are supposed to get the best prices and they were supposed to be rich. But in reality, this was far far away from the truth for three major reasons. Firstly, the mandis are about 30 to 50 kilometers far away from the farmers and more than 80% of the farmers in our country are still small farmers. So most of them either had storage facilities or could they afford transportation facilities. Therefore, they either had to rent a truck or they had to sell it to a junior contractor who then sold it to the senior contractor, who then took it to the mandi. So to put that straight, they either had to bear the cost of transportation or they had to sell their produce to the middlemen at an extremely low cost. Secondly, the farmers had no way to find out what exactly was a price being offered at a particular mandi on a particular day. As a result, they only had to rely on word of mouth and take the risk of traveling 50 kilometers with the hope that the word of mouth was true. And lastly, since no other trader was allowed to procure crops from the mandi, the licensed traders formed a cartel and instead of the auction for the highest price, they all quoted the same price which was way below the standard price of the produce. For example, if one quintal of soybean was supposed to be sold at a base price of 8000 rupees giving the farmer a profit of 2500 rupees per quintal, what the traders would do is all of them would quote a price of 6000 rupees only. Why? Because 1700 farmers have already traveled 50 kilometers and they cannot go back and they couldn't sell their products anywhere else. So the farmer had no other option but to sell his crops at a bare minimum profit of 500 rupees to the licensed traders. And the worst case, if the farmer sold it to the junior contractor, then the profits would go down further from 500 rupees to less than 100 rupees sometimes even at a loss. And to make matters worse, even after dragging the price down to a mere 500 rupees. The mandi traders did not pay the farmers right away, and they took the hard on produce at an unofficial credit and paid the farmers only when they made a profit. And this time of credit would range from one week to even one month. And this pathetic system put the farmers in a very very dangerous vicious cycle. Since the farmers did not have enough cash flow. It led to low investment in farming equipment and other essential inputs like pesticides and fertilizers. This led to low production leading to low margins, which again led to a cash crunch. Even today, this is the state of most of the farmers in our country. And at the end of the day, in 1999, the farmers were losing 60 to 70% of the potential value of their crop with the agricultural gains of only 25 to 30% of the global standards. But you know what, guys, this is when ITC came out with a revolutionary initiative called the E-chaupal initiative, and they installed a super amazing tool called the computer in the remotest villages of India in 1999 itself. And under this initiative, ITC supplied a Windows PC and internet connection and a dot matrix printer to all the village centers in its canopy. To take this forward, they launched a website called soyachaupal.com, which consisted of three of the most important information tabs needed for the farmers, data, and weather reports to help the farmers decide what is the best time to sow their seeds and to prevent them from sowing seeds at the wrong time. Number two was the best practices section. For example, 18-inch spacing was considered to be the best practice. However, many farmers were spacing the seed rows nine inches apart, which eventually resulted in less yield. And thirdly, they had the Market Information section that gave the important market metrics, including the daily price and volume traded at the mandis and the ITC centers. And this was supported by other important pages like the q&a section, the new section, and even the crop Information section. Secondly, they appointed a lead farmer called the sanchalak who was responsible for helping the farmers out with computer operations. And he was given a commission of 0.5% based on the farmer's productivity. So because of the incentive, he automatically worked hard to help the farmers out with the computer operation and to enable them to improve their productivity. And thirdly, ITC convinced the government to allow the company to procure the products directly from the farmers with the promise that they will provide reasonable cost and will build an efficient and profitable supply chain. And that is all Ladies and gentlemen, the implementation of the E-chaupal began in 1999. Back then ITC had five processing units in Madhya Pradesh and 39 warehouses making a total of 44 touchpoints, covering 80% of the farmers in Madhya Pradesh, to which the farmers could bring the soybean production. The best part was that these points were only 20 to 30 kilometers away from the farmers as compared to the 30 to 50-kilometer range of the mandis. And this amazing setup ladies and gentlemen changed the way the farmers of Madhya Pradesh traded soybeans. And this is how the system worked out. First of all, the farmers were given all the important information through the E-chaupal computers, which included everything from weather forecasts up to the seed sowing techniques. Therefore, the farmers were confidently able to invest in their crops. This reduced the risk of the spoiled crops and at the same time, it increased the yield. Then after the harvesting was done, they could directly have a look at the website to see how much price was being offered at the apmc and the ITC center daily. Eventually, they could compare the prices and then decide where to go to have higher profits. In this case, ITC even reimburse the transportation cost to the farmers because of this, they do not have to depend on the contractors to sell their yield at a bare minimum profit. After that, when they arrived at the ITC center, the processing facility also included a soil testing lab. And here's where top great scientists offered the best recommendation for fertilizers or additives based on the chemical composition of the farmer's soil sample. And lastly, the farmer was given cash on delivery for the sale of his products immediately and this was a very big deal because it enables him to buy fertilizer and other essential products that were needed for the next season. And this wonderful system, ladies and gentlemen, turn the disastrous, vicious cycle into a virtuous cycle by which the farmers had good cash flow, which led to high investment into farming equipment that led to high productivity, eventually giving them thicker margins and better cash flow. On top of that, despite all these reimbursements, this setup was so amazing that even ITC ended up saving $3 per tonne on transportation, and at the same time, the farmers can earn $8 extra per tonne. Furthermore, this move turned out to be extremely profitable for ITC, because they got raw materials from the farmers at a low cost. And we're able to use that for their FMCG division. And today, each E-chaupal initiative already has become the largest initiative among the internet-based interventions in rural India, reaching out to more than 4 million farmers across 35,000 villages in 10 different states. And today, these crops include soya beans, coffee, wheat, rice, pulses, and even shrimp. This is the incredible story of the E-chaupal initiative. And this brings me to the most important part of the chapter and that are the lessons from the case study and the business opportunities arising in the Indian agricultural space. Moving on to the lessons from the case study. There are three important lessons to learn from ITC's E-cahupal initiative. Number one, technological accessibility, government regulation, and cash-rich stakeholders are the three pillars that can catalyze the growth of rural sectors of India. In this case, the farm bill now legally allows companies to procure the products directly from the farmers without seeking special permission. And thanks to Jio kisaan, farmers can now witness the next level of the E-cahupal initiative. Secondly, we are seeing the rise of extremely cash-rich and not-so-profitable companies like zomato and swiggy, who are building a b2b supply chain to supply raw materials directly to the restaurants. And this is where projects like zomato hyper pure come in. And just like ITC cannot own the supply chain, but only make it super efficient and profitable both for themselves and for the farmers. If this is done by the rest of the companies, the inefficiency caused by the apmc traders will get eliminated resulting in huge profits for grofers, zomato, swiggy, and other companies. And lastly, most importantly, if you're someone who wants to invest in organic farming or hydroponics please read about something called contract farming because it's opening up new supply chains that will eventually present you with game-changing business and investment opportunities.

XXV

JioMart

Retail wars in india are rising to new peaks every single day on one side we have giants like reliance retail and demard who are obsessively focused on profits on the other side we have new eight startups like big basket grofers and udan who are riding the internet revolution using their scale and software but while every single news channel talks about these billion dollar companies very few actually talk about the poor state of kirana stores in our country with each passing year while demand shares keep going up the revenue and profits of kirana stores are touching new lows to make matters worse we have the pandemic that put thousands of small business owners in debt sinking them deeper into an already existing crisis but you know what guys this is where reliance is bringing a revolution and the instrument of this revolution is none other than jio malt which started its operation in 2020 and the supply chain that they are building is so powerful that they could have both the scale of big basket and the massive profits of dmart eventually jio mart has the potential to become the most powerful player in retail the best part is that unlike demart or big basket jiomart will not become powerful by killing the kirana stores but by empowering them to become as powerful as big basket and demult the question is how is it even possible that a kirana store can compete with giants like demart and big basket what exactly is Jiomart's master plan and most importantly as investors and students of business what are the most important factors that we need to keep an eye on to understand the iconic retail wars of india the first thing you need to understand is how do the players in retail market operate in the first place the first player we have is dmart and as we saw in the dmart case study demar uses the power of discounting to get the commodities at such low rates that demar selling price is lesser or equal to the cost price of kirana stores for example a kirana store places an order for 200 units of ghee at 450 rupees per kg and says it at an mrp of 485 rupees per kg whereas dmard places an order for 20 000 units and buys the same packet of ghee at 400 rupees per kg eventually sells it at 455 rupees per kg therefore if kirana stores want to compete with dmart they have to sell ghee at a bare minimum profit of 5 rupees which is practically impossible this is how dmard used its massive scale and cash flow to erode the business of kirana stores now fortunately or unfortunately going to dmart had not been convenient for everyone since they started their online very late the customer segment that preferred convenience over price still went to the nearest kirana stores this way the kira store still had an essential place in the market but that is where big basket came in with its online service and a robust supply chain now unlike dmart big basket did not just use its scale but also built a super efficient supply chain to deliver these products to every nook and corner of the city therefore customers did not just get the price of dmart but also got it home delivered that gave big basket the extra edge over tmart apart from that big basket has done an incredible job at designing the most sophisticated user interface in the market and the most powerful tool it has is big basket daily and big basket daily wants to become such an integral part of your life that it wants to eliminate the very possibility of you going to demand this is how big basket and dmart have taken away two of the most fundamental pillars of a kirana store business that are cost and accessibility and they did that using their superpowers of scale and software as a result our local kirana stores are facing a nightmare with their incomes dropping with each passing year but you know what guys this is where jio mart came in and like i said before if JioMart business plan is executed properly within some time even a small kirana store will become as powerful as demand and pick basket and within no time Jiomart could become bigger than dmart and big basket combined so the question is what is this master plan and what is Jiomart doing to enable kirana stores to compete with giants like dmart and pick basket the first thing Jiomart is working on is beating demart in terms of scale and purchase and like i said before the reason why kirana stores cannot compete with dmart is because they do not have the purchase power to buy 20 000 units of ghee which is why they do not have the bargaining power but this is where jio's master plan comes in Jiomart says instead of the kirana stores procuring goods in small quantities jio mart will procure the goods from the fncg company straight away and become a distributor to the kirana stores for example instead of 10 kirana stores individually buying 200 units of ghee from a wholesaler jio mart will procure 48 000 units of ghee directly from the fmcg companies on behalf of 200 kirana stores eventually it will transport them individually to each one of these stores this way just like dmart bought 20 000 units of ghee for 400 rupees using its purchase power jio mart will be able to buy 40 000 units of ghee at the same price from the fmcg companies and then it can sell to the canada stores at 420 rupees to 425 rupees per kg this will enable the kirana stores to sell the packet of ghee at 455 rupees which is the same price as demart and this time they do not have to set it at a bare minimum profit of 5 rupees but can get a healthy margin of 25 to 30 rupees now this begs the question how is this going to benefit Jiomant because if you see while demand makes a profit of 53 rupees per kg jio mart only makes a profit of 20 to 25 rupees and on top of that it also has to take care of transportation but you know what guys this is where we miss out on the huge scalability factor that Jiomart has over team art while dmarc is serving only 72 cities kirana stores are present in more than 2500 cities all across the country and unlike dmart jio does not have to set up a giant store it just needs to build a logistics system to supply goods to the kirana stores and another point to be noted over here is that these kirana stores will be complementary entities to the already existing 12 000 reliance retail outlets this is how reliance intends to empower small kirana stews to stand up against the likes of dmart by turning them into micro distribution centers now the question is how is Jiomart going to beat big basket well that is where the second wing comes in and that is software support of gmart if you search jio mart in the play store you will find two Jiomart apps one is Jiomartt for consumers and the other is jio mart for partners in the first app that is Jiomart for consumers jio has brought along a professional grade user interface to help users to place orders and the vision is that when a customer places an order in the app the order will be delivered from the nearest kirana store that has the commodity in stock and this kirana store will be a Jiomod partner the catch over here is that while big basket expects you to have a minimum basket value of 500 rupees jio mart has no minimum order value for home delivery this is how Jiomart intends to use software and aggressive pricing to empower kirana stores to compete with big basket similarly the second app enables kirana stores to place orders directly with Jiomart which will enable them to procure goods at a very low cost without having to visit the mandi and without worrying about transportation this is how Jiomart intends to deploy its impeccable scale and software to empower the small kiruna stores all across the country to beat the likes of dmart and brick basket in the next 5 to 10 years and it is expected that small businesses will be empowered enough to become 5 to 30 more profitable in spite of the competitive pricing and jio mart will be able to scale up their accessibility through the lens and breadths of the country so on paper it looks like Jio mart is on its way to become the undisputed king in the grocery market right well not really because on ground there are four critical challenges that kirana stores are facing with Jiomart and only if they solve this problem can they actually stand a chance against big basket and team art and this brings me to the most important part of the chapter and that is as investors and students of business what are the crucial factors that will dictate the success or failure of Jiomart in the ongoing retail war in india moving on here are four critical challenges ahead of Jiomod that will determine the success or the failure of the company in the market the first challenge is that as soon as kirana stores start ordering from Jiomard they naturally have to cut ties with their existing suppliers now this is a very big sacrifice because we are talking about a relationship that has been fostered for decades secondly one of the most crucial instruments of business for a kirana store is credit for example if you are a kirana store owner when you buy 30 000 rupees worth of products from a supplier the supplier gives you 15 to 20 days to pay back the money this way you can sell these products make a profit of 5000 rupees and then pay back the supplier and as soon as a supplier becomes familiar with you they even offer one to two lakh rupees of credit for 15 to 30 days without any pressure of an official contract so even with very less capital merely because of the trust factor the kirana store can do business seamlessly but in case of Jiomart when i spoke to the store owners in my circle they said that although Jiomart offers lower prices than the suppliers it does not give them credit therefore they need a lot of working capital in hand in order to operate their business at the same time udaan initially gives businesses 15 000 rupees of credit for 10 days and as the business grows with time the current amount keeps increasing but this also means that even if you are running a grocery store for 20 years you will be treated as a newbie with a credit of only 15 000 rupees for 10 days therefore credit amount and time are critical factors that Jio mart needs to handle thirdly as far as my research goes Jiomant is not fulfilling delivery for the kirana stores so rolling that out again is going to be an execution challenge but until then the small business owners will again need more working capital and lastly Jiomart is planning to onboard kirana stores to turn them into jio mart exclusive stores and in this partnership Jiomart will turn a small kirana store into a premium looking mini shopping center where customers can walk in and take products from the rack in return Jiomart will make sure that any online order within a particular radius from the Jiomart app will go to that particular Jiomod exclusive store this way small kirana stores will start acting as micro distribution hubs for reliance retail now again while this looks lucrative on paper it comes with the condition that business owners need to pay for the equipment needed for the transformation but along with that they also offer six years of emi option secondly all goods must be bought from Jiomart unless the prices are lower at the monday or other suppliers and thirdly there is nothing officially mentioned about the store credit system and lastly the delivery has to be fulfilled by the Jiomod partner himself so working capital plus emi plus extra delivery staff will be very difficult to offer for small business owners these are the four on ground challenges that Jiomart needs to tackle if it wants to beat the likes of big basket and dmart.

XXVI Lenskart

lenskart is one of the most revolutionary startups in the Indian business ecosystem what started as a garage startup by three engineering boys has now become such a strong player in the Indian Iowa space that today it has grown to serve more than four lakh customers on a monthly basis and claims to account for nearly 30 percent of India's organized eyewear market and what was stunning to me was that when the financial year ended in 2020 while titan I plus revenue grew by just six percent from 511 to 544 crores lenskart's revenue exploded by 98 going from 485 crores to over 963 crores and because of this lens car took a major lead in the eyewear market of India and not just that today they have more than 800 stores in 120 cities across the country and are valued at 2.5 billion dollars with their first year of profit in 2020. so the question is how lenskart beat the giants like titan in the eyewear industry what was lens card's business strategy was as an entrepreneur and investor what lessons do we need to learn from Piyush Bansal and his legendary team at lenskart. this is a story that dates back to early 2000s back in the day buying specs was a cumbersome procedure you first had to take time out and go to the optician select suitable frames from a limited collection check on various styles choose your glasses and then finally wait for nearly six to seven days before receiving your glasses now although it looks pretty simple on paper only the ones who have gone through this procedure will understand how cumbersome this is not just that if you look at the eyewear market of india back then while 95 percent of the market was filled with unorganized players selling cheap products with no guarantee or no warranty on the other side in the organized market although the service was good the cheaper specs you could buy used to start from 1500 rupees which was titan i plus entry product that too only from 2007 onwards and below this category that is below 1500 rupees price range there were barely any reputed brands now when you see this cost range most people would assume that the reason why the prices are so high is because of the high making cost or perhaps the low margins in the eyewear market right well guess what this is what the margins in the eyewear market look like if you look at a normal brand like warby parker while frames and lenses cost them ten dollars shipping costs them ten dollars trade and advertising costs five dollars the total cost of a typical product stands at twenty five dollars whereas their selling price is ninety five dollars which means you are looking at a crazy profit margin of 73 percent not just that if you look at luxortica which is secretly a monopoly in the eye-wide space of the world their royalties cost two dollars marketing and ads cost six dollars frames and lenses cost twenty four dollars which i already think is an exaggeration by the way and lastly their shipping costs two dollars so total cost is 34 but their typical selling price is 200 which is a margin of 83 now the obvious question over here is with the margins being so high and the cost being so exorbitant why don't these brands bring down the cost to make it affordable for the common man well there is a not so sweet capitalistic intent behind it you see guys whether you are a rickshaw driver or school teacher or even a businessman if you know that your child needs vision correction you will have to buy a pair of glasses and even if it costs 1500 rupees if a rickshaw driver knows that his kid cannot see without it he will shell out his entire life saving just so that the kid can study well so you see it's a mandatory high stake pain point that needs to be addressed and hence in spite of the high pricing people will stretch their limits to be able to offer them this is the same reason why diabetes meds are so costly and the same reason why colleges ask for exorbitant donations without bothering about the affordability of the opposite person because it is a mandatory high stake pain point but this is where our shark huge bunsel and his co-founders saw a mammoth business opportunity and they spotted three problems that needed to be addressed in the eyewear market of india the first problem was obviously the costing which gave them a huge scope to play in the 250 rupees to 1500 rupees segment number two was that iwa was still being treated like a medical equipment which did not make the people with glasses feel good it was very similar to how people with hearing aid feel today and lastly let alone affordability even accessibility to opticians was very very limited in india more than 500 million people need vision correction and yet not even 200 million people are actually doing something about it on top of that in the tier 2 tier 3 cities even today there is a dire need of opticians this is the reason why piyush bansal and his co-founders started lensguard with a vision to correct the vision of india so riding the ecommerce wave lenskart entered the prescription glasses market with three value propositions cost convenience and variety while the cheapest branded product which was tied in i plus was priced at 1500 rupees lens card cut its margins and started selling at a bare minimum price of 250 rupees while local options took six to seven days to deliver your glasses lens card started dollaring them in just 72 hours while local opticians had just a few hundred designs lens card had 5 000 designs to choose from while local opticians did not give any guarantee or warranty on unbranded products lens card gave away one year warranty on frames one year for lenses and to make it even better they even introduce the 14 days no questions asked return policy therefore lens car provided all the perks of a branded product at the cost of an unbranded product on top of that while the glasses from local opticians often had a margin of error lens card delivered their products with zero error tolerance and merely because of this massive scale lens squad was able to completely eliminate the middleman through its online model and was able to cut the cost by nearly 70 percent this is the reason why they could sell their products at such low prices and this is how lens card entered the indian market with a bang but just like any other new age business model lens car tackled the adoption challenges very very elegantly to lure the skeptics of e-commerce they rolled out crazy offers like a free frame and heavy discounts to tackle the lack of trial problem they came out with their revolutionary virtual try on feature and they spent a ton of money in making eyewear look cool with lifestyle marketing and most importantly they very very strategically eliminated the very need to go to the opticians to tell you about it when people doubted their vision they had to go to an optician who had equipments to check their vision and then she gives the power figures to the customers now since people have already stepped out of the house many people were more likely to order glasses from the same optician herself otherwise they have to come home open the computer because mobile internet wasn't that good back then then go online enter the power on lenscard.com and then place the order and this friction itself reduce the chances of people going to lenskart.com this is the reason why lens cards started making some strategic partnerships and investments in companies like 6 over 6 and this enabled them to do home visits for eye checkup so now lenskart's own eyewear specialist would visit the customer's house for a free trial carrying 100 best-selling frames this way using the lenso meter solution the field executors could run low cost vision test at home eventually eliminating the very possibility of customers going to opticians and now not only could the customers get the power checked but even the frames could be tried and the customers could make a purchase with the executive himself therefore lens card made it super easy to place orders and reduce the friction of the process of going to the optician coming back home and then placing the order this is how through variety cost getting and convenience and by carefully addressing the adoption challenges lens cards successfully got a huge chunk of the indian audience to add up to online shopping for iweb on top of that they even entered the semi premium and premium market with their brands like john jacobs and vincent chase but you know what guys what was absolutely astonishing to me was that their accuracy of giving the right product to the customers is so amazing that their return rate was as low as four percent this number is super crazy because in e-commerce even a 15 return rate is considered to be excellent but you know what guys something strange happened in 2014 as we saw suddenly lenskart started opening physical stores all across the country in 2014 itself lenskart launched 20 offline stores in partnership with optometrist in tier 2 and tier 3 cities of india but now the question is did lenskart become exactly what they were trying to disrupt and if not why did they open up stores well there are three reasons for that number one like we saw before 95 of india's ivy market was filled with unorganized brands which had no way of online access and still people bought from them and back in 2014 internet penetration itself was too low so by being adamant with the online only model lens card was missing out on a ton of customers in tier 2 tier 3 cities who were still shopping offline merely because of skepticism secondly because lens card was investing in their manufacturing they already had systems in place that could produce high quality glasses at dirt cheap cost and that too with the supply chain so robust that they could deliver to thousands of pin codes all across the country in just three days and lastly because of digital marketing and its delivery model the name of lenskart had already reached the corners of the country which by default made them far far superior as compared to unorganized brands and at the same time the organized players like lawrence and mayo did not have a strong presence in tier 2 tier 3 cities of india so the only thing needed for lens card was the touch and feel factor so you know what lens card adopted something called the endless aisle strategy which is a perfect mix of both online and offline models and this is how it works out just like you walk into a physical store you walk into a lens card store which has the best selling frames an online catalog and an executive who can help you make the perfect choice here you get your power checked choose the frame you love and the store manager will place an order through his online portal and when this is done your process is complete and the rest of the process that is fitting manufacturing and delivery of your product will come from lens carts conventional supply chain itself so to put that straight the physical store is merely being used to give you the sense of touch and feel and the rest of the supply chain is still the e-commerce supply chain only now the question is what exactly are the benefits of doing this number one while normal optician orders 2000 frames at a cost of 200 rupees average and has to do stock keeping in his physical store lens card could place an order of 2 lakh frames at barely 100 rupees average cost which is stocked up in its warehouse and this stock could be shipped all across the country so the lens card store itself does not have to worry about dead inventory number two while opticians only have 500 frame choices lens card stores can offer 5000 designs without worrying about dead inventory this way lens card can offer both lower prices and higher variety and lastly since both ways you have to wait for the glasses to be made lens card has a massive advantage here while lens card uses its superior manufacturing technology to manufacture its glasses and still delivers it early opticians do not have such advanced tech which results into both higher cost and less precision cherry on the cake because of this cost cutting and high margins of the industry lens card is able to give a healthy commission of 25 to 30 to its franchise owners which further makes it viable and desirable for local options to get converted into a lens card store and when this got combined with a 14 day return policy and a quick delivery system the barrier to entry for local opticians increased by a large extent as a result the number of customers of lens cards started peaking this laid such a strong foundation for lens card that when the pandemic hit while the opticians had to keep their shops closed while big brands like lawrence and mayu had limited reach lenskart was seamlessly able to deliver its products through the lens and breadths of the country this is the reason why lens car grew by 98 from 486 crores to 963 crores in revenue while tide and iplus grew by just six percent to just 544 crores and now they have already started dominating the premium iot space with john jacobs in the 3 000 plus base and vincent chase in the 1000 to

1500 range and if done right these brands could become the biggest eyewear brands in india and this brings me to the most important part of the chapter and that are the lessons from the case study let's move on to the lessons from the case study lesson number one every time there is a technological revolution more often than not you will either have to change your product or your supply chain or sometimes both of them in this case while the product which is a pair of glasses remain the same the supply chain of these glasses were revolutionized due to e-commerce and lens card happened to become an opportunist and built a low cost highly efficient supply chain to dominate the iwa market in india lesson number two every time you see a mandatory undisabled pain point that is being leveraged by corporations you are looking at a mammoth business opportunity in this case it was a pair of glasses but if you remember from the gillette case study it was the exorbitant cost of razor blades and lastly while most people think that brick and mortar stores will be dead the concept of endless isle is a breakthrough in retail that will redefine the way we shop and if you want to read about in detail please read about how warby parker is using the endless aisle concept to sell eyewear in the u.s.

LIC

In march 2022 india is about to witness its biggest ever ipo in the history of the stock market because the country's largest insurance company lic is about to give away five percent of the indian government's take to potentially raise nearly eight billion dollars lic is an iconic company in the indian business history that has been dominating the indian insurance sector since 66 years now and what blew our mind is that lic is so huge that in 2017 while government of india's budget was 383.93 billion dollars lic's assets under management itself was 403.44 billion dollars the customer base of lice is nearly six times the population of uk and with more than 280 million policies it is the fifth largest insurer in the world in terms of insurance premium collection as of 2020 and today lic is not just an insurer but a nation builder and employment generator and a critical financial conglomerate of india the question is what is the story of lic how did it become such an important engine in india's growth history and most importantly as investors what are the factors that you need to consider before you invest into lic or similar companies the story of lic dates back to 1956 india back then it had been just nine years since the britishers had left india and india was still recovering from the scars of colonialism after 200 years of ruling the brits had left behind in india that was not only economically poor but also lagged in self-confidence and believed to prosper in the mid-1950s while the leaders of us and uk were executing social security schemes indian poverty rates had reached a maxima wherein 61 of india's population was living in poverty in 1954 on top of that we saw multiple disease outbreaks like malaria and cholera during that time and with our healthcare system still in its prenatal stages mortality rates in india were very very high now at the micro level if you look at the indian households in 1950s most of them only had a single earning member with multiple dependents in some cases there were eight dependents in a family with just a single earning member so if anything happened to that one earning member the entire family was vulnerable to poverty as a result financial security in india was the need of the hour now the leaders of india knew that life insurance was very very important and there were already 245 insurance companies operating in india but the problem with these companies was that they only cater to the urban pockets as in they only cater to the rich people who could pay a heavy premium and it was quite understandable because if they wanted to make a profit that was the only way to operate this is the reason why insurance was out of the reach of those vulnerable segments of population that actually needed it which were the rural and lower economic start of india however from the government standpoint if these people did not get insured they were extremely vulnerable to poverty which in the long term was very very dangerous for the economy of india this is the reason why on 1st of september 1956 a new engine for indian economy was born which was known as the life insurance corporation of india lic was formed by bringing together two 45 small and big private life insurance companies and the vision was to make sure that insurance is accessible through the lens and breadth of the country regardless of the economic strata of the population all of these companies together amounted to 27 000 employees 50 lakh policies assets under management of 400 crores and insurance covers of 1 000 crores now the question over here is if 60 percent of india was living in poverty these people were already struggling for food and water right then during such a critical time during such an adverse condition how do you get someone to pay for something like life insurance well this is where we saw the rise of lic agents and in the 1950s 60s and 70s in the absence of any digital medium back then lic's huge sales force traveled to every nook and corner of the country by cars buses trains motorbikes and in some cases even bulla carts to achieve lic's vision of securing the poor families of india and mind you it wasn't easy at all it took lic not 5 not 10 not 15 but 30 long years to first educate the poor then to instill the importance of insurance among the poor and then to normalize spending on insurance so basically lic worked very hard and spent 30 long years in creating an industry for every other insurance company that entered the indian market this insane persistent and sheer genius in establishing the importance of insurance to the lower economic start of india is something that is an invaluable contribution of lic this is where the second phase came in and that was in 1999 when the government of india opened up the market for private players and it resulted into 10 entities entering the space which finally ended lic's monopoly of 44 years this is where most of these brands like hdfc and icsi which had a banking presence started entering the space in a joint venture with world's largest insurers who had a vast experience of cross-selling insurance and like we saw in sectors like airlines and telecom government-backed organizations like air india and bsnl often lost their shield when private players entered the market and this was majorly because they could not deliver on the aspect of customer experience and the same thing was also expected out of lic but you know what guys in case of lic in spite of the entry of many private players with deep pockets from insurers all across the world lic still stood tall as a dominating force in the indian market the question is what was so special about lic for starters the synonymity of lic with insurance was something that was very very difficult to break when you say insurance people by default thought about lic secondly lic was excellent with settling claims and boasted of a claim settlement ratio of 98.31 which meant that out of 100 people who applied for the policy and paid for it 98 people's families received the insurance money on the death of the earning member now usually if you've ever been to a government organization mostly the staff doesn't talk to you properly i'm not talking about all but mostly this does happen and because of the bureaucracy and extreme job security there is often a sense of lethargy that kicks in because of which even the smallest processes often take a lot of time but in case of lic that did not happen because lic instilled that attribute in its employees which was way more powerful than any protocol or incentive and that was the sense of empathy lic in spite of being so huge invested heavily into not just training its employees but also into making them realize that the work was no ordinary work at all the officers were taught that with each passing day of delay it is costing an entire family's life if they sat on papers and procrastinated it it meant that they were adding to the problems in the lives of those families who desperately needed the money and this sense of empathy and bias for action was a crucial factor to ensure speedy claim resolution back when automation did not exist thirdly lic became more and more agile with time for example at one given point in time lic knew that its central reporting structure was creating a bottleneck in quick resolution earlier branches were only business procurement centers and the claim settlement process always needed approval from the central and zonal offices and this approval procedure used to take a lot of time because of which the back and forth resulted into a lot of delays this is the reason why lic undertook a massive decentralization project to move decision making from the central office to the zonal office then to the divisional office and finally to the branches this is the reason why by 2013 41 of the 43 divisional offices were functioning almost independently this gave a rapid boost to the claim settlement process but all of this alone was not enough to counter competition back in the 1990s when reese killing and upskilling weren't buzzwords in the industry lic invested heavily into continuous learning of its agents to both educate the staff and to understand the needs of the market this feedback loop gave lic critical insights based on which they could refine their business and launch new products and you know what guys lic was one of the first companies to introduce the concept of big money through big sale what this means is that back then because agents were deployed on a commission basis their focus was on selling the smaller covers of 25 to 30 lakhs because your premiums was very less and they could easily push the sale and get the commission as a result even if the family gets the insurance of 25 to 30 lakhs if their earning member drew a salary of one lakh rupees per month this little cover of 25 lakhs was barely enough for just two years of her income so the insurance was barely effective in covering the needs of the family in the absence of the owner but this is where lic deployed a method called some assured on the basis of human value and in this method they said that the cover must be decided not just on the basis of the offerability but also on the basis of the financial needs of the family so if a person's family needs one like rupees per month for utilities and discretionary spends the insurance cover should be decided in a manner that in the event that a person dies his family should get this 1 lakh rupees per month or 12 lakh rupees a year for his insurance policy so basically an assured sum of 1.2 crores must be payable over the next 10 years this back of the hand calculation is what decides whether the total cover should be 50 lakhs 1 crore or two crore and this was deployed by lic to make sure that their customers get the real value of the insurance similarly when agents did not sell low ticket plans lic designed special rural plans to cater to the needs of the rural and semi-urban part of india by which both the agents and the customer could be benefited and eventually lic started selling a large number of low ticket policies to the economically weaker section of india this is how through intense effort into educating india in the past 60 years through agility and constant learning lic has remained a successful government entity without succumbing to the pressure of socialism and this brings me to another very very important factor and that is how did lic as an entity contribute to the economy of india to put that straight you see the beauty of insurance lies in risk pooling so at any given point of time let's say a life insurance company collects 500 rupees premium from 10 lakh customers that gives them a capital of 50 crudes out of which 20 to 30 girls might go into settlement and expenses but the remaining 20 crores would still lie idle which is why lic considered putting this money to task by investing into financial instruments so that they could generate better returns with this ideal money so in 1956 when lic was formed the government wanted to ensure that the nation's savings invested in insurance policies were directed towards building infrastructure and providing amenities to the masses in rural and urban areas so some regulations were designed wherein lic had to invest its money as per the following guidelines fifty percent of its aum had to be invested in government and government-backed securities thirty-five percent of its aum approved investments only through public or private sector bonds or equities and fifteen 15 could be invested on discretion and guess what this mobilizing of funds became such an important contribution to the indian economy that it gave lic the title of a nation builder itself why because out of its 25 lakh crows in assets 65 was invested towards the social sector especially in power water supply sewage and transportation and this humongous capital laid the foundations for the infrastructure of india in fact even when the road ministry under nitin gadkari sir had announced to increase the coverage of national highways to 2 lakh kilometers in 2016 they had outlined a budget of 2.5 lakh crores out of which 50 000 crews was to be pumped in by lic alone similarly lic played an important role in housing schemes even before hdfc even when housing was not even a priority for banks at all fun fact is that lic was also known to be a stock market stabilizer in 1986 when the kashmir conflict escalated to a full-scale war between india and pakistan the indian stock market had plummeted causing many prizes to be manipulated by speculators but in just a matter of few days under the direction of the government of india lic pumped in close to 5 crore rupees to provide some stability to the market and in the recent times lic has been pumping close to 50 000 crores in the equity market mainly in nifty 50 companies this is how lic has not just been an insurer but also an important pillar for the development of india and this brings me to the most important part of the episode and that is considering all the rosy picture about lic that you have now as investors what are the pointers of concern that you are supposed to consider while you invest in lic or similar companies there are three pointers that we need to keep in mind before you invest into lic number one lic even today is extremely dependent on agents now although this is an important pillar of growth with threats like covet that completely curbed traveling dependency on agents hasn't proven to be very very helpful and at the same time during covalent life insurance as a sector has grown rapidly so with the rise of internet penetration reliability on agents alone may not be the best for the company secondly you need to keep in mind that insurance is not like any other business so financial indicators need to be studied differently and in a much better manner in this case let's say today lic collects premium worth 50 crore rupees this 50 crore rupees cannot be considered as revenue right because next year if 100 people die this capital needs to be deployed similarly you can't expense this figure to derive profit and loss statements like we do for other companies which is why you need to learn about something called embedded value this is a little complex so i'll give you a link in the description so that you can understand this concept better and lastly one of the best ways to understand how a company is performing would be to keep an eye on the competitors and to draw a comparison based on their strategies in this case i would highly recommend you to keep an eye on the innovative solutions deployed by hdfc and icse

XXVIII
Lijjat Papad

This is a story of 7 ordinary women who had no background in business, and no significant educational qualification with just 80 rupees in the capital they were able to build a business empire worth 1600 crores which are spread across 69 branches and more than 42,000 employees. This home-grown brand that I'm talking about is none other than Shri Mahila Griha Udyog Lijjat Papad. Now, what's more, fascinating about this company is not the growth of the company but the fact that the business philosophies of this home-grown company somehow seem to have a very close resemblance to extraordinary companies like Starbucks and Apple also. The question is- What is so special about this papad company and how has it lasted for more than 62 years? And how did these 7 women manage to build a business empire out of just ?80 in the capital? The answer to this question lies in the incredible history of the Lijjat papad. This is a story that dates back to the late 1950s India when India was a fairly underdeveloped country. And back then let alone education, even literacy was considered to be a luxury. And even in terms of literacy during those times woman's literacy was not even considered important because of which only 8% of women in India could read and write while 92% of women in India were illiterates. On top of that, women were not even allowed to go out and work and the earning capacity of the families was not enough to afford a decent standard of living. That is when in 1959, Mumbai. A group of 7 amazing women from very ordinary backgrounds came together to discuss a business idea that wouldn't need them to step out of the house, wouldn't need education, and yet could produce a competitive product in the market. That is how the idea of Lijjat Papad was born with just ?80 of capital that was given to them by a social worker. They first started selling their papads at a local store and soon enough due to the superb quality and taste of the papad even other shops started buying their papads. And that's when they started scaling up. Now, when they started scaling they had the opportunity to hire women at a dearth cheap cost because they were one of the rarest avenues of income for women which allowed them to work from home. But you know what? When these women had their first board meeting they established the fact that the primary goal of their business wouldn't be to make money but to empower women from the smallest households in the country and to provide them with the livelihood to nurture their families. And more importantly, they also established the fact that money would only be used as fuel to scale their impact on the women of India and not be the sole purpose of their existence. So instead of hiring women, they started to give out ownership to every woman who joined their business and called them Lijjat Sisters rather than employees. This is what you call collective ownership, wherein every employee owns a small part of the company such that the profits and losses, both are shared by every single person in the organization. So regardless of your age, caste, or religion even if you were at the lowest hierarchy of the Lijjat Papad organization you'd still own a part of the business. Now, most of us might think that this is just another business move but I gotta tell you guys that this attribute of collective ownership is one of the foundational principles that make Starbucks an extraordinary company. Because you know what? Just like the sisters of Lijjat papad own a small part of the company regardless of their position in the organization, every employee at Starbucks is considered a partner in the business rather than an employee. Everyone starting from the baristas who serve coffee to the customers up to the senior management officers, each one of them is offered stock options of the company. So this way, just like the Lijjat sisters every employee in Starbucks could be a small owner of the company this move develops a deep sense of ownership which cultivates a culture of greatness wherein every employee is motivated to go out of the way and to contribute diligently towards the growth of the organization. But the only difference between both these companies is that while Starbucks ideated this with MBA masterminds and with a million dollar capital backing the 7 sisters of Lijjat did it way before Starbucks, in 1959 without even knowing what an MBA degree is. Such was the business acumen of these incredible women. The second phase of Lijjat was building a robust supply chain that would be cost-effective, would ensure quality production, and would fit the lifestyle of the women who work for the company. So instead of having huge office spaces, they used the houses of the sisters as their small centers of papad making. And this is what their supply chain looked like The flour would first arrive from the mills to the respective central location wherein the dough is made. And after the dough is made the sisters will be brought by a bus facility provided by the company. Over here they would collect the doughs and then go home, make papads dry them on the veranda, and then deliver the papads the next day. And lastly, after the delivery of the papads, they would collect their money and the dough for the next cycle. This would be followed by surprise visits by the supervisors to check the quality of oil they use, the hygiene check of the house, and most importantly the process of making papads. Now the sisters are also given aluminum papad makers to ensure that the papad is produced in a standardized manner. This happens at all the branches. If one of these branches do very well the profits are distributed among the sisters. And if not, the losses are borne by the branch members together. And after all of this comes the most challenging part of all and that is sticking to the vision and mission statement of the company. Now people, for most of us mission and vision statements are just stupid formalities and they have no real significance to us. Why? Because in a corporate everybody knows that mission, vision and values are just fancy words written on the wall. And at the end of the day if your boss wants to kick your @$$ he is going to do it anyway. At the same time in the case of colleges also even your principal wouldn't remember the vision and mission statement of your college and if he did it would only be because he mugged it up. After all, some committee was visiting to give your college some stupid certification or some accreditation. And this is the reason why most of us do not understand the importance of mission and vision statements. But here's a thing guys Mission and vision statements form the very foundations of every single organization. And when designed and followed the right way it can help the organization sustain itself for a century. At the same time, if not done right they can even bring down a million-dollar business. A classy example of the same is Apple. Now people, when Steve Jobs got fired from Apple in 1984, Apple was a million-dollar company. Until he was there at the company, the company stuck to its value. And it was a formidable player in the industry. But after he left, they started to derail from their values. And within just 10 years they were almost about to go bankrupt. That's when Steve Jobs got called back to Apple to fix things and get the company back on track. And you know what? After he took over the company, the first question he asked every single engineer every single designer, and every single manager was What does Apple stand for? And what are the values that we believe in as a company? Because the biggest mistake that Apple made was while he was not around they started to lose their identity and started to deviate from their values because of which they started making products with no sense of purpose. Eventually, the brand lost its unique identity and customer loyalty just faded away. So Steve baba comes back and asks this question and within some time the entire team is absolutely clear as to what exactly they were supposed to do. And this is what got them the 'Think Different' campaign that told the world what Apple truly stood for. And that is "Think Different". And within just 2 years the same company with the same engineers and the same resources then went on to create history to become a legendary company that made products that changed the world forever. And again as soon as Steve baba left we all know what was happening with Apple. This is the importance of mission and vision statements. And here's the most mind-blowing fact of all. In its 62 years of existence, not a single time Lijjat Papad has ever deviated from its core values. And even today After expanding to 67 branches and scaling up to 42,000 employees and exporting their products to 15 different countries. They still abide by the core philosophy of their business, that is, Sarvodaya, which means Progress for all. While we live in a world where billion-dollar corporates, even with the slightest change in the policies wouldn't think twice before firing thousands of employees and putting each one of their family's life at stake. On the other side, we have got Lijjat Papad wherein with every single piece of machinery they bring in for automation, they make sure that not a single woman is asked to leave the organization. Because they are 100% clear that their ultimate purpose of business is not to make money but the empowerment of women so that they can give their families and children a better quality of life. On one side where we have got these evil companies who would put the health of their frontline workers at stake just to maximize their profits. On the other hand, we have got Lijjat Papad wherein even if they have a great year, they make use of the extra profits to sponsor the education of the children of their frontline workers regardless of their age, caste, religion, or even position in the organization. And they do all of this just so that the next generation of these frontline workers can be given the opportunities that they truly deserve. And last and most importantly while despite being at the pinnacle of the technological revolution there are people like you and me who often keep doubting our capabilities. And here we see a standing example of 7 incredible women who had no educational qualification. no background in business and no fancy investor. And yet, they were able to build a business empire that is now empowering generations of women all across the country. And that too during a time when women had no scope of opportunities. If this isn't an epitome of greatness I don't know what is.

Maggie

Maggi is one of the most iconic brands in Indian business history. And for our generation, it's even more special because it has been an integral part of our childhood. But from the business standpoint, the most fascinating thing about Maggi is that way back in 1983, both Maggi and instant noodles were completely alien to the Indian culture. And yet, Nestle single-handedly created a Rs 937 crore market and has been a market leader in the domain for 38 years. And despite giant rivals like ITC, Marico, and Unilever, even today, Maggi has a whopping 60% market share in the instant noodle segment. The question is, how did Nestle create a market for a seemingly alien dish in India? How did it almost establish a monopoly in the instant noodles market? And what are the lessons that we need to learn from Nestle's genius marketing strategy? This is a story that dates back to the 1950s, in Japan.During that time, the country was still recovering from the downfall of World War Two. So noodles were one of the most affordable foods in the market. But because the demand was too high, and it took a lot of time to be prepared, it resulted in long lines and long wait times. This is when a curious Japanese man named Momofuku Ando decided to make a type of noodles that could be prepared quickly and cheaply. And after hundreds of iterations, he was finally successful in making a revolutionary product that we all know today as the instant Ramen noodles.Now although his newly invented instant ramen did not debut until 1958, the instant ramen noodles became a game-changing business during the economic boom in Japan. And as the country started developing rapidly, the instant ramen became such a big hit that despite costing six times more than the conventional noodles, the Japanese still bought instant ramen in large quantities. And soon enough, the instant ramen products started traveling abroad to the US to again become a massive hit. And even today, the parent company of ramen Nissin accounts for 50% of the billion-dollar instant noodle market in Japan. And while all of this was happening, Nestle was carefully observing the market and realized that instant noodles are a goldmine product in Japan. But very, very cleverly, Nestle chose not to pursue the Japanese market, despite knowing that there was a billion-dollar worth of market share still left to be capitalized in Japan. The question is when there was a clear market for a scalable product that too in a booming economy, why didn't Nestle enter the Japanese market? Now there are two seemingly logical reasons for that. Number one, Japan was not so liberal hence, it would have been very difficult to operate as a foreign company in Japan. And secondly, why go to war against a monopoly when you can create your monopoly? Right? Well, that is why Nestle started exploring every other market except Japan to create a market for instant noodles. And one of the biggest markets was India. And that is how Nestle entered the Indian market in 1983. And like I said before, both the concept of instant noodles and the Maggi brand were completely alien to us.We were still a closed country with hardly any foreign companies in the market. And the western influence over us was relatively very less. It's almost like asking our parents to eat lasagna every single day. Then the question is, how did Nestle turn Maggi into such an integral part of our lives? Well, that is because Nestle very clearly understood both its customer and the consumers. To tell you about it if you look at instant noodles as a product, anyone and everyone could have noodles, right? It doesn't matter whether it is a school kid or a 40-year-old man. And noodles by default are one of the most generic dishes on the market. So had it been some ordinary brands, they would have tried to capture the entire 740 million Indian customer base, and they would have tried to sell to every single Indian who could have had noodles. And on the outset, it does seem like an obvious choice, right? Well, Nestle was no ordinary brand. And they understood the fundamental marketing principle that if you try to sell to everyone, you will end up selling to no one. So Nestle's marketing team started finding the best niche profiles to see who could be their ideal target audience. And that is when they carefully picked two categories, and those were mothers and children. Now, this begs the question, what was the thinking behind this? Now listen to this very, very carefully. For the adoption of an alien product, it has to meaningfully cater to the pain of the audience and the interest of the audience. Now, in the case of Nestle, there were two primary stakeholders, there is the customer and there is the consumer. The consumer is the child who eats Maggi and the customer is the mother who buys Maggi.And during 1983 there were two categories of mothers, working mothers, and homemakers. Both of them had one major pain which is to give their child something tasty and healthy when they come back hungry from school. The problem with working parents was that they were not at home and with homemakers, after running all morning, after sending the kids and husbands to school and work, they needed some time to rest before they could start working again for dinner. On top of that, the child had just eaten chapati-bhaji in school, so giving them the same for evening snacks would not be good enough. And at the same time, they needed to make something that was less tedious, but the same time was tasty enough for the child to eat. So the two pains over here are working mothers who wanted something that the children could make themselves and homemakers who wanted something less tiring to make for their kids. And the interest was a tasty dish for their child to eat. And this is where Maggi became an opportunist and positioned itself as the perfect solution for mothers as a super easy and tasty meal alternative for their children. This is how the tagline "2-minute mein Maggi" was born. And as we've seen in the commercial it showcases an act of a mother preparing Maggi for the kids only to see them happy and delighted by the taste. Apart from that, Nestle reached out to school kids sponsored quizzes and events, and even gave them a free hamper of Maggi products. This was followed by a widespread sampling with over 4 million new contacts every year. And as time passed, Nestle even began advertising on TV channels during peak times when people like you and me were watching Power Rangers, Dragonball Z, and Ninja Hatori. This is how by positioning itself accurately to cater to the pain and interest of both its consumers and customers, Maggi established itself as an integral part of our lives. Now the question is if Maggi could establish a name in the market, so could others, right? Because there were already other big guns like ITC, Unilever, and Nissin. Then the question is, why couldn't they compete with Maggi? Well, there are three specific reasons for that. Number one, Nestle had evolved its supply chain for 25 long years, which was next to impossible to replicate. And on top of that, it controls the supply chain end to end. But when Nissin the parent company of ramen tried to enter the market, it struggled to find national distribution partners, and its alliances with both Hindustan Unilever and Mariko to solve this problem completely failed.

Secondly, Nestle achieved an unmatched level of penetration even in tier three and tier four cities of India. And more people knew the term Maggi than they knew about the actual product which is instant noodles. So no one asked for instant noodles they just asked for a packet of Maggi. This was because, from 2005 onwards, the marketers of Nestle conducted exclusive studies and did everything in their capacity to make Maggi accessible to the bottom of the pyramid of India. And in technical terms, based on socioeconomic status, the Indian audience could be categorized into eight categories, ranging from A-1 to E-2.The top segment consisted of SEC classes as in socio-economic classes of A-1, A-2, and B-1, the middle segment was B-2 and C and the bottom segment was D, E-1 one, and E-2. the top and middle segments were already captured by 2005 through Maggi's conventional marketing efforts, and they saw that the real opportunity was in SEC classes C and D that represented over 40% of the market. And after an extensive study, the first product to be launched was Chotu Maggi, which was priced at just Rs 5 and was aimed at penetrating the lower segment of the market. The communication was carefully designed in local vernacular languages, and the distribution system was intricately designed with strategic wholesalers and redistributors to reach up to 2.2 million outlets all across the country. And because of this extensive effort, the household penetration numbers of Maggi shot from just 45% to 71% for the C class, and from 31% to 62% for SEC classes D and E in just four years from 2006 to 2010. This is the reason why when ITC and Unilever entered the market, they found it very difficult to achieve this level of penetration and brand recall value. And lastly, it was the impeccable connection that Maggi had established with its customers. And this is something that does not need any explanation, but a classic demonstration of the same was seen in 2015 when this happened to Maggi. As soon as this bad happened, Maggi disappeared from the stores for five long months and their market share nosedived from 75% to 0% within no time. But you know what, guys? As soon as Maggi came back they came up with something called the '#WeMissYouToo' campaign wherein the brand asked fans to share their stories about how much they missed Maggi on social media. Now you see, this is not some Michael Jordan's Nike product or a revolutionary iPhone that we're talking about. It is just an instant noodle brand expecting fans to share their memories. But as we all saw, it turned out to be one of the most successful campaigns Nestle had ever executed, and fans from all across the country started pouring their love for Maggi. Snapdeal sold out a whopping 60,000 Maggi welcome kits within five minutes of the Maggi flash sale. And hashtags such as '#DilKiDealWithMAGGI' started trending on Twitter after the sale resumed. This was the extraordinary level of connection that Maggi had established with its audience. And not so surprisingly, it was very, very difficult for Unilever or Nissin to achieve this level of connection with a player like Maggi in the market. And guess what? By 2017, Maggi was back to the number one spot in the market with a whopping 60% market share in the instant noodles market. This is the iconic story of the Maggi brand. Now, this brings me to the most important part of the chapter, and that is the lessons from Maggi's genius marketing strategy. Moving on, there are four lessons that we need to learn from Nestle's incredible business strategy. Lesson number one is always remember while most brands spend time and resources to find out how to penetrate a market only a few brands spend time and money to find out which market to penetrate. And so the most revolutionary products in the market are more often than not the products that have created a market for themselves. And it's not just Nestle. Even Apple never tried to compete with Rolex to make mechanical watches, they instead created a market for smartwatches. And now they're way ahead of any other watch company in the world. Similarly, Henry Ford had the option to compete with luxury cars, but he instead created a market for the bottom of the pyramid. And in our case, Maggi created a market for instant noodles in India, instead of going head-on with Nissin in Japan. Lesson number two, if you're selling a generic product, your first instinct would be to sell to every single person in the market. But always remember, if you try to sell to everyone, you will end up selling to no one. So always try to find a specific target audience to sell your generic product. And for the people who have done the communication masterclass you already know which brand I'm talking about. Lesson number three the golden recipe to market penetration lies in identifying the pain and interest of the audience. And your accuracy in spotting this pain and interest is directly proportional to the ease of adoption of your product. In this case, it was Nestle's intricate understanding of the mother's pain of being too tired to make an evening meal for the children. And the interest was so beautifully captured through Nestle's initiatives to interact with children by the means of cartoon channels and school competitions. And lastly, like I've said many times before, while good brands sell you a product, great brands sell you an emotion. And even if you're selling something as simple as a dry cake of noodles, if you connect with the audience at an emotional level, you will stand out from the rest of the crowd. Like a legend once said, "people might forget what you said but they never forget how you made them feel".

Marlboro

On the historic date of 11th of January 1964, it was officially declared by the United States government that cigarette causes cancer. And within a day an 8 Billion dollar tobacco industry and the incomes of 7,50,000 families were at stake. While most companies saw their sales dropping down there was one company that miraculously went from having just 1% market share to becoming the 4th largest cigarette brand in the world in less than one year. And after 1970 when cigarette advertisements were permanently banned from televisions this brand became even more popular to go on to become the largest manufacturer of cigarettes in the world. This brand that I'm talking about goes by the name Marlboro. And Marlboro today is so huge that it has got more consumers than its next 10 competitors combined. The question is - What the hell did they do? because of this the very same cancer report and the ban which is essentially supposed to kill its business ended up becoming a stepping stone for Marlboro to become a $58 Billion brand. The answer to this question lies in one of the most iconic marketing strategies ever witnessed by mankind. which is called lifestyle marketing. Now let's try to understand this using a very simple example that is closer to home. If you are a 90s kid and you watched Sachin Tendulkar play I bet you that at some point in your life or someone in you're friend circle must have bought an MRF bat. And chances are that when you visited the store you knew nothing about English Willow, Kashmir Willow. You did not care which wood the bat was made of. You did not care whether it was original or duplicate, you just wanted a bat. And then you had two choices bats with no stickers or bats with MRF stickers. And you chose the MRF bat by default And then after that god knows after how many years later you realized that the full form of MRF is Madras Rubber Factory. And the fact that MRF is primarily a rubber tire manufacturing company that just happened to sponsor Sachin Tendulkar. Later on this very same thing happened to Reebok when Dhoni started using Reebok bats. Now here the question is - is it a coincidence that millions of children all across the country were so stupid to mindlessly buy a bat with a sticker of a rubber tire company? If not, then how the hell did this even happen? Well, here's where the magic of lifestyle marketing happens. We all idolized Sachin Tendulkar and we all wanted to be like Sachin Tendulkar. So subconsciously, the MRF bats made us feel as if we were holding the same bat like Sachin Tendulkar himself. So to put that straight, what we essentially bought when we bought MRF bats is not the bat itself but the connection that it had with our idol, that is, Sachin Tendulkar because we wanted to be like Sachin Tendulkar. Now in the US, the same thing happened to Nike's Air Jordan shoe lineup wherein when Nike signed up Michael Jordan the fascination for Air Jordan shoes became so crazy that even today, after 18 years of Michael Jordan's retirement he still makes 100 million dollars every single year just in royalty. This is what we call lifestyle marketing wherein consumers buy more into the lifestyle of the icon associated with the product than the product itself. And this is exactly what the marketeers of Marlboro cigarettes did to their brand. After the 1964 report, which was released by the surgeon general of the US, brands started to do everything in their capacity to keep their reputation. Some brands tried to justify cigarettes while some brands completely disapproved of the very research itself. Back then Marlboro was a very small company that made cigarettes only for women. But as soon as this news broke out the parent company of Marlboro, which is Philip Morris decided to shift their method of marketing and became an epitome of business propaganda in the 20th century So what the marketeers of Marlboro did is that instead of justifying smoking and using statistics that were difficult to understand they came out with a campaign called the Marlboro Man. wherein they introduced a character who was supposedly everything a man wanted to be like. and they named this character "The Marlboro Man". Marlboro Man was a cowboy who had a perfectly built-up body and the commercial showcased him as the ultimate archetype of manhood. He was tough, affectionate, and stylish and overall stood as the icon of freedom and manliness. And just as we kids bought into MRF batsmen of the 1960s were so fascinated by the Marlboro man and started buying Marlboro cigarettes that the commercial became a massive game-changer for the company. And within a year

Marlboro went from having less than 1% market share to become the 4th largest cigarette manufacturer in the world. And the fun fact is in all of those commercials cigarettes were not even the primary subject of focus. Cigarettes as a product got less than 10 seconds of time footage time in all of those commercials. And because of this even when cigarette commercials were permanently banned from television and brands couldn't show cigarettes in commercials or on TV, Marlboro was very easily able to navigate through that situation because their focus was anyways not on cigarettes but on Marlboro Man himself. And that is how they were able to communicate their emotion very easily even through print and magazines. And this is the reason why even after the 1970 ban Marlboro's business still kept growing. The sales skyrocketed because the rest of the brands were struggling to market their brands without showing their products. And that is how Marlboro became a legend in advertising and laid the foundation for Marlboro to become a $58 billion brand. Now, more than a business lesson there is a very very important life lesson that we all need to learn from this iconic case study. People, just like Marlboro in the 1960s, even today what we often fail to realize is that we are constantly being bombarded with lifestyle cigarette commercials that do not appear as ads but in the form of pop culture icons. Now, this includes a James Bond appearance wherein he appears in a tuck and symbolizes gentlemanliness or Kabir Singh who is portrayed as the epitome of manliness. Now, regardless of how lucrative they look what is important for us to understand is that they are merely tapping onto your insecurities to convince you to do something which will give you a feeling as if you are an elevated version of yourself. But the truth is because of your lack of self-awareness you don't realize that your insecurities are putting money into their pockets eventually to make those companies billions of dollars but to turn you into a sick, miserable addict of either cigarettes or social validation, depending on what you're buying into. So keep your eyes open and do not fall into these traps. And last and most importantly my big brother's advice to you is "Always remember that buying dumb sh*t will never make you feel happier or make you a better version of yourself. The only thing that will make you feel better is your acceptance of your insecurities and imperfections. And at the end of the day if you do not embrace your insecurities some billion-dollar brand will dig into your misery and make a fortune out of it." So think about it and if you think I make sense to you then help me spread this message by sharing this video with as many people as possible. And like once a great woman said,

"Imperfection is beauty, madness is genius and it is better to be ridiculous than to be boring." - Marilyn Monroe.

XXXI

Mensa brands is one such startup that has taken the indian startup ecosystem by surprise in just six months this company raised 300 million dollars to become the fastest growing unicorn in indian business history in these six months mensa has already acquired 12 consumer brands like villain and category and in the month of october itself these brands seem to have hit a growth of 250 percent and 140 respectively and what is even more mind blowing is that while every other startup in india is engaged in a cash drain incurring millions of dollars of losses mensa has claimed to become profitable within these six months itself the question is what exactly is mensa brands all about how does their business model work and most importantly as entrepreneurs in the indian startup space what are the opportunities that mensa brands is creating for small scale entrepreneurs like you and me and the answer to this question lies in a new age business model called the thracio model this name became popular because of the meteoric rise of an american startup called thracio trasi was a company that was founded in 2018 and within just two years it hit a billion dollars in valuation to become one of the fastest growing unicorns in the world the question is what do they do and how does the business model of tarsio work so let's start from the basics if you look at the amazon marketplace you will see that amazon operates through two types of sellers first party sellers and third-party sellers in case of first party seller relationship if amazon understands that your product is doing insanely well amazon itself invites you directly to establish you as a first party seller and this means that you sell your products directly to amazon and then amazon sells those products to customers taking care of everything from shipping product details listing pricing and even returns your role as a vendor is just to fulfill the purchase order send by amazon and ship the products to amazon basically you just make your product and let amazon sell it and pay you whatever amazon thinks is best whereas in a third-party relationship with amazon anyone and everyone can sell on amazon's marketplace and this way you get way more control over your operations in this arrangement you sell your products directly to the consumers on the amazon marketplace but the catch over here is you have to take care of everything starting from your product listing advertising pricing and even logistics and returns and in order to make this process a little bit easier amazon offers something called amazon's fulfillment service that is called as fulfilled by amazon or fba this is a shipping program to send your products to the customers through the logistics of amazon this is what you call as the direct to consumer model and you know what guys in the past 20 years amazon's third party sellers have done so well that in 1999 only three percent of the gross merchandise sales came from third-party sellers but as time passed the contribution of the third party sellers accelerated at such a pace that as of 2019 these third party sellers made up 58 of amazon's gross merchandise sales which means what amazon's third party sellers contributed more to amazon than amazon's own first party sellers this is how because of the visibility and accessibility of amazon even people like you and me have been able to sell our products across the country and according to rough estimates close to 50 000 of these third party sellers make more than one million dollars in revenue now although cumulatively it looks like amazon third-party sellers are doing very well if you look at the on-ground reality it is actually being run by small-scale entrepreneurs who manage everything from marketing listing manufacturing packaging to even shipping this is both extremely tedious and costly and especially in a place like amazon where there is cutthroat competition it becomes extremely difficult for small-scale brands to bring new products and scale their brand therefore in spite of having a great product these small-scale entrepreneurs reach a saturation point in fact market research even states that amazon sellers in most cases reach a saturation point when they are close to three to five million dollars in revenue and if they want to grow any further they either have to take in hefty loans or worst case they have to take up a personal debt and this saturation of growth is where thrasio comes in trashy is a company that was founded by the veterans of different industries who have both the credibility and insight on how to grow these small skill brands and using their credibility they raised a million dollars in funding and started offering an exit strategy to these great amazon sellers and once these third-party sellers got acquired by thrashior the company uses its scale capital and expertise to further grow the operations a classic example of the same is a company called angry orange after extensively serving through the amazon marketplace tracio found angry orange which is a company that makes pet older eliminator spray they had excellent customer rating and were clocking in an annual revenue of 2 million dollars but then after four years of running the company it was taking a lot out of its founder Mr. Adam both in terms of capital and management and taking the risk of growing the business any further did not look so lucrative to him and this is when tracio approached him and offered him an exit plan and within just one week tracio acquired the angry orange brand with a 100 payout to Mr. Adam and then they started the process of acceleration they rebranded the entire angry orange product lineup and revamp the packaging to give it a premium look they presented a better brand story did some excellent copywriting and brought in professional photographers and videographers to shoot world-class commercials and then started promoting it on amazon furthermore trasio's marketing team took it one step forward and instead of just focusing on amazon sales channel they invested heavily into other digital marketing channels and started generating leads through facebook and google also in fact all thanks to their million dollar funding they were even able to do influencer marketing and celebrity endorsements to gain more brand value and visibility to the angry orange brand and lastly the thras u team built an extensive supply chain to get the product into retail shelves like target walmart ace hardware and true value this is how angry orange which was once a small skill brand now became a national brand of the united states and the result well first of all the founder mr adam got a 100 payout secondly the average monthly pay-per-click sales increased by 1860 from 2019 to october 2021 and most importantly the revenue of the company skyrocketed from just 2.5 million dollars to a trailing 12-month revenue of 23.1 million dollars this is how by leveraging a world-class team to tell a brand story by backing it up with extensive digital marketing initiatives in multiple channels and most importantly by strategically investing into an efficient supply chain management system trasio turned angry orange into a national brand in the u.s and now that the brand has gained enough traction thoracio invested heavily into product innovation and started creating new products like the ready-to-use spray for stain removal or even a bathroom spray adding to the umbrella of the angry orange brand similarly they took up a company called trail buddy and increase their e-beta by 300 since acquisition they took up a company called this works and increased its training 12 month revenue by 785 percent since acquisition and lastly they even acquired a brand called crafts for all to increase the repeater by 148 within just two years of acquisition and until today thrasio has orchestrated more than 150 acquisitions worth 600 million dollars has over 22 000 products from 200 brands in its portfolio turning thracio into a giant company with a variety of brands under its umbrella this is how the thracio model works and it is very very similar to how mensa works just like thrashio mensah brands first surveys the market to understand the gaps that can be capitalized upon after that they survey to find small skill companies that have a digital first approach have quality founders loyal customers and between 1 to 10 million dollars in annual revenue digital first means companies that have largely built themselves over a digital ecosystem so after identifying a great product with immense potential they start negotiations to acquire these brands here's where there's a slight difference between how thrashio and mensa work while thrasio gives the founder 100 exit mensah still keeps the founders kin in the game with just a major stake in the company and they intend to fully acquire these brands gradually in the next five years after that just like thrashio mensah uses their digital marketing specialization sales channels and supply chain expertise to scale these brands both domestically and overseas this includes organization and optimization of all of their inventories in all popular marketplaces and even their official website and once the foundation is set they then invest heavily into product innovation to launch new product lines within the canopy of the brand and as of now mensa has 12 brands across three key categories which are fashion home decor and beauty and personal care the obvious reason for this is because like in Nykaa's case study the online penetration of bpc or beauty and personal care is just seven to eight percent so there's a huge market that's just waiting to be capitalized similarly fashion sector is largely untapped with an expected penetration of just 18 in 2021 which means 92 percent of the market in the bpc segment and 82 of the market in the fashion space is completely untapped hence presenting a huge market opportunity for mensa brands and the most amazing example of this acquisition is a story of a perfume brand called villain which has now become a leading men's fragrance and accessories company according to mensa, villain has grown by over 250 in october 2021 itself and then we have another brand called karigri which is a high-end designer sari brand that grew by 140 percent in october similarly according to mr ananth narayanan the founder of mensa brands a vast majority of mensa brands have grown over 100 and in the next five years mensa intends to grow these brands by another 1 000 this is how in the past six months through technology and digital marketing mensa has been able to grow their brands at a staggering rate of 100 and in the next one year the company plans to double down on its existing verticals by partnering with 30 more brands and what's more surprising is that 30 percent of mensa's revenue is already coming from overseas which clearly states that mensa is not building a brand for india but for the world itself this is the story of an iconic indian startup on the rise and this brings me to the most important part of the episode and that is considering the rise of mensa where is the e-commerce wave heading and what are the opportunities that are arising for small-scale entrepreneurs like you and me because of a brand like mensa. Here are the three points that you need to keep an eye on in order to find opportunity in this new e-commerce wave of India number one the d2c market as in the direct to consumer market is just getting started in India while mensa acquires just 12 brands there are hundreds of companies in India that have more than three to seven crores in revenue and while class u is planned to enter the Indian markets we have other players like global bees even flow brands 10 club and even powerhouse 91 that are operating in the same space as mensa number two the rise of these brands means that if you're a small scale digital-first brand if you have a wonderful product that fits the market with great reviews within the next two to three years these brands will start paying more and more to acquire you therefore it is a great time to be a small scale entrepreneur on amazon and last and most importantly mensa is clearly going to be a direct competition to Nike so keep a very close eye on how this rivalry plays out. the market is so huge that even if we have five to six more players in the BPC segment even then it would be less to cater to the demand that we have in India

Microsoft

On the 18th of May in 1998, the US Department of Justice and the Attorney Generals of 20 US states sued Microsoft for being a monopoly and illegally killing its competition in the computer market. And what followed next was one of the most historic cases in tech history, which lasted for two decades. And fast forward to 23 years later, even today, Microsoft is still killing its competition right in front of our eyes, and this could result in yet another historic lawsuit. The question is, how did Microsoft kill its competition? What exactly was their business strategy that turned Microsoft into such a powerful company? And most importantly, what are the lessons that we need to learn from this iconic case study. The Justice Department has charged Microsoft with engaging in anticompetitive and exclusionary practices designed to maintain its monopoly. Microsoft in secret finished up '95 and released it, and then provided no documentation. Forcing Microsoft to include Netscape's competing software and our operating system is like requiring Coca-Cola to include three cans of Pepsi in every six-pack it sells. Do you agree that Internet Explorer is defined here correctly as Microsoft's web browser? This is a story that dates back to 1994 America when the computer revolution was just catching fire. This was a time when multinational corporates had accepted that the computer was a powerful tool. And they already started having hundreds of computers in the offices, which were being used by the employees. And these computers had already skyrocketed the productivity of these companies. So practically, a computer has already become an integral part of the American business ecosystem. And long story short, here are the most important events that happened in the computer revolution of America. On the 12th of August 1981, IBM introduced its personal computer with Microsoft's 16-bit operating system, which was MS-DOS 1.0, and this made Microsoft a tonne of revenue through licensing. By 1985, Microsoft was already clocking in a revenue of 140 million dollars. Then on the 13th Of March 1986, Microsoft Stock goes public breaking all records and turning Bill Gates into the youngest billionaire ever, by 1987. Then in August 1989, Microsoft introduces the earliest version of Office suite applications, which then became the industry standard for businesses all across America. Followed by that, in May 1990, Microsoft launched Windows 3.0, which was a big leap into the graphical user interface. And this is what made computers accessible to the common man, which were back then used only by the techies through code. And as soon as this happened, the usage of computers exploded in the United States of America. And this is what made Microsoft the most powerful and the most dominating force in the computer world, with Windows 3.0, selling at the rate of 1 million copies per month in 1993. And nearly 90% of all PCs in the world ran on Microsoft operating system. And this is when another dimension of the computer industry opened up and that was the internet. Therefore, in the early 1990s, we saw the rise of the internet browser market. And one of the most revolutionary browsers at that time was a browser called Netscape Navigator, which was launched in 1994. Netscape at that time was loaded with features that were far ahead of its competition, they had the future of document streaming, which allowed users to view the documents while it was being downloaded. They have the feature of multiple downloads simultaneously. And they also supported JPEG image format. And this product was so revolutionary that even with a $49 subscription cost, they were able to capture up to 80% of the browser market share. Now the point to be noted over here is that, just like today, without the internet, your computer is mostly useless. Back then in 1995, people started using computers just to use web browsers to connect to the internet. And the operating system was just a bridge that connected the users to the web browsers. So practically, browsers were becoming more important than the operating system itself. And building upon this phenomenal success. Netscape went public on December 5th, 1995. And within a day, the company had hit a market cap of $2.2 billion. And just when they thought of becoming another legendary internet company, something happened in the same year that marked the beginning of Netscape's wall and within the next six years, the same billion-dollar company was almost reduced to nothing. The question is, how is it even possible that such a big and innovative company went down so quickly? Well, the answer to this question lies in an accurate phrase coming from the Department of Justice itself, which summarises how Microsoft kills its competition. And it says, embrace, extend and exterminate. To tell you about it, In 1994, Microsoft realized that they were too late for the internet boom, and the browsers are becoming more important than the operating system. So in August 1995, when Microsoft launched Windows 95, they also included their web browser called Internet Explorer, and they made it the default browser for every PC sold. So when you start your computer, you could see Internet Explorer right on your home screen. On top of that, Microsoft directly attack the most important features of Netscape by launching something called ActiveX controls. And this update made it impossible to easily download files on the internet, especially the Microsoft Office files. And this was a direct attack on Netscape's prime features. And because 90% of the computers used MS Office, it became more and more difficult for them to use Netscape and other browsers. And then, Microsoft also removed Internet Explorer from the ad and remove the tab, because of which neither the consumers nor the manufacturers could delete Internet Explorer from the computers, and the cherry on the cake, they made it available for free of cost. So this is how they first embraced the concept of internet browsers. Then they extended their products with features that do not support the competing products. And lastly, Microsoft used its dominance over the platform to promote its product over its competition, eventually, exterminating the need to use rival products. And not so surprisingly, this led to the downfall of Netscape Navigator. And by 2000, Internet Explorer had a 95% market share, making it the most dominating web browser in the market. And this is how Microsoft established an industry standard, which meant that if you wanted to make a living from software development, you had to make sure that your product worked in Internet Explorer. But if Microsoft things were making a lot of money, maybe the story could be over for you. Similarly, Microsoft's instant messaging platform, MSN Messenger, also tried to kill one of the most popular instant messaging platforms during that time, which was AIM, which was made by a company called America Online. And the way they did that was that they first embrace the concept of instant messaging by launching MSN Messenger. And this was installed on your PC by default. And then they extended the standard with proprietary Microsoft add-ons, which added new features but broke the compatibility with AOL software. And then they gained dominance by providing MSN Messenger for free.

And now the same thing is happening with zoom. Now, here's the catch, guys. Microsoft Teams has seen exponential growth since 2020 by 456%, and I couldn't find Zoom's monthly active users since the last April 2020. But when they release the numbers, you know exactly what to compare them to. On top of that, you might also see that Microsoft will build an insanely user-friendly file-sharing system for Microsoft Office files in Microsoft Teams. And soon enough, you could also see some hurdles, which might make zoom difficult to work with. Now, the point to be observed over here is that, in April 2020, while zoom had 300 million daily active users, one year later, Microsoft Teams already had 145 million active users. And these users, are the ones who could have used zoom or shifted from zoom to Microsoft Teams. So effectively, Microsoft has already started eating into zoom's customer base. This is how Microsoft kills its competition. There are three very important lessons to learn from Microsoft's iconic case. The first thing I want you to do is to take a step back and look at the story very, very carefully. Did you see that despite Microsoft sabotaging Netscape, Chrome was very easily able to beat Internet Explorer to become the most used browser in the world? Despite Microsoft killing AOL, using MSN Messenger, Facebook and WhatsApp have turned out to be the winner of the social media revolution. And it almost looks like Microsoft was so obsessed with killing its competition, that it completely lost sight of the evolving trends in the internet services like search engines, social media, and even the mobile revolution. And this tells us two very, very important lessons while good companies focus on their competition, great companies focus on their customers and the needs of the market. Number two, regardless of how powerful you are, if you don't build great products, the success you're going to achieve is always going to be short-lived. And lastly, while Microsoft always wanted to be the richest kid on the block, and tried to keep all the wealth to itself, Apple and Google built a platform for developers to empower them and build wealth for a large number of people. And in this process, they ended up making more money than Microsoft.

XXXIII

MTR

On the 25th of June 1975, the Indira Gandhi government officially declared a nationwide emergency. The fundamental rights were curbed, the press was censored and within a fortnight the livelihood of 620 million Indians was at stake. Little did they know that the next 21 months of their lives would be known as the darkest chapter in the history of Indian democracy. And all of this was happening during a time when India was already witnessing a socioeconomic crisis. During this time, let alone business prosperity even survival was considered to be a miracle. And the story that I'm about to tell you today is the story of one such miracle wherein amidst this economic nightmare while most businesses were shutting down there was one incredible businessman who turned this very same emergency into a business opportunity and built a business empire that now has a revenue of 1000 crores. This businessman is Mr. Sadananda Maiya and the company that I'm talking about is Mavalli Tiffin Room which is popularly known as MTR. The question is- What was so special about MTR and how was it able to turn an economic nightmare into a business opportunity? The answer to this question lies in the rich history of MTR that dates back to 1924. This is when the Maiya family started the MTR restaurant with the vision to serve the most authentic, hygienic, and tastiest South Indian food to its customers. And the entire family was so dedicated to their profession that even during the post-independence time when the country was witnessing political turmoil they still served the most authentic, hygienic, and tastiest South Indian food in town. Within a few years, the restaurant became so popular that it became a hotspot for tourists television personalities, and even film stars. But after 5 long decades of prosperity; in 1975 when the emergency was imposed the family hit a dead end due to the socio-economic crisis. During this time, apart from the emergency, India had already seen 2 bad agricultural years and due to the formation of OPEC the oil prices had quadrupled and the inflation in the country had skyrocketed to 15%. The situation was so bad that the government had to stop all new construction work they froze the wages and salaries in the public sectors And imposed compulsory savings on income taxpayers. And this meant that every single rupee was a lifesaver for a middle-class person and it meant that rarely anybody ever went to a restaurant. On top of that, the government required every restaurant to conform to prices set by the government and it was practically impossible to run a profitable restaurant business with those given prices. For example, under the President's rule, the price of Idli was clipped to 10p from 25p while a cup of coffee which cost one rupee was to be sold for just 25p. Now, people, when something like this happens most restaurant owners do either one or many of these 3 things to survive. And this is something that you would've seen even during the COVID-19 crisis. Number one, they do extreme cost-cutting and fire all of their employees. Number two, they indulge in adulteration and serve extremely low-quality food to their customers which eventually leads to health hazards. Or number three they just shut their shop altogether and wait for the situation to get back to normal. And this is exactly what the restaurant owners did in 1975 because they saw no other option to survive. But you know what? Even during this time MTR foods still served the most authentic, hygienic, and tastiest South Indian food to its customers without compromising on their quality. And not just that They retained most of their employees and built a supply chain that was so robust that when the emergency was lifted MTR went on to become one of the most successful food companies in the country. The question is- What exactly was this strategy and what was so special about it? As it turns out when the government imposed the prices the MTR restaurants started bleeding. They were losing out ?25,000 on weekdays and lost up to 1 lakh rupees during weekends. But even during that time, Sadanand Maiya sir was not willing to compromise on his family business values. At the same time, he did not want to fire any of the employees because they had stayed loyal to the business for decades So you know what? He took a bold step to shut down the restaurant altogether and made 3 strategic changes to its business. Number one, he realized that despite the emergency, the demand for food did not go down. It's just that the purchasing power of the customers had declined drastically. And the supply chain of the restaurant was too costly to cater to their demands. So, to reduce the cost he moved from cooked food to packed food. Because of this the heavy cost and loss due to perishable items were eliminated. On top of that instead of adulterating the costly ingredients, he changed the ingredients altogether. For example, they moved from rice idlis to Rava idlis to make idlis cost-effective. And even today, Rava Idli is one of MTR's signature dishes. Number two since he could not comply with the prices imposed by the government he turned the same restaurant into a grocery store and started selling food mixes via grocery sales. And last and most importantly he trained his entire staff to build an efficient supply chain to make packed food and sold it at an affordable price. In the corporate world, this is what we call reskilling. And that is how MTR was able to survive the emergency without compromising its business values. And guess what? As soon as the emergency was lifted MTR restaurant reopened but this time along with the restaurant they had a ready-to-fire manufacturing chain that produced nothing but high-quality products. Soon enough it extended to multiple food mixes like pickles, spices, and even special spice mixtures. Fast forward to today MTR has emerged as one of the finest food brands in the country with a revenue of almost 1000 crores. And MTR exports its products to 21 countries including the US, the UK, Australia, and Japan. And most importantly it has successfully stood the test of time for 97 years without ever compromising its values even during the COVID crisis, 10 years after Maiya sir stepped down The company is still setting very high standards for change management in the industry. While most companies were clueless and struggled to keep their supply chain intact during the COVID crisis; MTR foods had already doubled its inventory level from 14 days to 30 days capacity. And while the first lockdown was imposed on the 25th of March MTR rigorously started preparing for the crisis way back on 10th March itself. And this is when none of us had a clue that our lives were about to change forever. And that is how time and again by turning a business threat into a business opportunity MTR has consistently set a benchmark for other brands to follow and from entrepreneurs like you and me to learn. Now there are 3 very important lessons that we need to learn from this iconic case study. Number one and this is something that has been followed by Dhirubhai Ambani sir better than anybody else wherein his policy was every time you see a market crisis you need to realize that your competitors are facing the same crisis as you are. The question is are you going to see it as an obstacle and succumb to it or treat it as a business opportunity and get way ahead of your competition. Number two, money can build a company but it takes guts, quality, and values to build a brand. And last and most importantly as much as the Internet is filled with American and European business case studies we often fail to realize the fact that India has had a long history of political and economic crisis and the adversity has been so much that let alone business, even staying alive was considered to be a big deal. But even during these times, we have had some incredible entrepreneurs who were able to build a business empire and have established a golden legacy for us to follow and we being in the Indian markets need to pay very close attention to these lesser-known goldmines because they have got nuggets of wisdom that can turn us into extraordinary business leaders of this country.

PubG

In the past two years we've been hearing horrific stories of people who have been adversely affected because of over engaging with pubg while some people often think it to be as some digital chinese invasion strategy what most people miss out on is the fact that pubg is a work of a genius and pubg has got some critical business strategy lessons that these schools often don't teach us because you see in spite of the release of thousands of games designed by the most talented game studios in the world rarely do you see a game like pubg that takes the world by a storm within just 5 years of its launch this game today has 40 million daily active users has more than 400 million monthly active users and has a mind-boggling download count of 1 billion downloads as a result it has been able to make 2.8 billion dollars in revenue and like we saw with many people around us these players are so engaged in playing the game that they literally have to be pulled out of it so the underlying question over here is what is so unique and powerful about pubg's product design that it is able to achieve such an extraordinary level of engagement how does this model work out and most importantly as entrepreneurs and business strategists of the future how can you cultivate the skill of building a super engaging product like pubg and apply that to your business the answer to this lies in this incredible book called hooked and in this book the author explains a model called the hook model this model consists of four behavioral elements and if these elements are applied to your product your product by default becomes an addictive product these four elements are trigger action investment and variable reward the first and the most simplest element of all is trigger and this is an element that actually motivates you to start using the product these triggers are of two types internal trigger and external trigger internal triggers are those triggers that tempt you to use the product without any external force like an advertisement or a notification classic examples boldum is the trigger for instagram hunger is the trigger for zomato and the need to go out is the trigger for ola or uber whereas for external triggers we've got apps like bloomberg and gmail that get you to the app through a push notification about a news or an email and just like that for pubg the internal trigger is boredom and the external trigger could be your friends calling you to get online or a notification that tempts you to start playing pubg and if your friends do not call you pubg will send you a daily bonus as a reward just to tempt you to enter the game so that you have the motivation to start playing this is followed by the second element which is action in this case action is nothing but a simple act that you do in anticipation of the reward in case of pubg it's as simple as you starting to play the game in anticipation of getting an adrenaline rush and this is where the third element comes in which is by far the most powerful element that is capable of causing addiction and this is the variable reward system to understand this let me take you back to a very famous experiment that was conducted by an american psychologist named dr b.f skinner in the 1950s in this experiment dr skinner created a small box this box had a small button which can be pegged by a pigeon and along with that there was a small opening right below that button where the pigeon gets the reward with food so basically dr skinner was trying to find out if he could create a habit in the pigeons by using the reward of food so in the first set of experiments he rewarded the pigeon every time it pegged and he noticed that the pigeon actually started asking for food when it got hungry so after some time he decided to tweak this experiment slightly and this time he started rewarding the pigeon randomly both in terms of quantity of the food and the frequency in which they were rewarded so instead of the regular rhythm of one pack and immediate food this time he used to give them food after two packs sometimes after three packs sometimes after five packs and then used to give it after 12 packs and so on and so forth so this way the food was given to the pigeons in a random pattern and to his surprise he noticed something absolutely unbelievable as it turns out unlike the pigeons that received the same food at regular intervals the pigeons that received variable rewards went crazy these pigeons started continuously pecking at the button compulsively even after getting more food than needed in fact one of these pigeons hit the button 2.5 times every single second for the next 16 hours and another one packed the button 87 000 times in the next 14 hours and the pigeons did that in spite of getting the reward less than one percent of the time and as it turns out this exact same behavior was also shown by rats when they were put in a similar condition this is when dr skinner realized that when a creature is rewarded for its action in a random unpredictable pattern that creature will get addicted to carry of that action again and again this is what you call as the variable reward system and guess what the exact same system is very cleverly used in pubg to keep the gamers hooked every time you play the game you have no idea who you're playing with you have no idea what formation is going to be which weapons you will get and the box that drops down i don't know what you call it but then you have no idea when it's going to land or where it's going to land on top of that if you're going on a winning streak the algorithm will deliberately curate your player's lobby such that you will end up playing with players of higher caliber such that your possibility of losing increases similarly if you're on a losing streak you are put in a lobby of players of lesser caliber making you more likely to win therefore the reward of winning is deliberately made variable and this is the reason why it is so difficult to win 10 games in a row all of these attributes when deployed together they make pubg the product a complex version of many skinner boxes that keep you so hooked to the game that you completely lose track of time and just like the pigeons in the skinner box the players end up compulsively playing the game for a very very long duration if this is very very clear to you let's move on to the next powerful element and that is something called the infinite loop phenomenon people has it ever happened to you that you started scrolling through youtube shots and the next thing you know it's already been one hour the same thing must have also happened with you when you started scrolling through instagram reels and if you've been using tik tok you must have felt this very early similarly even while playing pop g people just decide to play one game but they end up playing for hours without even realizing it so the question over here is how is this happening and what is the secret recipe of this design the answer to this comes from an american professor named brian one sings most famous experiment called the bottomless bowl experiment in this experiment the participants were made to sit in groups of four and they were given a bowl of tomato soup they were given 20 minutes and they were asked to eat as much as they wanted and the catch over here was that while two of these participants were given a normal soup bowl secretly the other two bowls had a small pipe at the bottom that kept filling the soup as these participants were drinking it and the most astonishing thing that this professor found was that a typical person drinking soup from the bottomless bowl ended up consuming 73 more soup as compared to the people with the normal bull and guess what when these participants were asked if they were full they said how can i be full i still have half a bowl of soup left and this is how this experiment drew an important conclusion about human behavior that if there isn't a visual cue to indicate the quantity of consumption and if the experience is left unhindered then by default it will lead to excessive consumption and most importantly in spite of the excessive consumption the subject will still be unsatisfied leading to more consumption this is the reason why when you start watching youtube shots because it is a continuous unending loop leading to an unhindered experience you end up consuming it excessively and cherry on the cake is that you are still left unfulfilled by the way this is also the reason why when you take a shower you have no idea how much water you're consuming you lose track of time and you're always left with a slight urge to shower more this is also the reason why netflix plays the next episode before you get the time to think what to do next and in case of pubg if you watch closely the game in spite of being so complex with millions of players playing every single day it somehow gets the players into the next game as quick as possible to keep the experience unhindered this is done so that they do not get satisfied and do not get the time to quantify how many games or how much time they've spent and lastly we have the fourth element which is an investment into the game that increases the perceived value of the game so if you've reached a certain level in pubg if you have a certain number of coins if you have a particular set of weapons that you bought and if you made in-app purchases it by default increases the value of the game for non-gamers many of us do not use facebook and yet if i ask you to delete your facebook account today you will still be a little hesitant why because your account has 500 friends whom you might get in touch with in your entire lifetime which is quite unlikely and yet you are hesitant because the perceived value of facebook is increased because of the network that you've formed this is also the same reason why google photos gives you 15 gb of free backup so that when you backup your photos the value of your gmail account increases by a large extent this is how using the super powerful hooked model pubg as a product has been able to achieve extraordinary levels of user engagement and when this got combined with the elimination of the entry barrier through pubg mobile this game took the world by a storm becoming one of the most successful products in gaming history and many many games today have already adopted these kind of models to keep the players hooked to the game these were some of the most important attributes that turned pubg into an insane product now the question over here is pubg is a great product that is fine but how can you learn about the intricacies of product design and what are the sources that you have to refer to in order to apply these principles to your product let's move on to the study materials to help you become a genius in product design the first reference is obviously this book called hooked written by this legend called real i'll also attach the workbook that he gives out in his website and this workbook has got specific questions that will help you apply the techniques that you start in this book so don't just read the book also try to solve the workbook discuss it with your team if you really want to build insane products the second book is this book persuasive technology it is slightly expensive so only buy this book if you're damn serious or you are a professional product designer and lastly if you find this book too expensive please read this book called tiny habits written by bj fogg himself.

Reliance

Reliance and Amazon have officially entered into one of the biggest business wars in Indian history. We are looking at two of the most powerful companies locking horns to capture the 200 billion dollar Indian e-commerce market. While on one side, We've got Amazon, a trillion dollar company with a stellar record of destroying its competition in every sector and every country. While on the other side, we have the mighty Reliance, which is by far the most powerful company in India with a reputation for disruption. And we all saw that with the Jio Revolution that literally redefined India forever. And now that both these giants are going to be fighting the billion-dollar business war in India, the obvious question is, What exactly is their strategy? How are they planning to destroy their competition? And most importantly, as students of business, What are the business lessons that we need to learn from this iconic business war? The story of Amazon's dominance in India started way back in 2013 and as we saw in the previous episode, they are creating a very, very powerful ecosystem using the sun cost strategy of Amazon Prime video. And because of their 60+ Warehouses spread across 15 states, Amazon has the highest penetration in India, along with Flipkart, which enables it to deliver products upto 15000 PIN codes. And these PIN codes include all types of cities, starting from tier 1 cities to tier 4 cities. In addition to that, Amazon has a huge amount of data about what does each customer want and what they don't want. Apart from that, they've also got the best customer support in the world. So now the question is, while Amazon has spent eight long years in mastering this art of e-commerce in India to build a robust supply chain and customer loyalty, How is Reliance even planning to compete with

Amazon in the first place? The answer to that lies in the most important asset of any e-commerce company and that is the supply chain. Now if you compare the supply chain of both these companies, while Amazon has around 60 giant warehouses in 15 states, Reliance has more than 12000 micro warehouses in 7000 cities spread all across the country and these warehouses exist in the form of Reliance retail stores. Now this distribution chain gives Reliance three incredible superpowers over Amazon. Number one- while Amazon can give you a one-day delivery, Reliance can give you a two-hour delivery. For example- Both Reliance and Amazon have data that says that Chitale Bakarwadi or Sparx sandals sells very well in Pune. But while Amazon can bring it only up to the nearest warehouse that is hundreds of kilometres away from your house, Reliance can bring it to your closest reliance store, which is just a few kilometres away. Because of which, it can give you a two-hour delivery, whereas Amazon will take at least a day or two to come. And of course, the products that are not available in the Reliance retail store, they will take a day or two to come, which is same as Prime delivery. Secondly, because of the data accuracy, Reliance has been able to build such a robust supply chain that while Amazon e-commerce marketplaces reported a loss of 5849 crores, Reliance Retail has been extremely profitable with 9842 crores in profit and not just that, they also had a footfall of 640 million in their Reliance retail store. And thirdly, because of these two factors, there is a very big disadvantage that Amazon has over Reliance and that is customer returns, because this is what Amazon returns looks like- I'm scared to think about how much stuff is going back to landfills, because it's just it's endless amounts of this stuff everyday. Returns are the largest challenge to e-commerce for both retailers and manufacturers. So, slightly more than a hundred billion dollars in returns. In e-commerce, its twenty or thirty percent get returned. Seventy-nine percent of consumers want free return shipping. Five billion pounds of waste gets thrown away as a result of these returns that can't be resold. So long story short, the three points to be noted in this sequence is that, Number one- More than seventy percent of the customers look for the return policy, which makes it an essential feature of any e-commerce platform. Number two- If you ask your customers to pay for the return shipment, there is no way you're going to retain them. Therefore, the seller has to pay for the return shipment. And lastly, because a large chunk of the Amazon.in products are sold by Amazon itself, it comes at an exorbitant cost with 100 billion dollars worth of returns in Amazon America alone. So practically, the reverse supply chain of the return shipment is a billion dollar loss venture for Amazon, but not so much for Reliance. The question is, why is this only a loss venture for Amazon and not for Reliance? Well that is because, here's what the reverse supply chain of a conventional e-commerce return shipment looks like- When you place a return order, it first gets picked up by a delivery boy. Then, it gets transported to the hub. Over there it gets packed and then it is either sent to a local warehouse, or back to the seller. Over there it sits in the inventory, either to be destroyed, or until someone else places the order. This means a total waste of transportation, labour and packaging for both delivery to the customer and back to the warehouse. And this is not applicable for Reliance, because as far as Reliance is concerned, the delivery boy from the Reliance store could just collect it and keep it at the nearest Reliance store. And because the Is so close by, most of the products wouldn't even need to be packed, saving them tons of packaging material, millions of dollars in packaging costs and millions of dollars in the labor that is needed for packaging. On top of that, after the product goes to the store, if it is really faulty, it would go back to the seller or it would be thrown away. But, if it is fairly usable, it could either end up back on line or it could be featured in something called the refurbished section at the Reliance retail store, such that, all these return products could be available at a discount for the customers who are visiting the store. And these products could be made available at a dirt cheap price. In business terms, It's called the throwaway price, which is a prising that is specifically meant to move the product out of the inventory. And guess what, this throwaway pricing strategy will attract more people to the store by acting as a lost leader to get them to buy more from the store, eventually profiting Reliance again, even in the return shipment process. And you know what? I also see a possibility where in, Reliance will tell you that, if you shop for 500 Rupees at the store, you can access the refurbished section where in you can get JBL speakers and clothes at a 50% discount. And this is attractive enough to get people to spend more, which will rapidly move out Inventory. This is the superpower of integrating a high-traffic online platform with a high-traffic offline platform, like the brick and the mortar store. But fortunately, or unfortunately, this luxury is available only for Reliance and not for Amazon. Now this begs the question, When a billion-dollar company like Reliance can build 12000+ brick-and-mortar stores. Why can't a trillion dollar company like Amazon do it? I mean, they've got so much cash to burn. They could just build one Amazon retail store right next to every Reliance retail store, right? Well, not really. This is what brings me to the third segment of the episode and that is government regulation. And as it turns out, from 2018 onwards, the government regulations on foreign direct investments have become more and more strict. And now, international companies are not allowed to own more than 51% of the local brick-and-mortar supermarket chains. Therefore, it is extremely difficult for Amazon to build a supply chain as big, or as profitable as Reliance. Apart from that, one of the most profitable wings of Amazon is on the verge of being destroyed. And if this happens, there is also a possibility that Amazon might be forced to quit the Indian markets. To tell you about it, if you look at Amazon's operations in India, they operate with two models. The first is a Marketplace model, and the second is the Inventory model. The Marketplace model is a model wherein, there are independent buyers and independent sellers and Amazon merely acts as a platform to connect the buyers from the sellers, whereas, in the Inventory model, Amazon is going to place a bulk order with the seller, eventually having the bargaining advantage to place the order at a dirt cheap price and then, Amazon will markup the price and then sell it to the consumers by keeping the inventory to itself, For example, if a bookseller makes a book at 150 rupees and sells it on the e-commerce site at 450 rupees. In this case, if the e-commerce company acts as a platform, it will generate a revenue of 112-150 Rupees. But this includes the packaging cost and the transportation cost for national delivery, which eventually reduces the scope for commissions. But, if the e-commerce company operates with the inventory model, the platform will buy 10000 books from the bookseller at once, and will use its bargaining power of a bulk order to buy the book at just 200 rupees per piece. After that, all these books will be kept in the warehouse and then it will be listed in the e-commerce site at 450 Rupees. So if you see, this gives them 250 rupees in revenue as compared to 150 rupees in the previous case. Now although this includes the inventory cost, it gives them a wider scope of profit. In this case, is the 100 rupees where in there is a scope of profit for the e-commerce site. Now when it comes to books, it's just 100 Rupees. But when it comes to products that cost 10,000 and 20,000 Rupees, the difference in revenue that can be generated between both these models skyrockets by a billion dollars. Therefore, the inventory model is a billion dollars more profitable for Amazon as compared to a Marketplace model. This is the reason why Amazon entered into a strategic partnership to establish giant sellers like Cloudtail in 2014 and appario Retail in 2017. And using these sellers, Amazon has deployed the inventory model to generate a major chunk of its revenue. And according to a Reuters investigation report, in 2016, Cloudtail share of sales on Amazon.in was around 47% of the total Amazon sales. But that month, Amazon got some bad news because the Indian government announced new foreign investment rules wherein, it capped the online marketplace sales from a single seller at 25% of the total sales because of which, they had to bring down Cloudtail's share of sales on Amazon platform to less than 25%. Now, from here onwards, there are certain sensitive information that I cannot directly convey to you. So what I'm going to do is, I'm going to attach a link in the description that will help you understand the detailed report completely and from that you can draw your own conclusions. But long story short, while the government of India allows 100% foreign direct investment in the Marketplace model of e-commerce, it has not allowed FDI in the Inventory driven models of e-commerce. And the competition commission of India has also placed strict restrictions on Amazon selling its own products in the form of Amazon Basics. Therefore, three of the potentially most profitable channels of Amazon have been restricted to a large extent. So as of now, on the outside it seems as though Amazon cannot match the number of brick-and-mortar stores as Reliance. Number two, Amazon cannot use the Inventory model like they planned. And lastly, they cannot sell their own products as much as they planned. This is the state of the biggest business war in Indian history. With that, We move on to the most important part here and that is, considering all this drama as Investors and as students of business, What are the factors that we need to keep an eye on in order to understand the future of this retail war?. Here are three very important points that you need to study in order to understand this retail war better. Number one, there are seven major variables that will determine the success or the failure of any e-commerce company. From the consumer standpoint, there are three variables: cost, delivery and variety. And from the business standpoint, the three variables are customer retention, supply chain and profits. And lastly, the most crucial variable of all is nothing but government regulations. So as students of business, you need to keep an eye on these seven variables, because ultimately, this is going to be the scorecard of this billion dollar retail War. Number two, just like Reliance, even Tata and DMart have a huge advantage over Amazon and Flipkart, because they are Indian companies. So keep an eye on their retail ventures, because they've got some powerful strategies that can again lead to a retail disruption.

XXXVI

Rupay

On 15th of august 2014 the government of india made a revolutionary announcement about the pradhan mantri jandhan yujna and this gave rise to an iconic venture by the national payment corporation of india this venture that i'm talking about is none other than india's own card network that we all know today as rupee and rupee has taken such big strides in the indian payment industry that in 2013 rupee accounted for only 0.6 of all cards but in just four years by 2017 rupee had already surpassed visa as india's largest payment card with 375 million transactions and by 2020 it already commanded a market share of 60 in india's card market and this put visa under such big threat that it approached the us government to help them stand against rupe so the question is in just six years how did rupee kill the billion-dollar duo bully of visa and mastercard in india what is the government's strategy and intent behind this revolutionary initiative and most importantly as citizens of india what is it that we need to know about rupe as to how is it going to affect the lives of the people of india the first thing you need to understand is how does the payment ecosystem operate in order to carry out our transactions so let's try to understand this with very simple examples let's say i have an hdfc visa card with a one lakh rupees of credit limit and alan poly is this clothing merchant with her account in icici this makes hdfc the issuing bank and icici the acquiring bank and this is how the transaction between us gets executed in the backend when i enter my hdc card details to make a 10 000 rupees payment my card details get entered into the payment gateway of the website which in this case let's say is raise or pay here the value out of razer pay is that it will help the merchant receive payments from different sources like credit card debit card upi etc now since i am making a credit card transaction razer bay will collect my card information and the transaction amount and then it will pass it on to the merchant's bank which in this case is icse from then onwards icici will capture the transaction and forward the information to my credit card network which in this case is visa this is where visa routes the transaction to my bank which is hdfc and requests for an approval so basically visa is asking hdfc system whether i have enough funds and what is the status of my account so let's say my card is blocked then this transaction will be declined if i do not have enough credit limit then this transaction will be declined similarly in case of a debit card if i do not have enough balance then my card will be declined and if everything is all right and if i have the required credit limit then the transaction is authorized this approval process is known as authorization after that hdfc sends the response back to visa wherein hdfc says everything is perfect and assigns and transmits an authorization code along with its response and this way 10 000 rupees is put on hold from my hdfc account then visa sends this approval to the merchant's payment processor which in this case is razer pay and razer pay then sends the approval to the acquiring bank that is icici icsa then routes the approval code to the merchant's terminal and depending on the merchant or the transaction type the merchant's terminal will print a receipt for the customer to sign so if it's a website you will see a digital receipt if it's a swipe machine you will get the receipt printed this is how the transaction is processed now we come to the business part of this process to carry out this transaction the issuing bank or the customer's bank and the credit card network charged their fees which together accounts for 3 which is 300 rupees this percentage could range anywhere between 1 to 3 percent in this case considering three percent fees on ten thousand rupees three hundred rupees is reducted and nine thousand seven hundred rupees is transferred to the merchant's account now this transaction fees of 300 rupees is known as mdr or merchant discount rate apart from that razer pay will levy a charge of 0.5 percent which will eventually give the merchant 9650 rupees this is how the payment ecosystem works together to process our day-to-day transaction it's just that for debit cards there are two simple differences instead of the credit limit the amount gets deducted directly from the bank account so the repayment process is eliminated and secondly the mdr for credit card is way more than the debit cards so while debit card mdrs are capped at 0.9 percent for credit cards the mdr is typically one to three percent now listen to this very very carefully now this mdr rate majorly includes two variables the first variable is something called the interchange fee and the second is something called the switching fee now i know that this is information overload but don't worry it's very very simple to understand the interchange fee is the fee that the issuing bank charges the acquiring bank as in the customer's bank charges the merchant's bank which in this case hdfc is charging icici bank and then the switching fee is charged by the car network to the issuing bank in this case it's visa charging the customers bank which is htfc and up until 2014 visa and mastercard together were two of the most powerful players who had established almost a duo bully in the car network market of india but this is where something crazy happened this is where the government of india came up with a disruption using its very own card network which is known as rupee on 15th august 2014 the pradhan mantri jandan yojna was announced and this initiative mandated banks to enable zero balance accounts with deposit insurance and overdraft facility for the unbanked population of india so from 2014 onwards millions of bank accounts started opening up all across the country by january 2015 this number grew to 125 million and by january 2021 this number stood at 416.5 million bank accounts with women in rural areas accounting for more than half of this number and this is where rupay came in in order to make car transactions accessible to the lowest economic start of india instead of living a percentage charge like visa and mastercard for rupe a fixed mdr of just 90 pisces was charged which was 60 pisces to the issuer bank and 30 to the acquiring bank and according to the chief executive and managing director of ncpi mr ap hota this was a key differentiating factor that led to the enormous success of rupe and what followed next was nothing short of revolutionary all indian companies with an annual turnover exceeding 50 crores were required to offer rupee payment options to their customers and according to a data by the department of financial services under the ministry of finance 31.74 crore rupee debit cards have been issued until now and in just six to seven years the market share of rupees shot up to 34.5 percent out of the 90 crore debit cards issued in india but you know what then came another big announcement by the government of india wherein it was eventually declared that there will be zero merchant discount rate for rupee debit cards and this put visa in such deep trouble that now it is seeking the help of the us government itself now the question over here is how and why did the business war between visa and rupe come in and why did the government of india introduce the concept of zero mdr well the answer to this lies in the fundamental problems existing in the indian banking ecosystem and here are the most important ones that prompted the government of india to launch rupee if you go 11 years back in 2011 back then close to 557 million people which is close to 50 percent of india's population did not even have a bank account this was majorly because the banks demanded a minimum balance of three to five thousand rupees from their customers now this may seem relatively fair to us but for people like daily wage labor the contract labors or our mates this sum of money is their rental cost in the grocery budget for an entire month therefore most people in the unorganized sector like chai wall and bheburiwaras they refrain from opening bank accounts this meant that 557 million people were bereft of any financial support and facilities and even if the government wanted to provide support if fifty percent of your population that to the bottom of the pyramid is excluded from the banking system then it is nothing short of a disaster this is a reason why the government of india introduced the pradhan mantri jandan yojna and made sure that every citizen in india can be banked without having a minimum balance barrier and what was mind-blowing to most analysts was that the total estimated balance held in these accounts was estimated at 1 lakh 37 195.93 crore rupees which is equivalent to 18 billion dollars but this is where the government discovered a critical challenge you see when we open a new bank account we get a checkbook and a debit card as a part of the account opening process this debit card is crucial because it facilitates withdrawals from atms and enables us to make cashless transactions and because of this there was a dire need to have visa and mastercard like services but this is where the government discovered three critical challenges number one back then mastercard and visa had their offerings only with 55 banks out of the 500 plus banks that existed in india and they were predominantly catering to the private sector banks so there was a dire need of a car network that could serve the rest of the 500 banks in india number two offering debit and credit to the unbanked required customizations like giving credit lines to farmers or helping them procure grains and these facilities did not come under the ambit of players like mastercard and visa at all and thirdly the processing cost of these international players was very very high so while big merchants like tsar or mcdonald's have the luxury of having a 40 50 sometimes even 90 profit margins when it comes to small scale vendors like a grocery store or an electrical store their profit margins are ranging between 10 to 30 percent and in that case if you charge an mdr of one to three percent it goes very heavy on their profits this is the reason why zero mdr was introduced through rupee but now the question over here is are in the banks incurring losses because now that mdr is zero both interchange free and switching fee has to be zero right so the question is how is this even viable for the banks well for starters for the losses incurred due to the charges like the interchange fee wherein the acquiring bank pays the issuing bank to compensate for these type of fees the government has set aside 1300 crores to make sure that the stakeholders in the ecosystem are compensated for their losses this is how the government is on a cash drain to make sure that the bottom of the pyramid of india is included in the banking systems of india now the question is what is the benefit of spending 1300 crores into making a payment service free isn't that a reckless use of the tax base money so the question is why is the government spending so much money after all for a card network and how can it change the lives of the ordinary people of india the first thing this move has done is lay the foundation for financial inclusion such that it gives the government a pipeline to distribute schemes and services to the people of india secondly india can and is providing facilities to those segments of the population which will otherwise never be catered to by a company like visa or mastercard and rupee has already started doing that by the way with its five types of cards these card types includes a pm jdy debit card which comes with the added personal accident death and total disability coverage up to 2 lakh rupees the mudra card which can be used to make multiple withdrawals and avail credits to manage the working capital limit in an efficient and productive manner the pun grain card that can be used to avail automatic grain procurement facilities at the pun grain mondays and lastly we have the kisan credit card scheme which was implemented to provide need-based timely credit to support farmers for their cultivation needs as well as for their non-farming activities in a cost efficient manner this can help india take financial inclusion to the next level and can empower the common people of india if executed with persistence and consistency and lastly just like visa and mastercard being foreign entities became dominating forces in the indian ecosystem rupe and upi both are now venturing into the foreign soil with the vision to revolutionize payment industry not just in india but the world itself now what remains to be seen is how do we build up from here because in case of bsn and india both we saw that it's quite evident being the best and having the garments back alone cannot help you if you succumb to the challenges of capitalism and this brings me to the most important part of the episode and those are the study materials and the references to help you ponder over this concept and to help you understand the government initiatives better , moving on there are three things that i want you to think and read about to understand the government strategy with both rupe and upi number one check out the website of rupe and see how is it operating and study how rupe and upi are being leveraged for financial inclusion in india and more importantly study the importance of financial inclusion and its impact on a country's economy secondly do study how this move could go wrong in my site it could play out in two ways number one if this initiative is not executed properly then that 1300 crore number which is only going to keep going up will be nothing but a meaningless drain of cash number two since there are many stakeholders involved in the payment ecosystem until a certain point subsidizing makes sense but if it starts eating into the profits of the players like the payment gateways and the banks then the incentive that these entities have in order to spread digital payments will fade away and this will be nothing short of a socialistic nightmare.

XXXVII
Southwest Airlines

11th of septmeber 2001 turn out the most horrific event in the American history A group of terrorist hijacking 4 planes one of the struct the Pentagon and two of them collided write into the World Trade Centre And What followed next was Catastrophe that sent shockwaves all across the world All planes was grounded immediately people too scared to fly and the American emission sector was in such a terrible state that almost look like domestic air travel will be shut Down forever As a result all the major American Airlines started bleeding money resulting into millions of dollars of losses with each passing day 46000 job lost in condition of so bad that even major airlines like the United Airlines and the US airways start to file for bankruptcies but you know what gay's even during such a terrible time the world was shock to see that the one airline that remain profitable and did not registered the single a quarter of loss throughout 2001 and 2002 the question is which airlines is this and is so miracle about the airline that it had remain profitable even during such a terrible time to well this is no other than the legendary Southwest Airlines And the most astonishing thing about Southwest is that it had remain profitable 47 consecutive years until the pandemic hit and this 47 year include 2 oil crisies 9/11 attack and even 2008 recession so this beg a question what is so special about southwest airlines that it has remain profitable even during such terrible time of business what exactly is their business strategy And most importantly considering Mr Jhunjhunwala is latest venture and go air IPU announcement from the investor standpoint the first part of this answer is the incredible model of opertaion that southwest follows to tell about at in the aviation space there are two major model that airlines use in order to connect their destination the first is the hub and spoke model And the second model is the point-to-point model and hers they workout let see we have six destination A B C D E and F if you want to offer fight connecting all this destination using point to point model her's out it would workout you need to a flight to go from A to B B to C C to D D to E and E to F and F to A then you need to connect A to C A to D A to E A to F so on and so forth so in total if you want to contact all this 6 destination you need 15 planes but hub and spoke model this become relatively easier Insanf contacting all this destination using the separate flight you Creat hub o between such That if you want to contact A to C this is how to model workout thell we be plane A which will carry all the passenger who want to go B C D and E F and then when plane A lands of the hub All the passenger go to their respective flights which are B C D E F And when those plane fly back to their destination automatically All the customer will arrive their destination now on the outside this might look little complex but here of 4 incredible benefits that's this provides over the point-to-point model 1. you only need 6 plans as compaire to 15 plans in point to point model 2. Using the hub and spoke model planes are more ooccupied because now you are surving the same number of customer with only 6 flights 3. Dow to the present Central hub maintenance become extremely easy 4.its is very very easy to expand your network because all it do is just add another spoke to by adding another plane to network And then you well automatically gate connecting 6 destination using the hub Whereas if you want to add another destination to the point to point model you will need another 6 planes there for the hub and spoke model is that model which can connect people for anywhere to everywhere in the most efficient manner but surprisingly southwest doesn't use this hub and spoke model Instant it Usse the point to point model now the question is when hub and spoke model such a cost effective model why is southwest airlines useing point ot point model and more importantly how did generating profit out of aninefficient system well that is because the hub and spoke model has some key disadvantages that Southwest decided to minimise 1. the jermey Dam increasing by large extent because is not going to A to B you go form A to O and then O to B As a result of which the fuel prices also increases Which leave to higher prices and thirdly the passenger and luggage how to be move to one plane to anotherplane at the hub which take lots of time increases the down time at the aircraft then lead more cost and lastly if they emergency or storm delay the first flight the customer misses missing the connecting flight which again needs to be pad for by the Airlines now even southwest understood the enorde to connect 6 destination useing the point-to-point model they would need 12 aircraft but the caught her's is this match is 15 planes is been done with underline convention that the airline won't to connect all this destination let Traveller go from anywhere to everywhere but you know what gay's southwest decided that they will not connect citizen for anywhere to everywhere inset they decide select only those destination which have got height traffic so is having 5 planes that go to A to B C D E F they said we well connect only A B and C because they are high traffic points and her's we the exfactor of profit comes in If you looking comparison of two model in the hub and spoke model the filght well go form A to O and then O to B Where is southwest well directly go form A To B without any stop in between Therefore because of the long journey in hub and spoke model they will need more fuel which lead to more cost And also lead to more time as compared to point to point model So all the customer who want to travel between A B and C by default they were choose Southwest why Because it was both cheaper and faster therefore these master stroke of southwest got them all the benefit of point to point system like less downtime low cost and less fuel uses and at the same time the They escaped from the disadvantage of hub and spoke model like luggage transfer Costly Hubfees or the hasees of missing of connecting filght This is how southweast carefully choose their model and hit the sweet spot of both cost and convenience which eventually become a widal pillar to turn them into billion-dollar profitable airline And this inturn give them turn of cashflow That kept them even during the time of crisis like 9/11 and even during the 2008 recession Now question is southwest wasn't the only airline to use point to point model right? There were other Airlines to then why weren't thoes airline as profitable as Southwest Airlines Well this brings to me the second superpower that Southwest cultivated That is something called the oil/heding This is the story days by 1990 when the Gulf War had its peak And because of the war there was certain speaking oil pricess where in the price of the oil went up by 100% in less than 1 year Now in the contest of Aviation fuel is the second most expensive element in supply chain Therefore any increasing in oil prices directly lead to increasing ticket price and causes The lot of trouble to Airlines but immediately after the war was over the all prices came down drastically But even during this time while The Other Airlines was enjoying high profit margin in low ticket prices The CFO of Southwest Garry kelly being a history student took this event very very seriously Because he realise that the world is not too far from another oil spike So he decided to develop a strategy to oil heding in simple word It's call fuel insurance Where an Southwest would make a deal with financial institution such that they would pay a premium for there fuel today so that's tomorrow if they oil pricess suits they well Steel by there fuel pre determined price for example if today oil prices $20/barrel southwest would pay $35/barrel with the condition that tomorrow if the price of the suits up ot $60/barrel southwest would steel pay $35/barrel only so form 1994's on word southwest starting hedging 20 to 30 paresnt of its fuel and by 2001 they had hedg 100% of their fuel useing there state of the art hedging platform and guess what this oil hedging strategy turn out to be such a amazing move that form 1998 to 2008 southwest instant up saving 3.5 billion dollar over what it what to do if it paid the industry standard Jet fuel prices fun fact 13.5 million dollars translate to 83% of the prophet in the same span between 1998 to 2008 and while leading money of the oil prices shot of in 2008 Southwest was very comfortable enjoying their profits this is second reason why southwest Airlines is extremely profitable even during the times of Crisis now this beg the question how do they channelize all of their money in how to hack their Future Growth and finally this brings to me the thired perhaps the most important pillar of Southwest that is employee and customer satisfaction you now peoples sieman cine coffin speaks about this Legend called Bob Chapman he says that when your family you are 4 and if you get food only 3 what you do do you let one of your children starve so that other children can have belly full no right? you dived food amoung for 4 so tthat one of them doesn't starve Similarly great organisation build a culture weren't the organization just like a family Divide the heart shaped such that all of them suffering a little so that same of them don't suffer a lot This is how Southwest operate after 9/11 will all other Airlines engaged in layoffs leading to lose of 46000 job's The CEO of Southwest made a public statement in he said an I quote and as for as the customer were concerned many of airlines refused to give refund and try level best to make a hard for customer to get their refunds Because those airlines needed to cash flow but southwest only Airlines to offer no question asked full refund policy Such was the compensinate value that the wonderful companies by stood by even that it was bleeding money and what flow next was nothing short of fairy tail the decision inspired the entire company to work together to word gathering the planls in the air As quickly as possible when the grounding was lifted and from the very next day itself All the employees return to work and did everything in their capacity to get the plans in the air The finance team extendaly work no cost cutting and the insurance issues were rectified New flights schedules which usually took weeks to be created were just a few days Some employees violently pleasing a part of their income to help the company survive And give their profit share money just so that the company doesn't suffer losses The entire staff work in day in out to establish security protocol as quickly as possible Some work 18 to 20 hours a day to other did not take a weekend off You know that most touching instant was that some customer were writing $1000 check to the Airlines Saying that the just want to make a valuable contribution for the extra ordinary services Southwest provided You know that like you writing 20000 rupees check to hear India's saying that to you when to make valuable contributions so that Air India servives Therefore this extra ordinary level of consumption love persistency integration Unity unble Southwest Airlines to cut cost to remain profitable even during the 9/11 crises And even during the 2008 recession And this are bring us to the last part of chapter and that is what is the business lesson that we need to learn from this case study And what are the factor that we need to consider while we analyse and potential ssuccess or the failures of the players in the aviation industry Lesson no. 1 from a business standpoint always remain just because the industry is pointing on from a standard protocol You don't have to extend it into two in this case it was bold choice of southwest Choose the point-to-point model with the strategic for side of minimise and weakness and maximize the strength of both the model And from the investor standpoint you always need to keep finding out the strategies developed by the companies That separate them from the rest of world in this case that was the point-to-point model of southwest In case of Indigo it was the sales and less back model lesson n. 2 Herb kellener says at Southwest we manage in good times so that all of us will be protected from the bed time In this case it was the for sight for Gary Kelly about upcoming risk become of which they were able to use oil holding strategies to protect the day during the bad times Therefore as an entrepreneur during the good times you must work the hardest spot medicated and prepare for the risk During the times of crisis you are way ahead of your competition and from the investor standpoint you need Dig into the company specific to find out what a particular company is doing in order to prepare for upcoming risk As compared to the what the competition is doing in same market And last and most important always remember hold good leader focus on only profit great leader focus on channelizing those profit for the betterment of employees Just so that innocent family does not suffer just become business is not doing well.

XXXVIII
Starbucks

If you want to be an effective and powerful leader then this chapter is for you because the story that i'm about to tell you today is the story of an extraordinary leader who revived a billion dollar brand from failure and no matter which domain you belong to if you apply the lessons from this case study in your life even you can go on to become an extraordinary leader this legend that i'm talking about is harvard shoes and the company that he revived is none other than the iconic starbucks coffee chain and in 2007 starbucks was in such a pathetic state that the stock price had fallen by 50 percent the same store sales had hit a rock bottom of one percent growth and most importantly the perception of starbucks was almost like nokia wherein people perceived starbucks as a dying legend who's just waiting to go extinct on top of that this state of starbucks came in the worst possible period which was the 2008 recession in the united states so the question is why was starbucks failing how did hovershoe solve the starburst crisis and most importantly how can you apply the leadership lessons from this legend in your life to become a powerful leader the story of starbucks dates way back to 1971 when three friends started a coffee bean company called starbucks and long story short howard schulz was one of the employees who eventually bought the company and when he visited italy he became fascinated by the italian coffee culture where people came to the coffee house just to bond and hang out and the belongingness that he felt was something that he wanted to bring to the united states and that is how the concept of starbucks experience was born where people did not just come to drink coffee but came to feel comfortable and warm in a place that was their third place away from home and office and just like we indians fell in love with pisas americans fell in love with the coffee culture and in the next 15 years howard choose built a billion dollar company out of the starbucks brand with 13 000 stores in the united states and further extending the coffee culture to japan china and even dubai and finally after taking the company to an impeccable position he finally stepped down as ceo on 1st of june 2000 and as soon as he left the company in the next seven years on paper starbucks started to grow even faster with six stores opening every single day in 2007. but you know what guys on ground there were three critical problems that none of the financiers paid attention to number one the company was so obsessed with growth and pleasing the shareholders that they started compromising on the core principle of the company and that was the starbucks experience for example they replaced the semi-automatic machines with the fully automatic coffee machines now on paper this did help baristas make more coffees in lesser time but it killed the hallmark of starbucks which was the magnificent display of the baristas making coffee the board failed to realize that people did not come to starbucks to get a quick coffee they came there to have a magnificent experience of the coffee similarly in the race of expansion the company did not even bother to build a supply chain that could cope up with their skill as a result they did have a lot of stores but they did not have enough stock to serve all coffees in the menu and at the same time for some reason starbucks even started selling products like dvds now this confused the customers and dilated the essence of the starbucks brand number two the culture of the company had taken a very big hit when howard shoes was the ceo every barista was given extensive training on hospitality and the starbucks baristas had such a level of warmth and connection with the customers that the baristas used to remember the names of the customers their coffee and even their allergies and this connection over time became so wonderful that starbucks baristas used to get invited to their customers weddings this was the deep rooted connection that the starbucks brand was built upon this is the reason why people visited starbucks not with the intent to visit a coffee shop but a place that was next to home whereas by 2007 the condition was so bad that the baristas were just behaving like baristas who made you a cup of coffee and that's it there was no friendship no warmth left at the starbucks tour this is what howard schultz called the commoditization of the starbucks brand and lastly this deterioration that happened did not happen overnight it took eight years for the company to derail from its core to becoming commoditized and this happened because the leaders of starbucks were not listening to the demands of the customers as a result in spite of the rapid expansion the same store sales hit a rock bottom of 1 growth people started to switch to discount coffees from mcdonald's and dunkin donuts and the starbucks brand overall started failing miserably and when howard schulz saw all of this happening to his brainchild he decided to take matters in his own hands and returned as the ceo of the company this is how on 7th of january 2008 howard schultz came out of retirement and took over as the ceo of starbucks and you know what guys within the next three years starbucks was back on track with an incredible track record the sales growth went from just one percent in 2007 to nine percent in 2011. the profit of the company almost doubled from 673 million dollars to 1.24 billion dollars and the stock price shot up by 100 from just 20 to 40 dollars in 2011 and starbucks again returned to become one of the best performing companies in the world the question is what did howard do so special that he was able to bring in such an incredible transformation to the starbucks brand well as it turns out howard did the complete opposite of what they had done in the past seven years on first of july 2008 starbucks announced the closure of 600 stores and by 2009 they had to lay off 6 700 employees they threw off all automatic machines and got back the semi-automatic machines to make coffee and started their employee training from scratch in fact the entire country was shocked to see that even during recession while most businesses were doing everything in their capacity to save every dollar starbucks actually closed all their 7100 stores for 3 hours for employee training and they called it the art of espresso in these three hours the employees were taught the most basics of making a wonderful coffee this made headlines all across the country and costed starbucks 6 million dollars during the time of recession now while most experts saw this as a silly move it actually made a very bold statement to the customers of starbucks that they are damn serious about getting back on track this was the first phase of starbucks revival but unfortunately nothing actually tangible came out of it the brand was still incurring losses the recession started draining money even more faster and the stock price hit a rock bottom of 14.95 but this is where the second phase came in and that was about building an action-oriented culture for starbucks you know guys many times journalists often ask harvard shoes as to what exactly is a secret recipe of starbucks growth to which he often replies that we are not in the coffee business serving people we are in the people business serving coffee which means what when you're on the coffee business serving people your first priority is coffee but when you're in the people business serving coffee your top priority is the people and coffee becomes a mere instrument of your service and howard schulz wanted this message to be very very clear to every single employee in the company and you know what he did just one month after the september 2008 stock market crash when companies are again saving every penny that they could howard shoes called upon a leadership conference in a place called new orleans now this place was no ordinary place it was a place that was devastated by floods and hurricane and thousands of people needed help with the reconstruction of their neighborhood and as it turns out this leadership conference was not about sitting in a fancy room to watch motivational lectures but about actually helping the people of new orleans getting their lives back on track and guess what 10 000 starbucks employees collectively spent 50 000 hours painting houses planting grass cleaning trains and even constructing playgrounds that day ladies and gentlemen there were hundreds of hugs smiles and tears of joy and new audience as they saw 10 000 strangers coming together for a selfless act of service this costed starbucks a hefty 30 million during recession but at the same time it sent one message loud and clear to the customers and the employees of starbucks that starbucks was not a coffee company serving people but a people company serving coffee and even today starbucks brings out beautiful initiatives to reinforce its motive of bringing joy and service to mankind while most corporates try to find loopholes to escape government regulations starbucks spends millions of dollars to go beyond government regulations both for the environment and for the people it serves and one of my favorite initiatives is the sign language stores that they opened to make it tough and hard to hear people feel inclusive in the society this was the second pillar of starbucks explosive comeback and that was action-oriented culture and lastly the third pillar of starbucks transformation was inspired by michael dell and was known as something called my starbucks idea.com wherein the company literally asked customers for ideas to be executed at starbucks within no time this concept was a big hit with 7000 ideas and hundred thousand votes coming in just 24 hours the best part was that by february 2009 starbucks actually incorporated 25 of the most popular ideas of 2008 these ideas included a free coffee on a birthday free wi-fi in-store music changes and even the elimination of store receipts for purchases under 25 in order to reduce paper wastage and the most valuable idea that came out of it was the loyalty reward suggestion and you won't believe me when i say this but this idea alone made starbucks a billion dollars now in order to avoid information overload i'll get into this concept in a separate case study but until then here's a quick explanation of the same star wars announced a loyalty program wherein customers could instantly earn rewards like a free beverage or a size upgrade simply by registering their starbucks cards online and as soon as this announcement was made all loyal and frequent starbucks customers started loading their money into the cards and surprisingly within some time this amount in the starbucks cards amounted to 115 billion dollars and by 2008 this number was close to 1.2 billion dollars the catch over here is that since starbucks wallet money could only be spent on starbucks products it was practically a billion dollars in revenue lying with them with zero interest and that too during the times of recession and this kind of made starbucks the biggest bank in the world polymatter is a channel that actually made a beautiful video on it so if you find time do check that out this is how howard schools a legendary leader brought a billion dollar company back on track by choosing meaningful growth over mindless financial growth by choosing to be a people company rather than a coffee company and most importantly by choosing to build a great company over a big company and this brings me to the most important part of the chapterand that is with all this drama what are the most important leadership lessons that you need to learn from howard shoes in order to execute in your life let's move on to the lessons from the case study lesson number one financial growth must always be a factor but never the solution to evaluate the worthiness of a company in this case the starbucks management made a blunder by obsessing so much over financial growth that they lost sight of the very purpose of the brand's existence and that was the starbucks experience number two while ordinary companies flash their motto on walls and emails extraordinary companies actually act upon their core values to set a benchmark for others to follow in this case it was starbucks extraordinary initiative to spend 30 million dollars even during the times of recession for the service at new orleans to exhibit the true values of the starbucks brand and lastly always remember in this big bad world of digital connections the power of human touch and compassion are often undervalued but if a company learns how to practice and embrace these values the right way it can go on to become a memorable company for its customers and especially in today's world it's very easy to be big but it's very very difficult to be a memorable brand so my question to you is what are you doing to make your brand memorable for your customers.

XXXIX Tanishq

Tanishq is one of the most incredible brands in the indian business history , in the past 20 years the stock price of its parent company titan has shot up by not 10 not 20 but 33 000 going from just 7.11 rupees to 2700 rupees and a mere 10 000 rupees invested in titan 20 years back would be worth a minimum of 35 lakh rupees now although titan has a lot of brands under its canopy the jewelry division alone accounts for 75 percent of its total business and as of 2021 tanishq generated a net sales of 20 600 crores and today it is one of the biggest jewelry sellers in the country so the question is how did titan turn tanish into such a huge brand what were the business strategies that enabled them to disrupt the orthodox gold market of india and this is a story that dates back to late 1980s by this time it had been four to five years since the titan brand had started mr desa and his team had built an incredible company for the tatas in the tamil nadu government and now after cementing titan's position in india in the 1990s mr xerxes wanted to take titan to the european markets however this proposition did not take off at all why because the european watch market was crowded at all levels at the lower end they had local brands in the middle they had japanese companies like seco and then at the top they had swiss brands so while sales of west asia and asia pacific were good the euro business was incurring losses and eventually that division had to be shut down but you know what guys this is where suddenly titan decided to sell jewelry in europe now the question is why would a watch company suddenly start selling jewelry and that too in europe well that is because something crazy happened in the middle east during that time saddam had taken his gamble whether it was part of a plan to capture the world's oil supplies whether he would go marching on to saudi arabia america didn't wait to see iraq will not be permitted to annex the way that's not a threat just the way it's going to be the coalition took only a hundred hours to destroy the iraqi forces in kuwait in the hours before baghdad surrendered the oil wells of kuwait were set ablaze by saddam's retreating army kuwait which produced one and a half million barrels of oil a day before march of 1991 the united states had recently invaded iraq over saddam hussein's invasion of kuwait and in the build-up of invasion iraq and kuwait had been producing a combined 4.3 million barrels of oil a day but when the war tensions started rising it led to the 1990s oil shock wherein the price of oil shot up from just 21 dollars per barrel at the end of july to 46 dollars per barrel in mid october and this put nations all across the world in deep deep trouble and in case of india since india imported oil and paid for it in dollars or forex the high prices caused a significant burden on our forex resource by june 1991 india had less than one billion dollars of foreign reserves left which was just enough for three weeks of inputs this was a situation even after substantial borrowing from the imf so during this time any company that wanted forex had to generate it completely by themselves in simple words india said if you're a businessman who wants dollars don't come to india for exchange because we need to buy oil if you want to do any kind of import earn or borrow dollars from someone else and then spend it completely by yourself now in case of titan they needed dollars to import their watch components so they started swelling jewelry with the goal that they would make and sell jewelry in europe earn forex then use the money to import watch competence then use those components to make more watches in india and then sell them all across the world but this is when liberalization came into effect in india in 1991. as a result india's i.t companies like infosys and vipro started bringing an enormous amount of forex eventually the oil shop faded away and titan started focusing on the indian market under a different brand name this is how through another jugado method another iconic indian brand was born which we all know today as tanishq now the reason why mr desai and team pursue the jewelry market in india was because while visiting a jewelry exhibition at the taj hotel they made three important observations number one the indian household was extremely passionate about jewelry because it was an investment and not an expense and even an orthodox family did not mind spending tens of thousands of rupees into jewelry but secondly the jewellery designs in india were extremely mediocre and the purity of gold was quite questionable this was because impurity was a very good way for the local jewelers to expand their margins and make a ton of profits and lastly in spite of having such an enormous demand and a customer lifetime value in lakhs the margins in gold were extremely high because of both appreciation in value and more importantly because of cheap labor this is what propelled titan to enter the jewelry business now by the look of it considering the fact that titan had the cash for the tatas and the expertise to get world class tech it looks as if it must have been easy to crack the jewelry market of india right well not really in fact tanish in the initial few years was a loss-making unit and at one point in time the condition was so bad that they were in talks of selling it off and this happened because of two major reasons firstly the indian jewelry market was very very strongly established with the unorganized players why because the only dweller and indian family trusted were the local family dwellers i say local and family because if you ask your parents they'll tell you that even your grandparents and their siblings bought from the same dweller secondly back then 22 garrett gold was the de facto standard this is where you've got a product with ninety one point six percent gold and eight point five percent alloys but titan started out with 18 carat jewelry this was because the 18 carat was studio would not get scratches easily and would give a firmer grip to the gems and stones this way they could focus on innovative designs with started jewelry but guess what in india back then and even today design was secondary proportion of gold was primary why because gold for indians was an investment and not just a piece of jewelry so the weight of gold weight of diamond making charges appreciation value all of it mattered to the indian buyers and they didn't mind a simple design as long as it had more gold this is when mr xerxes and his team decided to introspect tanish very very closely so immediately the pricing system was changed the price tags now display the gold and the gem details that explain the price of each product to the customers and overall the focus shifted from design to purity and value and this is when tanishq made a game changing investment into something called the carrot meter and this investment completely changed titan's game forever to tell you about it like we discussed before most of the families in india trusted one family dweller who had been selling them gold and other jewels for 20 to 30 long years but at the same time tanishq understood that these dwellers were adulterating the products by a large extent and a common man can not actually differentiate these intricacies and this is also something that you cannot just tackle with marketing campaigns this is where the carrot meter came in carrot meter was an important machine from switzerland that actually used spectroscopy to measure the purity of gold this machine was installed in all tanish outlets and after that titan launched a special campaign wherein they invited customers to walk in with any piece of jewelry and measure its purity for free now since gold was very very important to indians people actually flocked to these stores to check the purity of their ornaments that they had actually bought from their family dweller out of blind trust and guess what majority of these people were shocked to discover that they had been cheated by their family dwellers for decades and this was because the gold was not as pure as the dwellers claimed and when lakhs of people felt betrayed or dissatisfied with their jewelry titan deployed another strategy called the 1922 strategy and in this scheme women could bring in their gold jewelry test it in the carrot meter and if the purity of the jewelry was lower than 22 karat and higher than 19 karat it could be exchanged for tanish 22 carat jewelry of their choice by paying only the manufacturing charges and tanish could bear the cost of gold yes you heard that right tanish could bear the cost of gold this was titan's customer acquisition strategy now although it might look like titan was draining cash by paying for the gold what we miss out on is the fact that when it comes to jewelry the customer lifetime value goes to lakhs of rupees and if done right just like local dwellers you could be looking at customers from three to four generations of the family as a result when this 1922 strategy was executed titan was very cleverly able to uproot the blind trust of the local dwellers and acquired lacks of customers from all across the country this is how tanishq laid the foundation to build its brand as a synonym of trust and purity and the result well by 2023 the jewelry division's operating income increased from 267.66 crores to 345 crores with profit before tax at 5.37 crores and this is where tanish rise as a blockbuster brand began because it tackled one of the most important batteries of customer acquisition and that is barrier of trust this is when they further moved ahead to tackle the second barrier which was the barrier of cost after the carried meter strategy tanish found another gap in the market for expansion they realized that because of their branding efforts the middle class indian family started to perceive tanishq as a brand that was too expensive for them and from the cost standpoint a middle class family that wanted to purchase gold could not shell out 6 to 7 lakhs at once but at the same time the desire to buy the set was there because after all it was an investment this is where tanishq launched the famous gold harvest investment scheme to buy jewelry in this game if you wanted to buy a gold chain worth 2.4 lakhs and you didn't have that kind of money now you could actually deposit 20 000 rupees per month for 11 months with tanishq and then tanish would pay your 12th installment of 20 000 rupees at the end of the year you would have 2.4 lakh rupees to buy your gold chain this is almost like an sip for gold and if you didn't want to buy gold after a year you could get the money back with the discount voucher for the additional amount this is how the barrier of cost was brought down as a result danish became more accessible to the middle class population of india and eventually they tackled yet another important barrier which was the barrier of cost and lastly what i personally love about these classic brands is that they often consider one factor that no other brand considers in order to identify intricate gaps in the market and this is the factor of empathy in this case tanishk actually observed that working women didn't want to wear very ornate jewelry to work because it looked too flashy at the same time they wanted something affordable elegant and easy to wear so tanishq launched the miya collection that specifically addressed this segment of the audience and started their pricing from 3999 onwards then they also found that the richest people in the society who had the purchasing power wanted to buy unique designs which would distinguish them from the crowd so they launched the zoya collection that starts from 70 000 rupees and goes all the way up to 70 lakh rupees then they also saw the digital wave rising so titan invested into carrot lane in 2016 which is an online jewellery company in fact even today if you go out in the market and you try to examine the competitions of tanishq you will see that there are very very few brands that actually cater to so many categories of audience like executive ultra rich traditional minimalistic designer etc this is how tanishq evolved to become one of the largest valerie sellers in the country and this brings me to the most important part of the chapter and that are the lessons on the case study , moving on the first lesson that we need to learn is that there is a thin line between what you think your customers like and what they actually like so always do your market research thoroughly before stepping into the market and the most powerful way to do that would be to study the data and then go and talk to people to understand the story behind the data the point we noted over here is talking to people is more important than analyzing data lesson number two sometimes you have to make people aware of the problem before providing the solution in this case although people are buying impure gold the blind trust of the local dwellers needed to be broken in order to establish the informed trust by tanishq this is where titan's carrot meter came in handy and lastly always remember empathy is that superpower that can turn a commoner into a king in this case the constant market assessment done by tanishq team gave them million dollar assets in the form of mia and zoya collections so always remember keep updating yourself about what your customers need otherwise they won't need you tomorrow.

XL
Tata Steel

Tata steel is one of the greatest companies in the history of india and the most astonishing thing about this company is that it has been a major pillar of india's economy for more than 114 years and these 114 years include the most turbulent times in world history including two world wars the great depression and four national wars but all throughout these times tata steel has stood tall and managed to become a dominating force in the world steel industry the question is how did tata steel become such a formidable company how did it manage to remain powerful even during the british raj and most importantly what are the lessons that we need to learn from the incredible house of the tatas this is a story that dates back to 1880s india when jamshee ji tata was traveling around the world to understand the different advancements in the textile industry during this time he attended a lecture by a british historian and philosopher by the name thomas kalail and in this lecture thomas kalil stated that a nation that understood the value of iron would reap its weight in gold and jamshi ji was so inspired by his lecture that for the next 30 years until his death jamshedji worked tirelessly to establish the iron and steel plant in india the question is why did thomas khalil say that and what was the underlying meaning of his statement well as it turns out the 1860s was the most important decade of the 19th century during this time although railways was a revolutionary invention its cost of operation and expansion was very very high this was mainly because cast iron that was being used to lay the tracks was extremely costly they could not carry a lot of load and they also needed a lot of maintenance this was because cast iron was susceptible to rust meanwhile steel production was even more costly because of which steel was only used in small quantities in tools like swords and cutlery but in the historic year of 1856 a british engineer named henry besmir invented a cost-effective and mass-producible technique to make steel and this process was such a breakthrough that during that time it reduced the cost of steel production by 82 from 40 pounds to just six to seven pounds per long ton and this invention ladies and gentlemen alone catalyze the entire industrial revolution in the western world and in the next 10 years steel became a general purpose material and was being used in every important aspect of development starting from construction all the way up to the railways and steel was not just revolutionary because of its cheap production but also because when it was used in railways it could withstand way more loads as compared to iron and more importantly the maintenance of railways became extremely cheap therefore steel became the most fundamental pillar of western nations development this is the reason why thomas khalil said a nation that understood the value of iron would reap its weight in gold and as soon as jamshedji understood this he spent the rest of his life in the pursuit of building an iron and steel plant for india during this time jamshedji tata had established the iconic empress mill in nagpur and within a very short span of time Tata had become a pioneer and a market leader in the textile industry but in spite of having all the wealth in the world jamshay jay tata was more keen on building a solid economic foundation for india than building his own fortune so as soon as he came to india he started reading every single report published by every renowned geologist so that he could find iron hole deposits in india and the craziest thing about this legend is that jamshedji and his team spent not 5 not 10 but the next 17 years in finding and collecting samples for iron ores at the same time he was also managing and growing his textile business and as the great saying goes fortune always favors the bold and persistent finally after 17 years of exploration in 1899 in the small village of sakchi jamshee ji tata's geologist perin ended up finding 3 billion tons of ore and the best part was that this ore was located just 45 miles away from the railway station and this is how ladies and gentlemen india embarked on its journey to participate in the steel revolution of the world but unfortunately jamshedji wasn't alive to see his dream come true while he passed away in 1904 his son dhurabji tata and brother aldi tata took his dream forward and finally the tata steel limited was incorporated in the year 1907 with the name tata iron and steel company limited and after five long years of preparation and fundraising in 1912 the first steel ingot rolled out to the factory now the question over here is all of this was happening when india was under the british raj right then the question is why and how did the british government allow these indian enterprises to grow well there were three reasons for that number one the britishers realized that the real profit was not in making steel but in making railways so that they could make money with trade expansion so the construction of the railways was more important than the steel plant secondly they realized that importing steel all the way from britain or the neighboring colonies was extremely costly and an extremely tedious procedure and obviously surveying the entire subcontinent was also not a viable option therefore they liberalized the mining laws so that people like jamshedji could use their resources and provide steel for the government and lastly on 28th of july 1914 world war 1 broke out and this turned the british empire's attitude towards indian enterprises from jealousy to positive encouragement now over here some people often ask me as to why the tatas help the britishers couldn't they just let the britishers lose the war well it's not as simple as that guys because had they done that the british empire would have easily taken over the plant forcefully which means what three billion tons of ore would belong to the britishers and on top of that they would have banned the tatas from building the other industries one of which was tata power which even to this day is one of india's most valuable assets so while most of us think of industries as just money making machines it is important for us to note that empires might rise and fall wars might come and go but if a nation strategically invest into industries these industries will act as the most important engines of a nation's economy and they will last for centuries in this case if you look carefully even during the british raj jamshedji tata laid the foundations of three of the most important industries in india that is textile steel and power and the absence of these industries would have left india in ruins during the post independence period a classic example of the same is the state of singapore in 1965. this is a reason why the tatas supported the britishers in that period tisco became the only supplier of steel in india and it enjoyed a terrific boom and tata steel alone supplied miles of rail and 300 000 tons of steel material and this created thousands of jobs for the indian workers and established tata company as an unshakable entity in the indian business ecosystem and just when everyone thought that disco was all set for the high the world war bubble burst and in 1920 the world witnessed something called the post-war recession and suddenly there was no longer a soaring demand for steel and no more jobs for the soldiers in fact in america alone the number of active soldiers fell from 29 lakhs to just 3.8 lakhs within just two years in 1920 and india was no different either as the war wrapped up the indian industries got badly affected and tata steals only regular customer japan was shaken up by an earthquake which again killed the demand for steel the condition was so bad that sbi which was back then known as the imperial bank of india they refused to extend loans to the tatas and to make matters worse on 29th of october 1929 the new york stock exchange collapse which pushed the world into one of the worst economic crisis in world history this was nothing but the period of great depression which lasted for 10 years from 1928 to 1938. now during such a time, the industrialists followed a very simple procedure they immediately fired all of their employees because they already made a ton of money during the war and all they needed to do was fire all the workers or sell the company to somebody else and just enjoy the massive wealth that they built for the rest of their life this is the reason why if you look at the timeline of the world from 1920 to 1939 every single major industry in the world starting from America to the British colonies all of them witnessed major labor strikes but amidst all of this chaos you know was the most surprising fact of all while every other industry in the world saw dozens of labor strikes throughout the great depression the tatas did not see a single labor strike throughout the great depression after 1929. the question is what was so special about the tatas that they did not witness single labor strike even during the worst economic crisis in world history well that is because the tatas were no ordinary industrialists in this case duranji also had the same option of letting the workers go to enjoy his fortunes but this is where the tatas stood out the tatas never saw their ventures as just money making machines they saw them as engines of india's economy that would stand as pillars of india's development so in spite of having 55 000 workers durabji and rd tata did everything in their capacity to not fire a single worker and duraji even put his personal assets for sale and asked his wife to pawn her dwells this way the tatas did everything in their capacity to pay every single worker on time in spite of the terrible market conditions on top of that to make workers feel secured they introduced several schemes for the workers family which included free medical aid the retirement graduate scheme and even the maternity benefit scheme it was even decided a few years later that the families of contract workers who suffered accidents at the tata steel premises would be provided cover and benefits through a scheme called the suraksha scheme all of this was being done in spite of the company bleeding money that was coming from the personal assets of durabji tata this was the true spirit of the tatas because of which they have not seen a single labor strike for 100 years now such was the legacy of the second generation of the house of tatters until another legend by the name jrd tata to go the company in 1938 but for now with all this information that we have let's move on to the most important part of the chapter and that is as future leaders what are the business lessons that we need to learn from the incredible house of the tatas and what are the study materials to help you dive deeper meanwhile if you're someone who loves the tatas as much as we do you can use the small case app to invest into the best tata companies by opting in for the house of tata small case small gaze is this wonderful company that designs a basket of stocks to help you make the best investments in any market conditions in this case the house of tata small case contains hand-picked stocks on the tata conglomerate that have got extremely high growth potential and the best part is that the small case manager will automatically rebalance the stocks as per the market conditions to give you the best returns possible and even if you do not want to make investments you could use my favorite feature in this app that is the new section and the newsletters these are again wonderful pieces of contents that will help you get the latest updates about the most important happenings in the market so if you love their idea download the small case app from the link in the description moving on to the lessons on the case study there are three very very important lessons that we need to learn from the house of tata's lesson number one no matter how big or small of an entrepreneur you are if you want to be the best in your sector you have to be a voracious reader and an ardent student of your industry in this case if you see at 40 years old most people often give up on learning but here we saw jamshedji tata at the age of 40 he was still attending lectures in spite of being a successful industrialist this is the reason why he was able to understand the importance of steel and eventually that information gave our country a billion dollar asset like disco lesson number two capitalism is the most powerful weapon of growth for any nation and like i said empires might rise and fall wars might come and go but if a nation strategically invests into industries they will act as the most important engines of the nation's economy in this case it was jamshedji's foresight to lay the foundations for india in spite of the british raj and the strategic investments made by the house of tatas in textile steel and power helped india get back on her feet even after the britishers left and last and most importantly while good businessmen grow their business to build their fortunes great businessmen like jamshedji tata and durabji tata grow their business as a service to their nation and more importantly as a service to mankind itself.

XLI
Tesla

We all know Tesla as the most powerful disrupter of the automobile revolution. And despite the pandemic, while all other automakers were struggling to make a profit, Tesla was very elegantly profitable with a profit of 721 million dollars. And as soon as it hit profitability, the stock price of the company shot up by 740 percent in 2020 alone. And not just that, even in q2 of 2021, Tesla reported a record profit of more than $1 billion. So at the outset, it looks like Tesla is on its way to becoming the undisputed king of the automobile revolution, right? Well, not, as it turns out, three critical indicators state that in 2021, Tesla is in deep, deep trouble, and how they navigate through this situation will eventually determine not just the stock price, but also the fate of the company in the automobile revolution. The question is, what exactly are these troubles? And from the investor's standpoint, what are the factors that you need to keep an eye on before you invest in Tesla or similar companies in the automobile market?.The first threat to Tesla is the overreliance on something called the regulatory credits. To tell you about it, ever since the carbon emission concerns have risen, Governments all around the world have introduced incentives for automakers to develop electric vehicles, which are also low carbon-emitting cars. In this regulation, car companies are required to produce a certain number of ZEVs or zero-emission vehicles. And this number is based on the total number of cars sold in a particular state. For example, if General Motors, Honda, and Toyota produce 100 cars, they are required to produce 10 zero-emission vehicles. And if they cannot produce 10 ZEVs by the end of the year, they will have to pay hefty fines to the respective government, whether that's the US government or the European government. But on the other side, if you look at Tesla, Tesla is producing hundreds of ZEVs already because all of its cars are electric vehicles. So technically, they have produced 90 ZEVs extra as compared to the mandate. Therefore, they earn Extra Credits equivalent to 90 ZEVs. Now, what General Motors, Toyota, and Honda could do is that, because they cannot produce ZEVs by themselves, they will buy 10 credits from Tesla, just so that they can comply with the regulations. So this way, nine companies can buy 10 ZEVs credits each from Tesla, for which Tesla will charge them fees. And these fees are nothing but pure profits for Tesla. This is how the regulatory credit system works. And you know what? These regulatory credits are so critical to Tesla, that in 2020, when they posted a profit of $721 million, $1.6 billion came from regulatory credits, which means, that had they not sold those regulatory credits, Tesla would have been in a massive loss. So practically, they made more money selling regulatory credits than they did by selling cars. And this is where the problem lies. The issue with this strategy is that while these credits may help Tesla in the short term, as soon as other companies enter the EV market, Tesla will no longer be able to make money through credits. For example, if you look at Atlantis, Atlantis is the largest buyer of Tesla's credits, and they bought $2.4 billion worth of credits from Tesla. But now, they are planning to roll out their electric vehicles by next year itself. Therefore, within just two years, this $2.4 billion of profits are going to be wiped out of Tesla's balance sheet. And even if you look at q1 2021, while the net profit of Tesla was $438 million, they got $518 million in revenue from sales of regulatory credits. And this is how Tesla has been over-dependent on regulatory credits to make its balance sheet look good. But that's where another twist came in. In the very next quarter itself, that's q2 of 2021. While Tesla recorded a net income of $1.14 billion, only $354 million came from the sales of regulatory credits. If you see, they have decreased their dependence on regulatory credits by a large extent. And just when everything looked fantastic on paper, and investors were happy about it, another big trouble began creeping in from the other side of the globe. And this is what brings me to the second part of this chapter, and that is Tesla's love affair with China. Now if you look at the Chinese EV market, it is by far one of the fastest-growing markets in the world. In fact, despite the pandemic, the global sales of EVs increased by 43% in 2020 in China, and China alone accounts for 1.3 million EVs, which is 41% of all EVs sold worldwide, and Tesla's story with China began in 2019 when they got exclusive permission to build their Giga factory, and Tesla became the first foreign manufacturer to own 100% of their factory in China. Secondly, Tesla was also given a loan of $614 million for the construction of the factory in China itself. Thirdly, the entire Giga factory was completed within a record time of just 160 days. That includes everything starting from getting the permits up to the construction of the plant. Whereas in the US, despite it being the home ground of Tesla, it took them close to two years to complete their Giga factory. On top of that, Tesla cars also bought a 10% tax exemption in China, which made them the first foreign manufacturer to receive this type of exemption without having a local joint venture partner. And even during the pandemic while all other companies were struggling to get N95 masks, Tesla was able to get N95 masks for its workers and the Chinese government itself provided buses for the workers to travel to the plants to keep them safe and keep the manufacturing going. Therefore, in 2020, Tesla was able to deliver almost half a million vehicles and set a quarterly record of delivery of 180,000 vehicles. As a result, Tesla's overall revenue increased from $24.6 billion in 2019 to $31.5 billion in 2020. And the revenue from China itself grew by 100%, from just $3 billion in 2019 to $6.6 billion in 2020. If you see, that's 20% of the entire revenue of Tesla in 2020. Until this point, everything looked like a fairy tale, right? Well, that's when as soon as 2021 started, China started behaving like China. In February 2021, a group of Chinese authorities held talks with Tesla after consumers complained about acceleration irregularities, battery fires, software upgrade failures, and other vehicle problems. In response, Tesla had no other option but to apologize and comply. In March 2021, China does a security review of the vehicles because they were concerned that, the information could be sent back to the United States. Why? Because Tesla's automated driving features relied on camera systems, the Chinese government did not know this at all. Then in April 2021, Tesla makes headlines at the Shanghai Auto Show. Why? Because a Tesla car owner out of nowhere starts protesting against Tesla. And this angry woman climbed on top of the model tree, and repeatedly yelled," Tesla's brakes don't work". And soon enough, the Chinese media, which is largely controlled by the government itself, starts posting this on social media, and eventually, it goes viral. And suddenly, Tesla is no longer the favorite brand of the Chinese people. As a result, Tesla sales in China start plummeting and goes down by 27% from March to April, and orders go down by 50% from April to May. And at the same time, its Chinese rivals like BYD are looking at a year-on-year growth of 189.62% and a month-on-month hike of 27%. Now this begs the question if at all China is doing this intentionally, why are they doing it and how is sabotaging Tesla going to benefit them? Well, there are two reasons. Number one, China has been known to steal intellectual property from foreign companies, especially American companies. This was one of the primary reasons why Donald Trump got angry and started a trade war between the US and China. Secondly, Tesla's entry into the Chinese market has compelled companies like NIO and BYD to enhance their performance and raise their standards. Eventually, it accelerated the EV revolution in China. This is the story of Tesla's affair with China. And apart from that, not just in China, but even in other places like the US and Europe, the competition has started eroding into its market share of Tesla. In February 2021, Tesla recorded a sales growth of only 5.4%. And when looking deeper, you will see that Ford's Mustang E is eating into Tesla's market share, as it became the third highest-selling electric car in the US in February 2021. Meanwhile, in Europe, Volkswagen's Electric model has beaten Tesla to become the top-selling EV maker in 2020. And lastly, General Motors announced that it will increase its EV and automated vehicle investment to $35 billion from 2020 to 2025. So all in all, Ford, General Motors, and Volkswagen, of them are racing towards the untapped market at the bottom of the pyramid. And this is a market segment that Tesla is not able to cater to, or is not willing to cater to. Therefore, the three threats looming over Tesla in 2021 are number one dependence on regulatory credits and number two is China's orchestrated threat towards Tesla, and lastly, giants like Ford, GM closing into the EV space with affordable vehicles for the bottom of the pyramid, which is eventually eroding into Tesla's market share. And this begs the question, as investors in the automobile space, what are the factors that you need to keep an eye on before you invest in Tesla or similar companies?. Number one, Tesla is in a crucial position in 2021. And had it been some normal automaker, you could directly say that it's in a bad state. But in this case, you are looking at Elon Musk, and you just cannot neglect the musk effect. Therefore, Tesla could come out with a game-changing business strategies to reduce its dependence on regulatory credits. And when they do, it's obvious that Tesla's stock price is going to shoot up. So from the investor standpoint, keep an eye on these business strategies, and as students of business take note of these business strategies because they are golden lessons that you can learn from and apply to your business. Number two, keep an eye on every single government subsidy that is being rolled out in India. Because while we have our eyes on Tesla, Mahindra and Tata are going to play a vital role in the EV revolution of India. And thirdly, keep an eye on the strategic partnerships that are being formed between automakers. For example, Toyota is partnering with Panasonic for batteries. Ford is partnering with redwood materials for battery recycling. Because people, these strategic partnerships and their outcomes will largely impact the future of these players in the market and eventually determine where they stand in the EV revolution. And yes, keep an eye on the US-China trade war, because there's something very interesting happening over there, which will help you learn some very important geopolitical lessons.

XLII
Titan

we are going to learn about one of the greatest consumer brands in the history of india and that is titan watches in the past 20 years the stock price of titan has shot up by not 10 not twenty but thirty six thousand two hundred and eighteen percent going from just seven point one one rupees to two thousand seven twenty one rupees and a mere ten thousand rupees invested in titan twenty years back would be worth a minimum of thirty eight lakh rupees in fact this is the biggest talk in mr rakesh involves portfolio which was valued at 11 0849 crores as of january 2022 but while most of us know that titan watches are great very few of us know how did titan watches lay the foundations for the iconic titan brand in india which is why in this chapter let's try to understand what is the story of titan watches what were the business strategies that laid the foundations for titan to become such a legendary brand in india and most importantly what are the business lessons that we need to learn from the iconic rise of titan this is a story that dates back to late 1970s when a project manager of the tata hotels named mr xerxes desai was looking to start a new venture for the tatas and generally the culture among the tatas is such that they constantly keep scouting and tracking for new industries to enter and in the 1970s mr desa and his quality made some critical observations about the watch market of india they saw that watch was such a fundamental accessory that every single person starting from a watchman to a student to an executive all of them were watches so obviously the watch market in india was very very huge but in spite of that most of this demand in india was being catered to by the unorganized players and in the premium space there was only one significant player which was a company called hindustan machine tools limited or hmt this company was a public sector company run by the government itself on top of that in the 1970s and 80s since liberalization had not happened in india foreign watchmakers like the swiss and the japanese could not enter the indian market so practically hmt was a monopoly in the market but when mr desai and his team did some ground level research they found something very very interesting number one they saw that although the swiss and the japanese watches were never sold in india surprisingly a lot of indians actually knew about these different watch brands all across the world secondly this fascination for watches was so much in india that people who had friends and relatives abroad actually smuggled swiss and japanese watches into india now i don't know how many of you remember or have experienced this but back in 2009-10 after iphone launched in the us the craze of iphone in india was so much that even though iphone was not being sold in india a lot of indians actually smuggled iphone from the us through relatives and friends and because iphone did not support the indian networks they did something called jailbreak by actually going to these small mobile shops just to make sure that they could use iphone in india and they do not care if it compromises security to the phone itself as long as they got to use an iphone so just like this iphone crazed in 2010 indians of the 70s and 80s were super fans of swiss and japanese watches and in a way a black market was formed for foreign watches in india and lastly since very few people had relatives abroad the only premium watchmaker they could opt for was hmt and out of 1.5 million watches produced in india 1 million watches were produced by hmd alone along with other small players contributing to the remaining 0.5 million but the demand was so much that hmd itself was not able to keep up and this resulted into long wait times just to buy a watch and this is when mr desai and team realized that the watch market of india was a gold mine so finally they decided to start a watch company that could cater to this untapped demand in indian market but you know what guys there was a slight problem since india was an extremely socialistic country watchmaking as an industry was open to either small-scale manufacturers or public sector companies so big private companies like the tatas were not at all welcome in this space so the tatas approached the tamilnadu industrial development corporation and back then even they were looking to find an indian partner for french watch manufacturing and as expected the government of india rejected their proposal so you know what they came up with a sneaky strategy wherein they set up a separate private company on paper called questar investments so that it would not draw the attention of the government and the project name of the company was derived from the two names of the organization tata industries and tamil nadu and when put together the name that came out was none other than titan and as luck would have it the government provided the clearance and the tatas immediately bought questar investments this is how in 1984 the tatas and the tamilnadu industrial development corporation together started an iconic brand from india through jugaad which we all know today as titan this is where the second phase came in and that was market research now as soon as the titan team was formed a team was sent abroad to study the watch market and to look for inspiration from watchmakers from france and switzerland and at the same time they very very cleverly set up a base in a place called hosuh why because hmd had its base in bengaluru and this place was just one hour away from bengaluru this way titan could easily draw in experts out of hmt and use their expertise to improve their operations and finally in 1987 titan officially started manufacturing watches secondly if you look at the watch revolution of the 1980s and 90s there were two types of watches on the rice mechanical watches and quads watches for those who don't know both these watch movements are literally engineering marvels and it wouldn't be too poetic to say that mechanical and quartz watches are an engineer's artworks to tell you about it a mechanical watch is driven by a mainspring and when this main spring is wound by the user its force is transmitted through a series of gears that work in conjunction together and eventually they move the hands of the clock and that is how you get to see the time whereas quas watches are battery powered and this battery sends an electrical current through a small piece of crystal called the quad's crystal and this crystal is embedded in the circuit this action then causes the crystal to vibrate exactly at 32 768 times per second then the circuit measures these vibrations and converts them into one pulse every second and this pulse drives the motor which then moves the watch hands eventually enabling the watch to keep time these were the two rival systems in the watch revolution of the world so when the titan team actually came back from market research they realized that quartz watches were the inevitable future of watchmaking this was because quads watches had three major advantages over mechanical watches firstly from the manufacturing standpoint quad's watches had 70-80 moving parts as compared to 100 to 120 moving parts in a mechanical watch this made it both easier and cheaper to manufacture a quads watch secondly from the consumer standpoint while mechanical watches had an error of 6 to 12 seconds a day quad's watches had an error of just 5-100 seconds in the entire year and quad's watches were also lighter and slimmer for the customer to carry around and lastly while mechanical watches of those days needed to be wound manually almost every single day quads watches just needed a battery replacement that too in a year or two this is a reason why quad's watches were the inevitable future of watchmaking but strangely in india until rajiv gandhi came in the government of india had a mandate that 80 of the watches manufactured must be mechanical watches which is why there were very less to none quads manufacturers in india but for titan this came at a very very accurate time because titan was founded in 1984 and all the base work they did enabled them to build their entire infrastructure around quads watches straight away this is how the titan team got the second and perhaps the most critical pillar right which was choosing the right technology and then came the third pillar which was the post manufacturing process and this included the store setup distribution and finances and here's how they carefully crafted each one of these attributes first of all for the distributors back then all the distributors were extremely reluctant to buy titan because like we saw hmd had an 80 market share and these distributors were extremely loyal to hmt and skeptical about titan so the titan team decided to directly tap into retailers by partnering with reputed businessmen in different cities all across the country and even if they did not have any experience in what selling titan conditioned them with great training and made them masters in what selling in return they bypassed the distributors and these retail businessmen were able to make way higher margins as compared to the industry standards and titan's training was so holistic that while a normal watt salesman is just taught to observe everything about watches a titan salesman was actually trained to study the market so broadly that he was expected to know the business of not just watchmakers but also other stores like a raymond store a premium sari store or even a jewelry store the question is why does a watch salesman have to know about raymond premium sorry stores and jewelry stores well that is because while most people thought watchmakers only compete with other watchmakers titan back then understood that a watch is also an instrument of love that could be bought with the intent of gifting like a wife would gift her husband a watch so titan understood that their competition was not just hmt but even other players in the gigantic gifting segment which included a jewelry store a sari store and many other stores that affluent customers would go and buy from and hence this proactive market research was instilled in the frontline workers of titan and for the customers they duly complemented their sales with a stupendous after sales service in fact at titan the act of repairing a watch was considered like the act of repairing a damaged relationship like repairing the company's reputation so they treated their customers with immense warmth and they even installed air conditioners in the waiting rooms in the 1980s just so that the customers would not feel inconvenienced while they come to the service centers secondly for marketing titan got hold of none other than the legendary marketers or gillian martha themselves and they helped them design such insane newspaper ads that back then when watches were always endorsed or showcased by a celebrity or a model titan placed half a page ad of just the magnificent watch design without a model at all and all they mentioned was just the brand identity and the price of the watch that's it and this method of marketing although quite counterintuitive it turned out to be such a big hit that people literally walked into a titan showroom with newspapers in their hands and said that i want this watch such was and still is the magnificence of their advertisement and lastly to keep their financials healthy titan just like pdlite did not offer a credit system at all and they took advanced payment for their supply and although it was met with initial resistance it contributed to titan's financial success this way titan's balance sheet was so healthy that they were able to show profits on the very first hit of the operation itself and the result well in 1987 88 that is just one year into the market titan earned a mammoth 19 crore rupees and sold 3.44 lac quads watches by 1989 titan had cornered nearly 55 percent of the quads watch market in the country and from here onwards the brand of titan only kept growing growing and growing and once they were able to build a brand identity and were able to showcase the results on their balance sheet their stock price just keep going up up and up this is how through titan watches the foundations of the titan brand was laid and in the next 20 years titan went on to build incredible brands like tanishq fast track sonata and titan i plus and each one of these brands today are more or less in the leading positions in their respective market and tanishq is actually a very very interesting story which i am not covering due to information overlord but if you want to know about it please drop a comment below and i'll try to release it in the next month's lineup and this brings me to the most important part of the chapter and that are the business lessons that we need to learn from the iconic titan brand moving on the first thing you need to understand is that when you are living in a developing or in an underdeveloped nation along with a lot of disadvantages as an entrepreneur you have the massive advantage of time because you can actually see what is happening in the developed world right now and incorporate that in a developing nation in the future and this is because technology often evolves in a similar trajectory , lesson number two an obstacle in business is often treated as an obstacle by the losers but the same obstacle is treated as a competition eliminator by a winner because you see the same obstacles are going to be faced by all the entrepreneurs in the field but the ones who choose to tackle it and overcome it will by default win against those who shrug their shoulders in this case the tatas tried for years to get an approval from the government and when they didn't they found a jugadoo way through quester investments to get into the business anyway and mind you this process took not one not two but almost 10 years just to start manufacturing and lastly jumping to the next curve is the easiest and perhaps the most powerful way to kill the dominance of a giant player in this case titan killed the dominance of hmd by jumping to quads and ironically now apple is rapidly killing the market of both titan and swiss watches by jumping to software-based watches and what remains to be seen now is how will titan watches tackle this mammoth challenge that lies ahead of them that's all from my side today guys if you learned something valuable please make sure to the like button you want to make youtube rubber happy and for more such insightful business and political case studies please subscribe to our channel thank you so much for watching i will see you in the next one bye bye [Music]

XLIII

Toyota

Toyota is one of the most extraordinary companies in the world. And the attribute that makes it so incredible is the fact that Toyota is a company that had every possible obstacle to failure. First of all, Japan is such a small country had very less natural resources and a very less population. Therefore, both raw materials and labor were extremely costly. In addition to that, Japan is a land of natural disasters where earthquakes and tsunamis are frequent, and could destroy your plant within a minute. Thirdly, when Toyota was just two years into the business, WorldWar2 happened where bombs were dropping from the sky. And during such a time, let alone business, even survival was a very big deal. On top of that, after the Hiroshima Nagasaki bombing and the World War 2, Japan's economy was in complete ruins. And lastly, with all these odds against them, they were in direct competition with the giants of the United States, like General Motors and Ford motors. And yet, in spite of these obstacles, Toyota has emerged as one of the most successful automobile companies in the world. In fact, in 2008, it even became the largest car manufacturer in the world. In 2016, Toyota's market capitalization was more than Ford, General Motors and Honda combined. Now, this begs the question, how did Toyota become such a successful company amidst such terrible market conditions? What exactly was their business strategy? And more importantly, what can we learn from this incredible case study? Before we move on, I want to introduce you to a wonderful language app called Duolingo. Duolingo is an app wherein you can learn more than 40 languages for free. Now, this obviously includes English but that's not why it is the top 10 free learning app in the Play Store. Duolingo is extremely popular because they have gamified the entire process of learning any language., I was kind of fidgeting around the application to see if I could learn some Japanese words. And trust me guys, it's surprisingly fun and surprisingly easy. This is a story that dates back to 1950 Japan, now it's already been 13 years since Toyota has been founded, and Japan was in complete ruins after the World War 2. During the war, Toyota barely survived by pivoting between making trucks and cars for the military needs. The condition of the company was so bad that even after 13 years of efforts, while Toyota motors produced just 11,000 automobiles in the entire year. On the other side, Ford motors produced more than 1 million automobiles in the exact same year. And this massive disparity in production prompted Toyota top manager EG Toyota and several of his engineers, to visit the Ford rouge plant, in an attempt to learn how do they exactly improve their manufacturing processes. But after this visit, they realised, that simply copying and improving the rouge system would not really work in Japan. Why? Because Toyota was in a very, very poor financial condition. On top of that, Japan was just recovering from the ill effects of the World War, which left the country starving for both capital and foreign exchange. Therefore, Toyota could not buy the latest western production that was needed to improve the production efficiency and to scale up the production. So practically speaking, there was no way Toyota could compete with the American companies in two of the most crucial aspects of manufacturing and that are capital and machinery. Now during such a time any ordinary engineer would give up and declare that there is no way he could compete with the Americans. But EG Toyota was no ordinary engineer. In spite of knowing that all odds were against him, he and his team work day in and day out to understand how could they build a competitive system against the American manufacturers. And that is when they realised that, although they could not compete with the Americans with capital and machinery, there was one very crucial aspect that they could beat the Americans with and that aspect was nothing but efficiency. So he came up with the idea of something called the lean manufacturing system. To tell you about it, EG Toyota understood that the standard method of operation of the US manufacturers was that, they first forecasted the demand up to a certain extent, and then placed bulk orders so that they can save up on the cost of machine parts and raw materials. So if there are three colours of cars that needed to be sold red, black and grey, the company will produce 200 red cars, 500 black cars and 300 grey cars and these cars will be ready to be delivered, but will be stored in the inventory until the order comes up. And as soon as the customer places the order, they are immediately moved out and delivered to the customer. But in this process, the Toyota team identified that there is a major problem that in turn led to a series of four major inefficiencies. And the fixing of these inefficiencies is what turned Toyota into a billion dollar company. In fact, it did not just change the way the automobile industry worked, it changed the way the entire world's supply chain worked. The question is, what were these inefficiencies and how did the Toyota team fix it? Number one, the Toyota team realised that when the demand forecasting happened in the United States, the production always used to produce cars in surplus and never in deficit. Therefore, more often than not, it lead to excessive resource allocation. This meant that unnecessary people were hired, more equipments were purchased and more materials and products were stocked up in the inventory. And this in turn, led to an increase in the overall cash costs without adding any value. Secondly, the presence of unnecessary people, equipment and materials automatically lead to overproduction. And then overproduction further lead to the third type of waste, which is excessive inventory of the final products. In this case, if there are 1000 cars that are overproduced, that is a huge amount of land that is being utilised, leading to very high maintenance costs, labour costs and transportation cost. And lastly, when all these ways come together, it leads to the fourth type of waste which is unnecessary capital investment. For example, if 1000 crore loan has been taken out, and if it is utilised in overproduction, Do you realise it's going to stack up a crazy amount of interest cost lead into very high cost with zero return on investment. And this further leads to more administrative costs, depreciation cost, etc. Now, on the outset, it looks like a lot of things need to be changed, right. But when the team of Toyota actually understood the root cause of this problem, it was all about just one thing. Forecasting of demand lead to excessive inventory, which in turn led to a chain effect resulting into the four types of waste. So you know what, Toyota decided to eliminate two of the most fundamental elements of the supply chain and that are inventory and demand forecast. Yes, you heard that right. Toyota built a supply chain where there was no demand forecasting and zero inventory. And this is how the world class just-in-time system was born. And this system revolutionised not just the automobile industry, but also became the world standard for supply chain management in every field you can think about, and this is how it worked out. Instead of having the cars manufactured and stored into the inventory, the cars used to be available for the customers in the pamphlets, and they used to be available in the showroom. And only after the customer placed the order, Toyota started manufacturing the car. Now this on the outside seems very simple, right? Well, here's what even an oversimplified process of Toyota's production look like. Once the ideation and booking dates are finalised, the machinery and technology are acquired in three months. After that, the parts and components arrive in seven days of the production centre. After the booking starts coming from several dealers all across the country, the production actually starts and the path start moving to the assembly. Now, when this moment happens, based on the demand, the exact same number of parts are set to arrive every single day. So, if 9871 components have been taken to the assembly, the next day, only 9871 components will arrive. And this happened not just for one component, but the hundreds of components that were being used for the assembly, this is followed by assembly activities and finally, the quality check is done. The vehicles that are assembled arrive at the dispatch zone and immediately, immediately they are shipped to the dealers based on their respective orders. And this entire process is set to happen in five days as for the stated source in 2016. Therefore, the entire supply chain of the company starts functioning on the basis of demand and not demand forecast. This is how the just-in-time production of Toyota works wherein, even a single delay can cause the company millions of dollars in losses. And this insane precision gave Toyota three incredible superpowers for the rest of the competition. Number one, in case of less demand or even if an earthquake shatters the plant Toyota would incur only minimum damage because they had less stock of components and close to zero inventory. Furthermore, Toyota even asked its suppliers to follow the just-in-time principle for their systems, which again reduced the cost of the overall supply chain without creating a bottleneck for the suppliers. Secondly, all four types of waste were eliminated resulting into extreme cost cutting and this cost cutting turned out to be is so amazing that even when other companies applied JIT, they saw a 50% reduction in their inventory itself, and a lead time reduction of more than 80%, eventually resulting into massive cost cutting and drastic increase in profit margins. And lastly, in case of Toyota, from 1955 onwards, Toyota's production started shooting up, they made 22,786 vehicles in 1955, 46,417 in 1956, 70,856, in 1957 and by 1965, they achieved a growth of almost 2,000%, producing 477,643 units in 1965. This is how by striking a perfect balance between extreme efficiency and extreme risk, Toyota and its engineers built an iconic supply chain that turned them into the largest and one of the most profitable automobile companies in the world. Now, the question is, as an entrepreneur, how can you apply the just-in-time concept to your company? And what are the lessons that we need to learn from a legend like EG Toyota? Number one, adversity is always the breeding ground of innovation. So if you want to learn to build the most efficient system, go back in history, and find scenarios where people did not have the choice of inefficiency. Because here's where you will see the most remarkable innovations taking place that will help you beat your competition. In this case, it was the adversity of the Japanese, which enabled Toyota to build a just-in-time system that helped it beat the likes of Ford and General Motors. Lesson number two, whenever you study the systems of your competitors, or even your ideal companies, never ever copy paste the same system to solve your problems. Always look deeper, and try and see how your constraints are different from their constraints, and then choose every step of execution very, very carefully. In this case, instead of just being fascinated by the just-in-time concept, I would urge you to look deeper into the risk involved with the strategy, which will kind of make you rethink if this strategy is even worth it. And that is when you will see that there are three more strategies of Toyota that helped them survive along with the JIT principle. And these principles are the Kanban system, the Kaizen model and the Jidoka method. ., please do a study about Toyota's risk mitigation strategies during the 1997 Aisin Seiki fire and 2016 Kumamoto earthquake. And you will see that Toyota's entire supply chain got disrupted only because they used just-in-time, but the way they reacted to it might have a very important lesson for you to learn.

XLIV
Volvo

The automobile industry has historically been one of the most competitive industries in the world. Inspite of being an extremely captial intensive industry the margins are thin, the risk is high and the industry, in general is extremely vulnerable to both technologicaal disruptions and global forces. While on one hand you'll see that even the biggest companies in the automotive industry fail within no time On the other hand we've got companies that will even indulge in malpractices just to be ahead in the game. But even in this super competitive market there is one extraordinary company that has stood by its ethics and is even gone one step ahead to help its competition just so that normal people like you and me can be saved from being killed. And the generosity of this company is responsible for saving 1 million lives already. This wonderful company that I'm talking about is none other than the swedish car maker Volvo and regardless of which domain you belong to if you only learn and apply Volvo's business strategies to your business you will be able to build, if not the biggest, at least the most valuable brand in your domain. The iconic story of Volvo dates back to the 1950s when the automotive industry was as revolutionary as Internet today. But the major problem was that with the increase in the number of vehicles, the number of accidents was rising. And every now and then, these accidents even made headlines. So, every automobile company was spending millions of dollars just to make cars safer. Because they knew if their invetion clicked it would be the perfect opportunity for them to become the number one company in the market. But after working day in day out and after hundreds of failed iterations. A Volvo engineer by the name Nils Bohlin came out with the invention of something called the three-point seat belt. And as soon as it came to the market every automaker in the market knew that considering the fear in the minds of the people Volvo could easily use the invention of the three-point seat belt to prove and project itself as the safest car manufacturer in the world. Eventually, it can go on to become the number one player in the market, effortlessly. But you know what? Volvo gave away its patent for the seat belt at no cost at all. In fact, they gifted it to their competitors and even encouraged mass adoption. Now, just to put that into perspective; a standard industrial norm is that great patents offer you a defensible advantage over your rivals which gives you 20 years of monopoly rights in the US. If you remember, these patents are the reason why Gillete was able to become a billion dollar company and was able to remain a market leader for 20 years. In this case even if Volvo charged a nominal $10 in royalty for every car that their competitor manufactured with 40 million cars coming on-road that would make them $400 million in profit without manufacturing a single car. And yet, they chose to give it away And since then the three point seat belt has saved more than 1 million lives which makes it one of the most important inventions of the century. And since then they have made pioneering inventions like the laminated glass plate that doesn't shatter when broken; like the booster cushion that could save the lives of 4 year old children during the times of accident. And fast forward to the modern day, they are now sharing 40 years of their accident and design research data with all of their competitors, just so that regardless of their rivalry, every brand could make safr cars for everyone. This is what brings us to the first lesson to be learnt from Volvo and that is conscious capitalism. As in, you can go on to make a ton of money by building a business, that's completely fine but the one thing you need to make sure is that the money that you're making should not come due to the harm caused to the society. This is very important because in today's world while we have got highly dangerous and toxic companies like *Bhai Chod* We desperately need companies that can maintain their ethical standards while they do business. The second aspect of Volvo's safety obssession is branding. If you look at the safety measures that Volvo takes, you will be stunned to realize that Volvo abides by such high safety standards that even the safety boards do not conduct any such test for that level of safety. This is the reason why Volvo is one of the rare companies to get 5 star ratings for their safety. And the reason why Volvo does all of this is because their vision is that safety should become synonymous with the name of Volvo. As in, the first brand that a customer must think about when they think about safety must be Volvo. This is what we call as establishing the determinant benefit of the brand, as in the singular attribute that separates you from the competition. And they have done such amazing work that time and again YouTube videos go viral wherein Volvo cars and trucks have saved people who are in such an extreme scenario that had it been some other vehicle they would've been killed within a blink of an eye. And the most astonishing fact of all is that After selling 50,000 units since the past 16 years no one has died in the Volvo XC90 model and this is what brings me to the third aspect of extraordinary brand building and that is going the extra mile. In 2015, Volvo took its idea of safety beyond cars when they realized that every year 19,000 cyclists in the UK encounter accidental situations and this was because the car drivers were not able to see the cyclists. So, they partnered with a startup company and designed something called 'Life Paint' This was a special reflective paint which reacted to the car lights and could make cyclists visible even during night time. And they gave away a lot of these paints for free at the most popular cycle outlets. And guess what? Within a week they sold 20,000 Life Paints and the campaign generated so much online buzz that the YouTube video got 4 million views in just 21 days and the campaign generated 130 million global media impressions with no media expenditure. And now Volvo has the vision to extend its initiative towards the safety of the planet by adopting to clean fuel. This is the reason why Volvo commands a ton of brand loyalty among the Eurpoean consumers. And they have positioned themselves so well that tomorrow, if a father wants to gift a car to his daughter the first brand that he is going to prefer would be Volvo. Now, there are 3 very important lessons that we can learn and apply to our domain to build an extraordinary brand. The first lesson is abiding by conscious capitalism. We all as entrepreneurs need to realize that as much as it is important to leverage the internet and the global economy to build and scale our business. It is equally important that we take responsibility to not make money through unethical means. And if you want to build a great brand money should always be used as a fuel to grow your business rather than being the fundamental purpose of its existence. So, do make a ton of money; just do it the right way. Secondly, you need to constantly keep asking yourself throughout your business journey as to how are you reinforcing the idea of your determinant brand benefit in the minds of your consumers. And when you execute upon those pointers you will begin to realize that slowly and steadily, your customers are becoming more and more loyal towards your brand. And last and most importantly, while every single player in the market is trying to be the best in the game by more or less doing similar things you've gotta ask yourself how are you going the extra mile to serve your customers. And trust me it doesn't matter how small or big that move is. If you go the extra mile, that is enough to separate you from the herd because at the end of the day the only difference between ordinary and extraordinary is that little extra. In this case, it would be that one gesture, one act of service towards your customers that will make all the difference in the world.

XLV
Walmart

XLVI
Wipro

Azeem premgi is undoubtedly one of the most respected businessmen in india in the past 40 years wipro has had such an exclusive growth that a 1 000 rupees investment in wipro in 1980 would be worth 45.2 crore rupees today but while most of us are familiar with azimsa's philanthropic moves hardly any of us know that wipro in the early days was a vegetable products company which went by the name western india vegetable products limited but today it has transformed into such a humongous it giant that it recruits more than 200 000 employees is located in more than 110 countries and gendered a revenue of 8 billion in 2020 alone the question is how did a vegetable products company go on to become such a big it giant what exactly was assumed sir's business strategy and more importantly what are the business lessons that we need to learn from this extraordinary businessman this is a story that dates back to 1966 when just before primeji was about to complete his engineering at stanford his father passed away unexpectedly postponing his graduation he returned to india to lead his family business which back then was mainly based on producing vanaspati immediately after arriving he started diversifying his business and started dwelling into consumer products such as soaps shoes light bulbs and even hydraulic cylinders and in 1977 he also renamed the company as wipro later on in 1979 when the indian government asked ibm to leave the country he began steering the company towards the computer business because ibm had left a huge market that needed to be captured so wipro started establishing a number of successful international partnerships in the 1980s to help it build the computer hardware for sale in india but during the same time in 1978 liberalization happened in china because of which the chinese started to offer an ultra cheap labor rate which made it extremely difficult for the players in the hardware market to survive and that is when ladies and gentlemen azim premji started to diversify into software development now if you take a step back and look at the timeline of these it giants like wipro infosys and even tech mahindra you will see that they began to witness exponential growth somewhere in the late 80s and in the early 90s if you see if something gives rise to a series of billion dollar companies in the same time period it is definitely not a coincidence there is always something very special about that time that turned these companies into billion dollar companies the question is what was this gold rush all about well as it turns out during that time the cost of human resource in the computer industry in the united states started to increase rapidly as a result outsourcing became very very important for the american companies to survive in the market now if you observe closely this did not just happen with coding or development but with every other industry that has achieved maturity every industry first originates in the home ground and as it achieves accelerated growth the cost of labor increases drastically which eventually decreases their profit margins making outsourcing extremely important and whichever country or company is able to make this outsourcing possible for these companies goes on to it a gold mine and makes a billion dollars in the 40s and the 50s when the textile industry needed outsourcing hong kong and south korea became opportunist and made a billion dollars in the 1980s when the electronics and manufacturing based industries needed outsourcing china became an opportunist and made a trillion dollars to turn itself into a superpower in just 40 years similarly when the computer industry needed outsourcing azim sir and narayan muttiso were two of the few people who could build an extraordinary system to make outsourcing possible for american companies and they delivered world-class service at the cheapest rate possible using something called the global delivery model the question is what exactly does it mean and how does the global delivery model work now this concept is an extremely complex concept but i'm going to give you an oversimplified example to help you understand this model easily so the global delivery model is a model wherein a project is divided into discrete processes and those processes are executed by different teams spread all across the world such that the project is delivered by a skilled labor force in the most cost effective way and in the quickest possible time for example let's say there is a media company that needs custom designed mics now this company has hundreds of journalists traveling all throughout the world they've got reporters in war stick in places like afghanistan they've got people reporting from protests and they've even got people reporting from disaster hit places like the katrina in the united states so let's say they need a special mic that can be used in all these conditions this is when they will go on to approach an audio technology company to get these special mics designed and this is how the project will be executed firstly the sales and market research team from europe will meet with the media company to know all of their requirements they will start taking notes that the media company wants a waterproof mic that needs to be sturdy enough to withstand a lot of falls and at the same time it also needs to capture the voice of the anchor without recording the noise from the background apart from that it also must be small enough to plug into the collar and should have very less wires to avoid entanglement then all these requirements are sent to the engineering team in the united states where they designed the mic in order to meet the accurate specifications using their r d and product design skills and then based on the design of the mic the engineering team would present a list of materials that are needed to manufacture the mic and this will include transistors capacitors carbon granules metal and so on and so forth and this is when the global supply chain unit will come in and will start procuring raw materials from suppliers all across the world for example they will procure metals from china semiconductors from hong kong and transistors from singapore and after that all these materials will be shipped to china for assembly why because china has the cheapest labor rates in the world after that testing will also be done in china itself eventually 40 pieces will be eliminated and after quality check the final products are sent to the media company in europe then the media company will run a pilot and eventually the audio tech company will also give them a 24 7 support team that will operate from india to help them with any difficulty or problems that they are facing along with that they will also give them an annual follow-up to upgrade or to add more mics as per their changing requirements therefore if you look at this system it was not executed by one team but by a series of teams located in different places as per the cost and expertise such that they all coordinate together to deliver the final product to the client this is what you call as the global delivery model and just like this azim ramji specialized in establishing a super efficient global delivery model for software development such that when the market in america matured and liberalization happened in india due to low labor costs azeem so was able to establish a major chunk of his workforce in india which dealt with development customer support and testing and today u.s and europe serve as major hubs for artificial intelligence and cloud computing for wipro and since cloud computing databases are located in europe even the infrastructure management team and hardware teams of wipro also operate from europe customer support is majorly located in philippines china and india and low technical development and hardware comes from china and today as per the requirements of the clients teams from 110 countries come together in different permutation and combination to deliver the software services to the client as per the cost and expertise in the quickest possible manner this is one of the primary reasons that turned wipro and infosys into billion dollar i.t giants and eventually turned india into a major beneficiary of the iit revolution generating more than 4.5 million jobs and this is what brings me to the most important part of the chapter and that is what are the business lessons that we need to learn from a legend like azim sir . let's move on to the lessons from the case study lesson number one as an entrepreneur in this fast-paced hyper-connected world it is very very important that you keep an eye on what exactly is happening in the global markets and more importantly how every single major global event is going to be affecting your industry in particular in this case it was the Chinese evolution that posed as a threat to the hardware industry and the business acumen of Azeem sir to be able to spot the opportunity in the software outsourcing industry is what enabled him to build a billion-dollar i.t empire lesson number two whenever you spot a series of billion-dollar companies coming up in one particular time always remember you are looking at a gold mine that very few people will bother to explore in this case it was a textile revolution in the 40s it was the electronics and Chinese revolution in the 80s and the 1990s it was nothing but the global delivery model that gave rise to the Indian.

XLVII
Zerodha

Zerodha is by far one of the most fascinating business case studies in the Indian startup ecosystem. In just 10 years, Zerodha went from 0 to $1 billion in valuation. On one side where tech companies are on a cash drain wherein they are incurring million-dollar losses, Zerodha has been very elegantly profitable with a profit of more than ?400 crores. And here's why it is mindblowing. all of this was done with zero funding and zero marketing. I REPEAT. Zerodha went from zero to $1 billion in valuation with zero marketing and zero funding. The question is- In this noisy world wherein companies are pouring in millions of dollars just to survive in the market how is it possible that Zerodha has been able to achieve something so incredible with zero funding and zero marketing. The answer to this question comes from one of the most legendary entrepreneurs in the Indian startup ecosystem who goes by the name Kunal Shah. In 2016, Kunal Shah delivered an INKtalk wherein he proposed a very interesting theory that more or less explains the root cause of the success of some of the biggest startups in the world. According to Kunal Shah, in this world, there are a ton of systems that have a ton of inefficiencies and hurdles which often prevent ordinary people like you and me from moving into a more efficient system. But we human beings once we find an efficient system we have this innate ability to move on from where we never come back. As a result of which if an entrepreneur can build a startup in such a way that he can fix these inefficiencies and can help ordinary people overcome the hurdle. He/she will be able to build a startup that will bring about a revolution. And their startup will be such a revolution that it'll bring about an irreversible paradigm shift in the behavior of the consumers. And once this is done that startup will gain 3 massive superpowers which will boost that startup to another level altogether. These 3 superpowers are Number one, high consumer tolerance. Number two is a unique brand proposition that will result in word of mouth. And thirdly, it will result in an irreversible shift. A very simple example that is closer to home is WhatsApp. If you see, all of us are using WhatsApp but none of us are using WhatsApp because of an advertisement. If you look at WhatsApp as a system, back then, before WhatsApp even sent a local text we used to think twice because 1 message used to cost us 1 rupee. And forget international calls, even to make a normal call we used to think twice because you'd run out of balance. But then when WhatsApp arrived, it took off all these hurdles, and today. texting has become completely effortless, that's the reason why we spam a lot of people and that's the reason why you receive 'Good Morning' texts. And if you look at calls, even making international calls does not look like a big deal today. And most importantly if you see, you cannot even imagine going back to your texting days. So, you see there are 3 major superpowers that WhatsApp gained as a startup. which boosted WhatsApp to another level altogether. Number one is the unique brand proposition which resulted in word of mouth. As in, WhatsApp gave you something that you had never seen before, as a result of which customers were screaming at each other to use WhatsApp a result which WhatsApp was able to go from 0 to 400 million users in less than 5 years. And today, WhatsApp has more than 2 billion users. Number two, like I said we cannot even imagine going back to our old texting days, as a result of which there is an irreversible change in our behavior. And lastly, when we come to high tolerance if you see, despite the creepy WhatsApp Privacy Policy you are still using WhatsApp. Despite our understanding of the dangers of WhatsApp forwards we are still using WhatsApp. And despite call lagging, we still do make WhatsApp calls. So if you see, we have developed a very high tolerance towards WhatsApp wherein even if they make big mistakes, we are extremely tolerant towards it. And we will still keep using the service as a result of which customer retention-which is one of the most difficult things to do- is done in a way that nobody can even imagine. So, this is how by fixing the inefficiencies of the texting system the founders of WhatsApp were able to claim their pot of gold as a result of which they were able to create massive wealth and eventually sold WhatsApp for $19 billion to Facebook. And the founders of Zerodha did the same. Before Zerodha Nikhil Kamath observed that 3 major hurdles were troubling the existing investors and were also preventing the common people of India from investing in the stock market. And these 3 hurdles were: Number one, lack of knowledge and awareness. As you all know, in India we make more life decisions based on myths and emotions rather than knowledge and strategy. The second hurdle they observed was that of brokerage fees as the conventional brokerage firms were charging a percentage commission on the amount of investment the investor was making which resulted in exorbitant brokerage fees. And third and most importantly, the entire process of investment was very very tedious and very complex for a common man to understand. And that is the reason why they came out with 3 unique solutions which turned Zerodha into a billion-dollar company. The first solution they came out with was to tackle the lack of knowledge and awareness as a result of which to educate the Indian population, they gave came out with something called Zerodha Varsity which is an extensive collection of the stock market and financial lessons wherein anybody can go out there and understand how the market functions eventually, to gain enough knowledge to make a strategic investment. And after learning from here any newbie can go out there and make a confident investment as a result of which then and there itself Zerodha started commanding the loyalty of the newbies. The second solution they came out with was to discount the brokerage fees to such a large extent that it resulted in a revolution. Like I said before, most firms were charging a percentage commission as in, if you were investing a few lakhs you'd have to pay tens of thousands of just brokerage. And guess what? Zerodha turned this into a super-efficient and super affordable system wherein they charged ?20 or 0.03% whichever is less for all intraday trades. And guess what? they charged zero fees for all equity and direct mutual fund investments. And third and most importantly to resolve the tedious and complex process of investment they used the internet and came out with a beautiful website and a very simple user interface for their mobile application. Using this any common man can get familiar with the entire process of investment without any hassles and with 100% transparency. And if you're also a newbie in the world of investment you can use the link below to create your Zerodha account today and jumpstart your investment journey. And that is how by fixing these 3 problems the founders of Zerodha claimed their pot of gold as a result of which today Zerodha is a billion-dollar company with zero investment in marketing because the consumers were screaming at each other to use Zerodha. And today, 4 million investors are making their investments using the platform Zerodha. Now, the question is- What do we as entrepreneurs have to learn from this incredible case study. People, we all need to understand that funding is one of the ways to accelerate your startup but not the only way to do so. So, if you are reluctant to pursue your idea because you are waiting for funding I would highly recommend you to do some introspection and see how you can proceed ahead without funding. And last and most importantly, we all need to realize the fact that there are hundreds if not thousands of pots of gold all around us in the form of inefficient systems. And each one of them offers ordinary people like you and me the opportunity to go out there and claim our pot of gold and eventually build a business empire out of it. The only question that we've gotta ask ourselves is Are we going to crib about the problem or are we going to fix the problem? And this attitude of crib or fix will eventually decide our destiny.

XLVIII
Zoho

This is the story of a man who went from being an ordinary employee to becoming one of the biggest social entrepreneurs in India. and he has a net worth of $2.6 Billion This is the story of a man who is running a revolutionary experiment that can solve the unemployment crisis in India by turning the remotest villages of India into the tech hubs of the world.This person that I'm talking about is the CEO of ZOHO Corporation and goes by the name Sridhar Vembu Sridhar Sir is a Princeton graduate who had the perfect job in the silicon valley startup Qualcomm and that is when he realized that there are so many Indian engineers working at crucial positions at multiple billion-dollar companies all across the world, and yet very few Indian companies were strong contenders in the software industry. So, he decided to step into the ring with a vision to build a software company that can empower the youth of India and that is how he started AdventNet which then became ZOHO Corporation. and since the past 22 years, ZOHO has gone from an ordinary startup to becoming a billion-dollar company with an estimated market value of $5 Billion but what's more astounding is not the growth of ZOHO but what Sridhar Vembu sir is doing with his company's massive influence He decided to start a revolutionary experiment to solve the unemployment crisis in India. Now, we all know that there is a huge gap between the teachings of the college and the requirement of the industry and even after 4 years of engineering, millions of engineering students severely lack the skill to work in the industry. Now, every politician and billionaire in this country knows about this and many have even spoken about it. But very few have done something proactively to fix this problem. This is why in 2004, the founders of ZOHO started something called ZOHO University. and here's where they started to onboard and train students with skillsets and abilities at a very young age. Now what is unique about this system is that instead of asking for fees and donations from the students, ZOHO pays the student a stipend of ?10,000 per month throughout the tenure of the 2-year course. and during this extensive training, students are taught Mathematics, English, Programming, and every other subject that is needed to turn an ordinary kid into an employable candidate. And after the course, they get recruited in ZOHO itself with an amazing package regardless of their degree. And through this job, these students get the golden opportunity to uplift their families from all economic challenges forever. and guess what? These schools have been designed specially to empower the youngsters from the villages of India where let alone employment, even education is considered to be a luxury. because ZOHO believes that skillsets and abilities are far more valuable than paper credentials. and one of the most successful stories of the ZOHO system is this boy names Abdul Alim who was an ordinary security guard working 12-hour shifts at ZOHO but one fine day, one of his seniors decided to tap into his potential and started training him. Fast forward to a few months later, today, this boy works as an engineer and takes up technical projects in the very same company wherein he was working as a security guard today close to 10% of the entire workforce of ZOHO consists of ordinary kids like Abdul Alim who became capable engineers after hailing from the remotest villages of the country. and not just that, today ZOHO is experimenting with these models in 10 villages in Tamil Nadu wherein 200 of its engineers 20 in each village will collaborate and build software for the world. And the leaders of ZOHO are working very hard to extend its empowerment models to the villages of Kerala and Andhra Pradesh also Now people, most of us dream about having corner offices in the city of Manhattan. Vembu sir believes that village offices would be the future of work, as village economies begin to prosper. This is why despite having his offices in 21 countries, including America, China, and Australia. Sridhar sir stays in a small village named Mathalamparai which is about 650 km away from Chennai. And he operates his $5B company from this village itself Now this is what you call 'practicing what you preach'. Now, the reason why Sridhar sir is a legend is that the model that he is building is a scalable model that can be replicated by several billion-dollar companies all across the country. And instead of giving out donations for a short-term impact through this model, companies can create a long-term impact and also make a ton of profit. This is how they can create a win-win scenario wherein companies can get capable employees and people can get opportunities. Now if many such billion-dollar companies start setting up institutions like ZOHO to build a direct bridge between academics and employment, can you imagine what kind of a magical revolution could come up. This is the reason why we need to start promoting incredible ideas like these. So that, we can have many such leaders like Sridhar sir, who don't just talk about the problems but also act on the solutions and this is what will make India a truly incredible country.

XLIX
Zomato

On the 14th of July 2021, Zomato will officially go public. With 9000cr about to be raised, this is by far one of the biggest and perhaps the most awaited IPO of 2021. But as far as the numbers of the company are concerned, Zomato seems to be in deep deep trouble! From 2018 to 2020 while the revenue of the company went from just 65 million to 368 million dollars during the same time, the losses exploded by 20 times from just 15 million dollars to more than 300 million dollars. And every time Zomato tried to become profitable it has to lead to nothing but outrage. They first tried to launch Zomato Gold to lock in the customers from going to Swiggy but that lead to massive losses to restaurants which forced them to shut the service down. Then they tried increasing the prices of their dishes but that ended up making the customers unhappy! So from the outside, it almost looks like the company is stuck in a vicious cycle of cash drain which is leading to nothing but more and more losses. And this is what every single expert and fundamental analyst, more or less, has to say. But you know what? There is one very very important factor that very few people are taking into consideration and this factor could turn Zomato into a gold mine if you only understand this factor you can go on to make the most strategic investments into the food tech space in the next 5 years. The question is What exactly is this X factor and how can Zomato or Swiggy turn into a goldmine investment. The answer to this question lies in a particular case of a Silicon Valley start-up called June. This is a story that dates back to 2013 when June became one of the pioneers to develop something called the smart oven. This oven was so amazing that back in 2013 itself had a screen for viewing recipes, could be controlled over Wi-Fi and it was also

Alexa-compatible which allowed voice command control back in 2013 itself! The company was doing so well that it was able to raise a series of funding from heavyweight investors. And in 2018 June also secured an investment from Amazon Alexa Fund and the company grew rapidly from 2015-to 2019. And just when everything looked perfect something crazy happened. Just a year later, Amazon launched its smart oven which had the same features as that of June including Wi-Fi connectivity and Alexa integration. But the highlight over here was that Amazon Smart Oven was priced at half the price of June Ovens. While June was selling its oven for about $499-$699 Amazon's oven would have cost you only $250 back then that is how this rising startup became a competitor of its prime investor and amazon started eating into profits of its bestseller. Now the story of June is not the only incident. Every year, Amazon unveils hundreds of products and they have developed an intricate playbook to put every competitor out of business. And if you look at the procedure as to how exactly this is done, it's pretty straightforward. Step 1, they find the best-selling product. Use the data from the seller's profile and make a list of all the specifications that makes that product the best-selling product. Step 2, they read through the reviews and find out what exactly customers love about that product. And then, they buy a manufacturing unit to get them to make the same product, and then they aggressively price it at 30–40% lesser than the best-selling product. And this is how without trial and error Amazon takes a cakewalk to make millions of dollars by selling products from all categories by successfully eliminating the bestseller himself. And all of this is being done because Amazon has 3 incredible superpowers. Number one, it has consumer data. So, Amazon knows exactly how much the customer can afford and what kind of products the customer wants to buy. Number two, it has the data of every seller. So they know what features make a product the best selling product. And last and most importantly Amazon has the superpower of digital real estate by which it can give special preference and rank its products at the number 1 position and make million-dollar sales. This is what makes consumer and seller data practically a GOLD MINE for Amazon! And guess what? This is exactly the case with Zomato! In this case, Zomato has all the data about thousands of restaurants and millions of consumers who have used Zomato to order food. Zomato knows exactly which dishes are in high demand in which area. And on top of that Zomato also knows what is the optimum price for a particular dish. They even know what is the best time to sell a particular dish. For example, Zomato knows that in Hinjewadi Pune Biriyani priced at ?150 will go on to become the best seller, er and the best season for biryani is from November to December. So this way, Zomato, and Swiggy are practically sitting on a data gold mine and they can use it very easily to launch their food chain eventually undercutting the existing food chains to make millions of dollars in profits. And this can turn Zomato and Swiggy both into super profitable businesses in no time. Fun fact: both Zomato and Swiggy have already ventured into it using something called the concept of "Cloud Kitchen". And there are 2 Zomato services that very few people are talking about. And those are Zomato Kitchen and Zomato Hyper pure. To understand the depth of this you first need to understand what is a cloud kitchen. In simple words, cloud kitchen is nothing but a super-efficient restaurant that only gives out take-way orders and has no dining space. It's just the kitchen of the restaurant that takes online orders and gives them out for delivery. A simple example of the same is Behrouz biryani. It's got no outlets but has got a fantastic digital presence. And this concept of cloud kitchen ladies and gentlemen is a revolution in the making. Why? Because it has got some game-changing cost benefits over a conventional restaurant. Now, just to put that on paper with standard assumptions and costing here's what the comparison with the conventional restaurant looks like. If you take a conventional 50 seater restaurant it would require 6 lakhs of rental cost considering that you would need 2000 sqft of area. 20 Lakhs in rental deposit, 8–10 Lakhs for licenses, 8–15 Lakhs for equipment, and working capital which includes inventory, salary, and a light bill will require about 20 lakhs. And most importantly, the monthly revenue needed to break even in 2 years is about 20 lakhs. On the contrary, if you look at a cloud kitchen the space needed would reduce significantly and would cost you just about 50,000 to 1 lakh in rent. Apart from that, you just have to pay 1 lakh in rental deposit licenses would cost you the same, equipment would cost you the same but the working capital needed to operate a cloud kitchen will go down by 50% as compared to a restaurant to just 10 lakhs and most importantly the revenue needed to break even in 2 years also goes down by 50% again to just 8-10 lakhs. And the benefits? Well, you're looking at saving 5 lakhs in rent per month. You save 19 lakhs in rental deposits, and 10 lakhs in working capital which results in the best part which is 10 lakh rupees less is needed as a monthly revenue to break even in 2 years. And this is the insane cost benefit that a cloud kitchen has over a conventional restaurant. And here's where most people underestimate the power of digital marketing.

People, instead of investing in infrastructure heavily even if a fraction of the money, in this case, even if 1 lakh rupees is rotated in marketing it is more than enough to drive an insane amount of traffic to the cloud kitchen, and on paper what looks like 2 years can even be achieved in 1 year. A standing example of the same is Rebel Foods. Now, this is the company that owns Faasos and Behrouz Biryani. And you know what? Both these brands, individually, bring in about 16-17 crores worth of business per month! And they have about 300 cloud kitchens across 35 cities in the country. The best part: all of this was done in less than 10 years from 2011 to 2020. and here's where Zomato Kitchens come in. And all these brands like Fasoos, Behrouz, Good Bowl, and Box8 are all using Zomato or Swiggy to sell their dishes, right? Well, in that case, if you see Faasos and Zomato, Behrouz and Zomato share the same relationship as of June oven and Amazon. So just like Amazon had sellers' data and knew everything about what worked for June and what did not. Zomato knows exactly which Behrouz cloud kitchen is doing well and which is not. Just like Amazon had customer data and knew exactly what is the purchasing power of the audience and who wants to buy an oven. Zomato knows exactly who is more inclined to buy a sandwich who is more inclined to buy a roll and who is more inclined to buy a biryani. And most importantly just like Amazon had the superpower of digital real estate to enlist its products on top Zomato can particularly open up its cloud kitchen and list its products at the top with an aggressive pricing model and undercut its best-sellers like Behrouz and Fassos And the best part is instead of being so evil Zomato and Swiggy are doing it more ethically now which is where ventures like Zomato Kitchens and Swiggy Access come into play. Zomato kitchen is this wonderful partnership between Zomato and a bunch of hand-picked brands across the country wherein Zomato uses its superpower of data and chooses the most profitable location in a particular area. And then based on what works best in that location certain brands are chosen. And Zomato will provide them with everything starting from raw materials to kitchen infrastructure. And this kitchen will have multiple sellers from specific categories and this space will be shared by all the cloud kitchens together which will maximize their profits and optimize their costs. And what most people do not know is that this concept is a profit machine because this system will give rise to something called a super cloud kitchen which will be so efficient (2X) that in just 2000 sqft space, that is, in the space of just one restaurant a cloud kitchen can accommodate more than 50 brands. And process more than 3000 orders a day. A standing example of the same is the Dubai-based start-up called KITOPI which has these super cloud kitchens that can accommodate about 40–70 brands in just 2000 sqft and can process 3000+ orders in a day. The cherry on the cake, KITOPI plans to go fully automated and will run these super cloud kitchens without human intervention by next year. If this is very very clear to you, now let's have a look at the economics of the cloud kitchen in India and see where Zomato has its gold mine. This is what the economics of a conventional cloud kitchen in India, today, looks like. We've got 3 kinds of costs. The raw material is about 40%. Commissions to the aggregator, that is, Zomato plus logistics is about 25%. Fixed cost like wages and energy is about 25% and profit is very less at just 10%. And most people look at this thin margin of just about 10% and then jump to the conclusion that it's not profitable enough and the fact that it's not viable enough for Zomato. Well, that's because they don't realize that this is a super inefficient model. After all, cloud kitchen is still at the baby stage in India. And just 3–4 years down the line this is what it is going to look like. Even if I use Kitopi's trajectory and use that as a reference for what it has achieved by January 2019. Here's what the figures look like. Raw material expenses are just about 20%, fixed costs which include labor cost, order processing, production overhead, and sales discount account for about 21%, brand royalty is about 7%, commission to aggregator is about 28% and this makes the profits stand at 16%. And here's where the X factor comes in because the fun fact is Kitopi is also a middleman which is why in the case of Zomato, the profits will shoot up. Why? Because Zomato does not have to pay aggregator commission because Zomato is the aggregator. And in the case of raw materials, Zomato is already building a robust supply with something called Hypepure. And this is a supply chain that will connect the cloud kitchen directly with the source which will bring down the cost of the raw material further from 28% to even less than 25%. And now if you look at the figures, you will see that Zomato's commission alone stands at 44% even if you neglect the margins from hyperpure. And with a healthy 10% commission on delivery, we are still looking at 34% profit. And if you follow Kitopi's trajectory this profit margin could easily go above 50% in the next 10 years. So in short by 2025, looking at Kitopi's numbers the same ?200 roll where Zomato is incurring a loss of ?20-?30 will eventually go on to give a profit of ?50–?100. This point is where Zomato and Swiggy both will go on to become super profitable businesses with super profitable cloud kitchens across the country. And I sense that Zomato is raising these 1 billion dollars to transition to this next curve of cloud kitchen. So now the question is- Should you invest in Zomato or not? Well, I don't want to tell you anything specific about the IPO but whenever you look forward to investing in Zomato or similar companies please, remember these important lessons. Lesson 1, always remember as much as people are obsessed with numbers and math it is important for you to understand that more than the numbers it's the story behind those numbers that is important. In this case, there are so many people out there on the Internet itself who are so engrossed in the fundamental analysis and the present numbers of the company that they have completely lost sight of the fact that we are living in the 21st century wherein the next disruption is less than 3 years away. And we as ordinary people are looking at the present and the next 2 years of the company the investors like the Sequoia Capital are looking at a 10-year trajectory. And as soon as we start putting ourselves in their shoes and look at a 10-year trajectory it will help us better understand these companies eventually, it will give us more clarity for our investment. Lesson 2, if you want to find these trajectories, the best way would be to do some extensive research about companies all across the world and find out those companies which are already in the next curve. In this case, if you see, an understanding of how Kitopi is operating gave us a very good understanding of how Zomato will be operating. And that is how you can derive some very valuable insights about what's gonna happen in the future. And last and most importantly keep a close eye on how Zomato and Swiggy keep pivoting to the next curve because these kinds of transition periods have got some very very valuable business lessons for each one of us. And always remember, once a great man said, Innovation always happens in the next curve and those who look for it will end up owning the future. In this case, it is the rise of the next generation of food-tech startups and Zomato's IPO will mark the beginning of this revolution in India.

Thanks to Appa, Miiee and Kubi Appa, Sangavi Akka , Krishna mama, Padhma Aaya, and my family for their support.

Thanks to my co-author Hitesh Subramanyam, without him this book would haven't been possible.

We promise fifty percent of this book's profit would go to trusts to support and help underprivileged students.

please visit agency.euteks.eu for Materials and worksheets @ Creative Commons.

www.ingramcontent.com/pod-product-compliance
Ingram Content Group UK Ltd.
Pitfield, Milton Keynes, MK11 3LW, UK
UKHW041856190726
13854UKWH00002B/943